JENN RUBEN

I Wanted Sunshine

But Ran . . . Sideways

ICKYNICKS

I WANTED SUNSHINE BUT RAN . . . SIDEWAYS

For information address:
Ickynicks
PO Box 722
Okemos, MI 48805

First trade paperback edition published 2010

ISBN: 978-0-97-54590-0-3

Printed in the United States of America.

Acknowledgements

To my family and friends, especially my mother

I Wanted Sunshine

But Ran . . . Sideways

One

I'm 24 years old, I just graduated from college, I have a job, I have a boyfriend and I have my own place. Everything is great. My life is wonderful! Couldn't be better!

Not quite. Unfortunately, my boyfriend's in school and has limited time for me, our roommate has Asperger's Syndrome, my parents are divorced and my job sucks. Did I miss anything? Oh yes, and well, I'm Jewish, which explains everything or nothing.

I have the thick, curly hair, big brown eyes, huge breasts (are they known for having that? No, I think that's the Hungarian genes). Anyway, I have the glamorous glasses (no, *not* sunglasses) and I have an entire closet filled with black outfits (which seems to be a Jewish thing or a Jewish grandma thing).

I'm sitting on the living room floor of our apartment listening to Yoga music. This is about the most relaxed I've been in a month. I hear keys jerking up and down in the doorknob outside our apartment door.

Yay, someone's home. It's probably Adrian, my boyfriend. I bet he got out of his exam early!

I hear keys falling down on the cement. Then I wait. Someone's picking them up and fidgeting with the doorknob. Nope, it's not Adrian. It's Jason, our roommate.

Grrr.

I have decided that Jason is either, a) Autistic with Asperger's Syndrome, b) just a jerk, or, c) needs to get the hell out of our apartment if he dares ask me one more time to fill the toilet paper holder!

Like, *hello*! Are we living in the 1950's? Um, welcome to the 21st century Jason, where women drink beer and sit on the couch while *men* do the cooking and cleaning. Wouldn't that be a revelation?

I hear Jason opening the front door as he clomps into the apartment wearing his basketball shorts and sleeveless basketball jersey and his backpack sloping to one side of his shoulder. He always wears basketball clothes and he's not even a basketball player, at least he's not built like one.

"Hey, Jason," I manage to smile.

He glares at me and throws his backpack on our living room floor. He walks down the hall and slams the bathroom door.

Well, so much for conversation starters.

I hear the toilet flushing. Already? It's amazing how fast a man can pee.

I hear the bathroom door open and Jason comes back out to the living room.

"Jenn," he looks over at me.

I look up from where I'm sitting. "Yeah, what's up?" Does he want to have our first conversation together? Oh, this could be exciting, or maybe we could talk about his annoying girlfriend Lisa—

"Jenn, uh . . . could . . . could you . . . could you buy . . . buy toilet paper . . . for the bathroom?" He stammers.

I'm sorry?

"Oh," I say. "Um, well, there's some toilet paper over there." I point to a bag of toilet paper under the dining room table.

He glances over at the table and then turns back to me. "Yeah, . . . could . . . could you maybe," he pauses.

I hope to God he isn't going to say what I think he's going to say.

"Could you maybe," Jason begins again.

Jason has issues with repeating his words. I think it's some sort of speech impairment and part of his Asperger's.

"Could you . . . could you," he stumbles over his words, yet again.

You're almost there Jason, just a little bit more.

"Could you . . . could you put . . . put the toilet paper on the holder? Because . . . because I can't . . . can't use the bathroom."

Huh?

"Um," is all I can manage to say, I'm dumbfounded. This is something he has never asked me to do. I'm honored. He has asked me, a woman, to do the honors of placing the roll of toilet paper on the toilet paper holder! Apparently, he can't use the potty unless a *woman* puts toilet paper on the toilet paper holder.

Unfortunately, for Jason, today is his not-so-lucky day. I have decided, as a Hungarian woman of charm and glamour, that today I need to declare my role as a woman.

"Listen, Jason," I begin. I don't really want to sound mean so I utter my friendliest voice. "If you want, you could just do it yourself?" I decide to ask it as more of a question.

This seems to work well for people like Jason who have Asperger's, a type of Autism resulting in a total lack of common sense. They can't understand anyone else's point of view.

"Um, OK?" Jason ignores me and grabs a roll of toilet paper from under the table and walks back to the bathroom.

People with Asperger's have a terrible time communicating with others. But everyone has trouble communicating at some point in life. For instance, my father David had trouble communicating with my mom Linda that he wanted a divorce.

One time my father said to my mother, "What's good for the goose is good for the gander."

She told him she wasn't interested in living like that.

"Oh, Linda," my dad said to my mother emphasizing her resistance, "the world is filled with so *many* beautiful women. Don't you want me to be *happy*?"

In the end, she filed for divorce.

Since the divorce, my parents have gotten along better. Yes, it's true. They make better friends than lovers. Which brings me to my next point! You see Jason, women *can* be nice if you learn to communicate with them!

"Um, Jenn. Is it . . . is it OK if . . . if Lisa comes over?" Jason peers out of the bathroom, looking down the hall at me.

"That depends—" I begin as he cuts me off.

"That depends on what? Why can't she come over? You and Adrian always get to have—"

Isn't it funny how he doesn't stutter his words when he's upset?

"Fine!" I yell over his voice and he goes back inside the bathroom. That's one way to silence an Autistic adult male. Otherwise, as I've learned the hard way, Jason will keep going and going and going and going, kind of like the Energizer bunny. Except, he's not cute or furry or pink. He's more smelly, and dirty and bald.

"I'm taking a shower." He yells out. "I told . . . I told Lisa to . . . to come over."

"Fine." I call back.

As he slams the bathroom door, I hear the shower being turned on.

Never ask what a man does in the shower for forty minutes. I've come to learn, that Jason is by far the *only* (and maybe the only man on this planet) who takes longer showers than women!

But I have to ask myself, what *does* he do in there? No, wait, on second thought, maybe I don't want to know. No, I must get these images out of my head!

"Jenn? I'm a little stuck here. Can you help me?"

Jason? Oh. My. God.

"Jenn, please help me," a voice repeats.

Who does he think he is? Is he really asking me to go in there, like, while he's, you know . . .

"JENN?" The voice screams. "I'm *outside*. Please let me in!"

Oh, Adrian! That's who's calling me!

"Jenn!" Adrian yells from outside the front door.

"Coming, sweetie, sorry! So sorry!" I run over, unlock the front door and swing it open. "Hey you, I'm sorry. I thought you were Jason." I grab Adrian and hug him.

"Oops, I forgot my keys," Adrian says, rolling his eyes and laughing.

"Ew, what *is* that awful smell?" I ask. I grab him closer and sniff his dirty, gray, sweater. "It's that, isn't it? When was the last time you washed this sweater?" I ask, pointing to his sweater.

"It's not the sweater," he shakes his head and smiles. "If I told you, you would kill me." He pulls me closer and kisses me.

I pull away, teasing him. "Tell me!"

"I forgot to put on deodorant! I'm sorry!" He says and gives me another hug.

"That's so disgusting, Adrian." I say, teasing him. He always forgets to put on deodorant. I think it's a guy thing. "But honestly, you went the whole day without putting on deodorant and smelling like that?" I ask, looking up at him.

"Well, it's a good thing for you! At least there won't be any girls attracted to me." He says.

"That's a relief!" I giggle. I take off his heavy laptop bag, which he carries practically everything in (except a laptop) and throw it on the dining room table. I grab him and we pull each other on the couch and start kissing each other like two star-crossed lovers. Wow, that *was* Romeo and Juliet!

TWO

I wake up to the sound of my cell phone buzzing to the ring-tone of, "Father is calling. Father is calling."

I get up off the mattress which serves as a bed, and search frantically for my phone, but it's too dark. One of these days we really need to open the blinds in this bedroom.

I find my eyeglasses on the nightstand, which is more like a book with a small lamp resting on it, and I shove them against my face. My ringtone keeps getting louder and louder. Eventually I hear a noise, like a phone dropping to the floor.

The computer! I rush over and search the floor beneath the computer, until I find my phone.

"Hello?" I say as I walk slowly out of the bedroom and close the door behind me so as not to wake Adrian.

"Jennifer?" It's Dad. "Hi, honey, I'm calling to see how your job's going?"

"Dad, do you know what time it is?"

"No, what time is it?" He asks.

I have no idea. I do know that it's really, really early in the morning. It feels like 5AM! So maybe it's 5AM!

"Dad, it's too early, why are you calling?"

"Oh, well, I didn't mean to wake you dear."

I hurry into the kitchen and look at the clock. It reads 9AM. Really?

"So, tell me about this job." My father continues. "Have they made you producer yet? How about director? I know my Jewish daughter will make me proud."

I feel my eyes rolling in the back of my head.

Here's the problem. I never did quite get around to telling my parents the truth about what I'm actually doing out here in California. They both think I have a job, a *real* job, which is more or less true.

I'm working for AmeriCorps, which means, I get paid nominally to help the local community. My mother didn't want me to work for AmeriCorps. She said it was a skanky government program that took advantage of gullible college students.

But nonetheless, my father thinks I'm here working on a film set, which could be true depending on how you look at it. I haven't quite decided . . . OK, well, it's not true.

"What position did they give you on the set?" My dad persists.

"Dad, it's just a low paying job, that's all." I try making my answers as generic as possible so I don't feel guiltier than I already do about lying through my teeth. So, I tell him the only thing I can think of, that would make him proud, and actually, it was kind of my father's idea. He's the one who suggested I should go out to California to make movies.

After all, you can't tell a Jewish father you're living all the way across the country volunteering for a job that pays what illegal immigrants earn picking crops. Any normal Jewish father would have killed me by now! I'm lucky mine lets me live this long!

"So, what movie are you guys working on?" He inquires.

"Actually Dad, it's still the same one," I say.

"What? Jennifer, I don't understand you sometimes. How can you begin to enjoy working on independent films, when you could go to Los Angeles and be a famous director, like Steven Spielberg?"

Why does everyone compare themselves to Spielberg? Why not Tim Burton? He's way better!

"Jennifer, why not start your own movie in Fresno?" Dad asks.

So here's the thing. Yes, I told the lie. But, at least I made it sound believable. Telling him I work on Hollywood films just wouldn't cut it, especially if he knew I lived in Fresno. I can't very well say I live in Los Angeles and have him send my mail there, can I?

Since my dad still sends me cards and gift baskets every now and then, I have to put my address on everything. And I live in Fresno, not Los Angeles. So this is my dilemma.

I had to tell someone eventually, as the guilt was getting to me! So I told Adrian and he laughed. He thought it was one of the best jokes in the world and he couldn't wait for me to break the news to my parents. Ha! That's what he thinks. I could never bring myself to tell my parents what I'm *actually* doing out here! How stupid does Adrian think I am?

"Is this film going to be in the theaters, at least?" My father asks hopefully.

"No, Dad. They're all low budget movies, remember?" I remind him.

"I know. But a father can wish. I really want you working on more professional stuff. Can't they get any Hollywood films made in Fresno?"

That's another reason why I can't tell my Dad. He gave me money to help me move to California for this job. He thought I would make it big in Hollywood, that is, after I landed a few jobs working on movies in Fresno. I guess he thought I would eventually venture down to Los Angeles. Boy, was he wrong. I already feel the guilt bleeding through me.

"Honey, I forgot to tell you!" He says with enthusiasm. "They're working on a Hollywood film in Lansing, Michigan! Isn't that great? If they can do it in Lansing, they can do it in Fresno!" He says a little over confidently.

Except, they aren't actually *making* the film in Lansing (no one would). It's being produced in Grand Rapids, which is like two hours away! Yes, I heard the news. Adrian told me.

"Dad, most of the movies being produced in Fresno are 'B' movies," which I can't tell if this is a total lie or not, who knows? I'm not even working on films out here!

"Well, when you find out, let me know! I'm anxious to hear from you!"

So soon?

"OK, well, thanks for calling. I think I'm going to get back to bed, OK?" I mention.

"Are you sure? It's almost lunchtime," he announces.

"Dad, there's a three hour time difference between here and there!" I persist.

"Oh, I forgot!" He says apologetically.

Then there's a pause, which isn't a good sign since he's probably looking over at a clock.

"Jennifer!" He says, coming back on the line. "Did you know it's almost 9AM over there? Why aren't you up already?"

Damn it!

If we don't talk about films, then this is usually where the conversation leads. Either way, it's bad for me.

"You're right, Dad." I lie. "I think I'm going to head out for a jog," I say.

"Good girl! I'll let you go then. Enjoy your morning run."

"Thanks. Bye." I hang up.

Ha! Who would really go for a run this early in the morning? Come to think of it, who would go running, *ever*?

After I talked with Dad, I went back to bed and now, here I am, enjoying my morning-lunch.

A few hours later, I'm sitting on the couch in the living room watching the television show "The Office." This is the most fun I've had in a few days. That is, until Jason walks through the front door, carrying a huge pile of mail.

"Here," Jason says, walking over to me and tossing two pieces of mail in my lap.

I hit the "pause" button on the remote and glance over at the mail.

"Regal Loans," I read from the envelope.

"What?" Jason asks.

"Re . . . gal . . . Lo . . . ans," I repeat slower.

"Oh," he says.

"I wonder what this is all about," I say, peeling open the envelope.

"*What?*" He asks.

"Nothing Jason!" I call back.

"Whatever." He says, walking to his bedroom.

I pull out the sheets of paper and find numbers stretched across the page with accumulated interest owed. Oh, this is bad.

I look down at the page and it reads, "Your next payment is due on the 25th of the month for $156.00." I squint back at the numbers. How much?

"My next payment? But I never even had a first one," I say aloud.

"Are you . . . are you talking to yourself?"

I almost jump out of my skin. I look up and Jason is standing directly behind the couch, breathing over me.

"Are you . . . are you talking to yourself?" He repeats again, as if I didn't hear him the first time.

"Yes, and I have to make a phone call," I whisper under my breath.

"What . . . whatever," Jason says and walks back to his bedroom.

At least, I *think* he's going back to his bedroom this time. I glance over the couch to make sure, and that's when I hear his bedroom door close. Good!

Jason is sooo creepy! I mean, I didn't even hear him come out of his bedroom! I'm telling you, this guy is either a stalker, or he's checking up on me to make sure I'm cleaning the kitchen and putting toilet paper in the bathroom!

I hate all those choices! But if I had to choose . . . no, definitely not.

I get up from the couch and grab my phone from the dining room table. I call the 1-800 number shown on the Regal Loans payment form.

I wait as the phone rings. An automated voice comes over the line.

"Please type in your social security number," the voice says slowly.

I do as instructed.

"Thank you. Please type in your date of birth, two digit month, two digit day and four digit year," the voice says.

I type in my birthday.

"Thank you. Please hold and a representative will be with you shortly," the voice announces.

I hear the sounds of classical music playing in the background and then a human voice answers. "Hello, Regal Loan Lenders, how can I help you?"

"Yes, I have a question regarding my—"

"Please provide your name and social security number," the woman says rapidly.

Didn't I already do that? I type in my number one more time and wait, while I hear clicking noises on the other end of the phone.

"Hello, Jennifer, what can I do for you?" She asks politely.

"Hi, yes, um . . . I received a letter in the mail regarding a bill for my student loans. And I'm in AmeriCorps and I was told I don't have to pay for any of this until my term of service ends," I ramble on.

I wait for her to say something and silence falls on the other line.

"Ma'am, it says here," she pauses, "you have a balance of $10,666.00 that needs to be paid off from one of your student loans. We ask that you start your payments as early as possible to avoid additional late payments—"

"But I'm in AmeriCorps! Doesn't that mean I *don't* have to pay back my loans? Can't I postpone my payments?" I inquire.

"You said you're in the Peace Corps?" She asks.

"No, I'm in AmeriCorps," I say.

"The Peace Corps?" She repeats.

"A-mer-i-Corps," I say slowly. Does she not get it?

"And how long have you been in the Peace Corps?" She states.

Oh, for crissakes.

"No, I'm not in the Peace Corps!" I want to yell at this woman!

"So, you're not in the Peace Corps?" She asks with confusion.

"Yes—"

"So, you *are* in the Peace Corps?" She repeats.

Oh. My. God.

"I . . . am . . . not . . . in . . . the . . . Peace Corps." Do you think she understood, now that I'm saying it a hundred times over?

Gosh, I feel like I'm talking to Jason.

"OK, so how can I help you today?" She asks.

Really? Do we have to start *this* part of the conversation over again?

I take a deep breath to calm my nerves. "I would like to request postponement on my student loans," I finally manage to say.

"Are you currently a full time student?" She asks.

Yay, a new question I haven't already answered!

"No." I reply, I graduated two years ago.

"Are you currently working full time?" She continues.

"Well, no." Although come to think of it, Ameri-Corps is a forty hour a week job that pays less than minimum wage. Does that count? "Actually, yes, I do have a full time job." I say at last.

"You do? And what is it, Ma'am?" She inquires.

"I'm in the AmeriCorps Program."

"The America Program? I'm sorry, Ma'am but I'm not familiar with that."

Oh, for crissakes. Not this again.

"No, it's called . . . AmeriCorps." Why is it that everyone knows about the Peace Corps, but no one has heard of AmeriCorps?

"Let me ask you an easier question," she says. "What is your biweekly paycheck?"

Um . . . I start crunching numbers in my head. Well, let's see, I get a little over $4 an hour which is like half of minimum wage, that comes out to about . . . .

I run over to the computer, open up Firefox and quickly type in, www.AmeriCorps.gov. Once the screen appears, I login. I scroll to the side bar and find a link for "view latest earnings." I open the PDF file and scan my last pay stub, it reads, $389.

"Ma'am, are you there?" The woman asks over the phone.

"Yes," I say into the phone. "I'm here." I read off the numbers. "I earn $389 every two weeks."

"Really?" She asks with confusion. "Are you sure that's not every *week*?"

"I'm sure. I'm looking at my last paycheck right now." I glance back to make sure I have the numbers right.

"I'm sorry, Ma'am, but you don't qualify for the economic hardship program."

Come again? Is she saying I earn *too little* to qualify as a hardship case?

"In order to be eligible for economic hardship, you have to be working at least full time with an average income of $560 every two weeks. If you qualify for the economic hardship, you could have your loans deferred for one year."

Wait, she's seriously going to reject me since I earn *less* than minimum wage for a fulltime employee? You've got to be kidding me. Where's the democracy in that?

"But I make less than minimum wage!" I remind her.

"I'm sorry, Ma'am, but there's nothing I can do. It says that you owe—"

I cut her off. "But I'm a volunteer!"

"So you are in the Peace Corps?" She asks surprisingly.

Oh no!

"Ma'am," she inquires, "why didn't you say something? If you're a volunteer, then we can have a form sent to you that will defer your loan payment for one year. All Peace Corps volunteers are eligible."

Perfect! "Yes, I actually am in the Peace Corps. Sorry for the confusion." I say.

"Great! I will make sure we mail out a form to you, and please sign it on the back and have it mailed back to us within two weeks time and the paperwork will be processed."

"Thank you so much." I close the cell phone. Ha! So telling the truth isn't always the best approach with the student loan company or my parents!

Plus, what does it matter if I'm not really in the Peace Corps anyway? Regal Loans will never know! What's the difference?

Well, I mean, the Peace Corps is practically the same thing as AmeriCorps, except, well, I'm not living in another country or surrounded by people who don't speak English, unless you count the illegal Mexicans who live in California, and I haven't learned another language in order to interact with the natives, unless you count my four week course in basic Spanish at the local community college, and I haven't spent 2 years in a volunteer program unless I reapply for AmeriCorps next year.

"Jenn?"

I jump up from the couch and find Jason standing right behind me.

How does Jason do that? Sneak up and scare me like that? I swear, this man is plotting to kill me.

I turn around to look at him. "Yeah, what's up?"

"Are . . . are . . . are you," he stutters, "Are you," he points to the TV. "The TV. You done?"

Come again?

"The TV," he points out. "Are you . . . are you done . . . done using it?" He finally gets it off his chest.

"Oh, I'm not using it. You can have it." That's what he meant!

"Cool," he immediately says before jumping over the couch, and plopping down into the seat next to me.

This couch is *not* made for two people. OK, well, it's made for three, but still, he takes up like half the couch (his smell included).

He plugs in his video game, turns on the TV and starts killing a bunch of zombies.

I never did understand the fun of playing video games, especially the shoot 'em up stuff. I do find it a bit odd and kind of amusing how someone like Jason acts overexcitedly to play video games. It's like he's an impoverished child who's never seen a TV before, or played a video game in his life.

I'm too weirded out by Jason's creepiness so I get up from the couch and walk over to the kitchen. I happen to glance at the clock and realize I'm already running late. Grrr.

I was supposed to be at the high school for tutoring orientation like five minutes ago and it's about a fifteen minute drive to get there!

I quickly pull out a few cookies from the top shelf and throw them in a Ziploc bag. I then grab my purse and stuff my wallet and keys inside and open the front door.

"Jenn! Um, Jenn!" Jason yells from behind.

Really Jason? Now? Do you really think it's a good time? "What?" I call from behind the front door. I try not to sound totally aggravated but come on, I'm already running late. What could he possibly want now? More toilet paper?

"Are you . . . are you going . . . going out . . . to get . . . to get the groceries?"

"No!" I yell back at him, "I have to go now!" I slam the door, race down the stairs and run over to my car.

I get inside, turn up my music, "Power Yoga," and pull out of the parking lot stall.

As I'm backing out of the stall, I look up in my rear view mirror and almost jump out of the front seat.

Jason is standing over the balcony at our two-bedroom apartment staring at me. And he's waving. Why is he waving at me? No, wait, he's not waving, he's gesturing me to come back. Why?

Oh, screw him.

I pull forward, hit the gas pedal and speed out of the lot toward the highway.

Three

I slam the car door and race across the parking lot and head toward the administration building. This school is so confusing. I mean, there's like six different buildings and it's only a high school! I thought I was on a college campus the first time I was here. There's a tall black fence surrounding the campus and police cars patrol the front building.

I swing open the doors to the administration building and almost bump into one of the teachers.

"Excuse me, I'm so sorry." I almost spill his coffee onto the floor.

"Please, do watch where you're going," he says and gives me a nasty glare. He lifts his chin and walks off.

Gosh, I'm really sorry.

I'm a tutor, or well, I guess you could say, I work in the Career Center of the high school. I'm part of the high school program called, "Upward Bound." It's a program to tutor and help high school students during and after school.

I was actually hired by Reading and Beyond and that's how I landed the job with the Upward Bound Program. Apparently, it is a nationwide, well-known program.

Anyway, I'm not the only tutor who works here. Actually, I don't really work here, it's more like I "volunteer" here since the AmeriCorps Program (or rather, the government) pays me to be here.

But the other tutors actually get paid, so they like "work" here for *real*. I'm totally jealous.

As an advisor, I'm scheduled to help students prepare for college, FAFSA and all standardized tests.

I'm almost about to open the door to the Career Center when I realize the door is jammed. I start pulling at the knob.

"What are you doing?" A kid of about five-foot-six and dirty hair stares up at me.

"Um, do you know why the door won't open?" I ask politely.

"Are you stupid?" He shakes his head and walks off.

Wow. Is this how all California students act? So much for getting any help around here.

I keep tugging at the doorknob and glance back at the clock near the secretary's desk by the front entrance. I'm already ten minutes late for my tutoring orientation and I wanted to get here early to set up.

I go around the side to another entrance of the Career Center. I glance into the room through the window in the door. It's filled with computers, tables and chairs for students and tutors. College posters decorate the walls with a collage of colorful signs announcing "Scholarships!" My supervisor's office is near the front of the room.

"Excuse me, miss, can I help you?" An older man of about fifty pokes his head out of the Career Center door.

"Yes, actually, I'm here for my tutoring orientation," I announce.

The man looks at me quizzically. "I'm sorry?"

"I'm the AmeriCorps volunteer here. I'm a tutor, actually I'm—"

"Oh, can you please step back?" He asks, shoving his hands against the door.

"I'm sorry, you see, I was just trying to—"

The man points to a sign next to the door. "My students are doing their AP Testing now. Can you come back later?"

Oh! Now why didn't I see that? It clearly reads, "AP TESTING. DOOR IS TO REMAIN CLOSED AT ALL TIMES."

Wow, now I really feel stupid.

I turn back toward the man to apologize but he's already shut the door in my face. How rude!

I look through the window of the door and I spot the old man taking a seat at one of the student tables in the corner. I'm left standing there in the hallway looking lost.

I decide to walk over to the secretary's counter. Maybe she knows what to do. And where is my supervisor Jackie? I didn't even see her in there! And what about the other tutors? Did everyone get a memo not to show up except me?

"Hello," I say cheerfully looking down at a gray haired woman scribbling something on a notepad.

"How can I help you?" She asks in a drone, not looking up.

"Do you know what's going on in the Career Center today?

"Testing. Don't interrupt."

I'm not sure if she means not to interrupt *her* or the testing going on. She continues concentrating on her notepad, completely absorbed in what she's writing.

"Do you know where I could find Jackie Hernandez?" I decide to ask about my supervisor.

"What? Who?" The secretary finally looks up at me.

Yay, I finally got her attention!

"Jackie Hernandez?" I repeat.

The secretary stares at me like I'm an idiot. What's with California people anyway? I mean, this isn't the first time someone has stared at me like I wasn't worthy of their time.

"Jackie Hernandez, from the Career Center?" I ask again.

"She's a student, right?" The secretary flips through hall passes on her desk. "Were you the young lady who brought me these?" She asks, holding up the hall passes.

I have absolutely no idea what she's talking about. I look up at the clock. I've been here for ten minutes and there is no one here for my tutoring orientation during lunch.

"Hmm," the secretary murmurs.

"Excuse me, when is lunch?" I ask.

"They already had lunch," she looks up at me.

They already *had* lunch?

"What else can I help you with?" She asks.

"I'm looking for Jackie," I say.

"Well, go ask the other secretary. Maybe she can help you." She indicates a desk around the corner.

I thought this woman was *the* secretary! How many are there? Does the other secretary work for this secretary?

"Turn right and her desk is along the wall. You can't miss it," she says, continuing to scribble on her notepad.

I turn away from the counter and walk down the hall to the right. Wow, there really are two secretaries here. I had no idea this high school was this big!

"Hi!" I say as I approach a woman sitting behind a counter with a name card that says, "Karen."

The woman named Karen has long brown hair. She seems friendly. She looks up at me and smiles.

Yay, someone smiled at me!

"Yes, what can I do for you?" Karen asks.

"Hi, I'm looking for Jackie—" I begin.

Karen cuts me off. "Oh, if you're looking for someone than you should ask Susan, the secretary. She knows where everyone is." Karen stands up and leans her head around the corner. "SUSAN!" She yells down the hall.

Oh, this is so embarrassing.

"WHAT?" I hear Susan calling back.

Karen glances at me and points down the hall. "Susan can help you find who you're looking for," Karen says, sitting back down and resumes typing at the computer.

I walk back around the same corner toward Susan's desk. What a coincidence. Susan happens to be the secretary with whom I just spoke.

"Hi, I was told you could help me," I say to Susan, wondering if she's done writing on her notepad.

Susan doesn't even bother looking up at me.

"I'm really sorry to bother you again," I say, "but I really need to find my supervisor, Jackie Hernandez." There's a long silence while I wait for her to speak.

"I told you, I don't know anyone named Jackie," Susan says, still writing on her notepad.

Do these California people give everyone a hard time or just with Michigan people?

"So, you don't know Jacqueline Hernandez?" I ask, feeling more like a prosecuting attorney in a courtroom.

"Jacqueline?" Susan jerks her head up and raises her brow as if hearing the name for the first time. "Did you say, Jacqueline? Jacqueline Hernandez?"

"Yes, that's her!" I exclaim, relieved we have communicated in English. "Do you know where I could find her?"

Honestly, what's the difference between *Jackie* and *Jacqueline*?

"Why didn't you just say you were looking for her?" Susan snaps.

"Well, I did—"

She cuts me off. "Jacqueline is out for the day, unfortunately," Susan says. "Did you need to leave a message for her? If so, than Karen can help you with that."

Susan immediately punches in a number on the desk phone and calls Karen.

"Karen, I have a young woman, oh wait, yes, that's right, you just met her. Well I can send her over to you."

Susan clicks some buttons and hangs up the phone. "Karen will see you now."

Wait, what? I feel like everything is happening too fast. I must be in one of those movies where I keep seeing the same two people over and over again.

"I'm sorry, I actually don't need to leave a message for Jackie. I was just wondering where she was, that's all."

"Jacqueline's home sick. She'll be back in tomorrow," Susan says.

I realize I've been leaning against her counter just pondering to myself. "What time does school get it?" I ask, trying to appear nonchalant.

"Didn't you see the schedule this morning?" Susan points to a bulletin board filled with many typed sheets of paper.

I try squinting to see the postings, but the words are too small. Or maybe I just need new eyeglasses. Or maybe I just don't want to look like an idiot since I'm not sure which posting is the schedule.

"Do you know when tutoring will resume?" I ask, knowing I will never find it among the postings.

"Have you talked to Jacqueline? Isn't she in charge of tutoring for the students?" Susan asks still glaring at me.

I don't get these people. How can I talk with Jackie if I can't even find Jackie, let alone, contact her, and if I could, then why would I be standing here asking Susan about her? I mean, come on!

"Is that *all*?" Susan states her question like an answer meaning, *no more questions.*

"Well, thanks," I say, racing out the front doors.

Note to self: I probably should make a point of never interrupting Susan again. Ever.

I don't like these California people and I haven't even started my new job yet. The student called me stupid when the door wouldn't open. The old dude slammed the door in my face. The secretaries bounced me back and forth like a volleyball. None of the other tutors showed up and it's like everyone else knew today's *mystery* schedule, except me.

I go out to the parking lot and sit lazily in my car, with the seatbelt strapped around my waist. I'm feeling really alone. I grab a Kleenex from the backseat and flip the mirror down by my face and wipe my tears.

I look out of the driver's side window and see three male students staring at me and pointing. They're leaning against one of the trees by the sidewalk.

Wait a second! Are they in the Upward Bound Program and they're—wait, wait a minute. Are they looking for me?

Oh, my God! They're laughing at me! They're elbowing each other and laughing! I glance at my face in the mirror. My eyes and nose are red and puffy. Can they see I'm crying?

This is so humiliating! I'm just this sad, pathetic, Michigan girl who cries about everything. What if they tell the other tutors, or worse, what if they tell Jackie?

I immediately put the keys in the ignition and pull out. I race out of that parking lot as fast as I can, hoping there're no police cars nearby.

I glance in my rear view mirror and luckily no one's behind me. I pull out onto the road from the parking lot and head straight toward the highway where I can go home and curl up on my warm mattress and have a good cry.

As I pass by the intersection, I notice a series of orange construction signs on the right that read, "Survey Crew" and "Be Prepared to Stop."

I glance at the car in front of me and they start to slow down. I look around and notice everyone is merging into one lane. I see another sign to my left, "Survey Crew." I don't get it. What's a "Survey Crew?"

There's a construction worker to my left dressed in slacks and wearing a green neon vest and waving the cars, indicating for them to move over to the left side.

I glance to my right and spot a pickup truck resting on some weird vehicle platform lifted up about three feet in the air. And there's a parked police car behind him.

I start to follow the car in front of me. Just as I'm about to get into the left lane, the worker in the neon vest puts his hand out in front of me, motioning for me to stop.

Oh, come on! Can't I just go home and cry?

He indicates for me to pull over to the righthand side. I do, watching the cars behind me pass by. I look in my rear view mirror and a police car pulls up behind me!

Oh shoot! I was at the DMV the other day, but I didn't have time to apply for a California driver's license! I was picking something up for a friend and I totally forgot to come back!

Surely, there must be tons of college students in California from out of state who forget to apply. Do the police know I don't actually have a California driver's license?

I see a police officer walking over to my car. Yikes! I'm going to Jail! I know it. I start crying, the tears spilling down my cheeks, again.

I grab my cell phone from my purse and start dialing Mom in Michigan but I hear a loud tapping at my car window. I jerk up, dropping my phone. Oh no!

I can't look, it's too unbearable! It's the police! Oh, no! Please, go away, leave me alone! I don't want to go to Jail today unless they give me a laptop and an internet connection!

I hear another tapping at the window and I look up, tears filling my eyes. I roll my window down and the officer stares down at me with his black visor and cop hat.

"Excuse me, Ma'am?" The officer asks.

Shoot! "Yes, sir?" I try to sound overly polite.

"Are you a legal resident of California?" He asks seriously.

No, I'm not.

Actually, yes, officer I am. You see, I've been living here for several months but I just got too lazy to stop off at

the DMV and get my California driver's license. You know
how it is . . . right?

"Yes, I'm a legal resident of California." Why did I
just lie to the police? Now I'll have to show my California
driver's license and I only have my Michigan driver's license.
I'm *sooo* going to Jail.

"Ma'am, we're doing a survey here and if you
wouldn't mind, we'd like to ask you a few questions."

"Um, sure, why not!" Really? Since when do police
pull cars over for a *survey?* I thought their job was to issue
tickets and make people cry.

"If you could please pull over here," the officer says,
twirling around, yelling at a construction worker across the
road. "Oh, all right, thanks, Jim." The officer looks back at
me. "Ma'am, are you aware you're driving with a Michigan
license plate?"

I start sobbing silently, feeling the tears trickling down
my face. I'm going straight to *Jail.*

"Ma'am, are you all right?" The officer asks me.

Does he feel sorry for me?

I look down at my feet. "Yes, I'm aware I have
Michigan plates." I think I'm going to die. Just cremate me
now.

"Well I'm sorry Ma'am, but—"

My life flashes before me. I'll end up in Jail. I'll be the
butch of a bitch, no, I mean the bitch of a butch! Nobody
will visit me! I'll lose all my friends! Adrian will break up with
me if I'm someone else's bitch! Jason will be upset when he
has to find a replacement woman to buy his groceries and
refill the toilet paper holder.

"Ma'am, you're free to go," the officer says.

"Really?" Wait, what? So I'm not going to Jail and I
don't have to give up the internet or be someone's bitch?

"Ma'am, we can't survey your car since you have Michigan license plates. Thank you for your time and have a nice day." The officer waves me forward.

I pull out and merge with the other cars and head toward the highway. Yay, I'm not going to Jail! I can have my own laptop and internet and my friends back and Adrian will still love me! Yay the world is my oyster.

I catch up to the cars in front of me and merge onto the highway. It's packed. Every highway out here in Fresno has at least four lanes in each direction, crammed with cars, trucks, semi-trucks, and SUV's.

As I merge into a lane, I catch a glimpse of the mountains in the background. Wow. The view is gorgeous. It's absolutely breathtaking.

I merge into another lane to get a better view of the mountains. I see brown mountain tops with a hint of snow peaking out of the clouds. The mountains are far away, yet they look so close, I feel like I could reach out and touch them—

HONK

"Hey, watch it!" I yell, except nobody can hear me with my windows rolled up.

The driver passes me and gives me the middle finger, indicating *up yours.*

What's his problem? And why can't he let me enjoy the beautiful view of the mountains?

I absolutely love telling people I live in California, they get a thrill out of it, well, until of course they finally ask me the dreaded question, "So, where in Los Angeles are you living?"

Come on! Does everyone think "Los Angeles" is spread over the entire state when you say you live in California? Actually, yes, considering, most of the time it's my friends, neighbors, or family members from Michigan.

I guess it's assumed that I live in the "awesome-but-too much-pollution" city, rather than the "I've-never-heard-of-that-city" called *Fresno.* Apparently Fresno isn't as popular as the natives think. And this is the point where the conversation usually dies. After all, if you don't live in Los Angeles, why are you still talking?

I glance out my side car window and take notice again of the mountains. It's so weird being out here. I guess it's because I'm used to the flat farmland of Michigan, the cold weather, and the road construction. Yes, definitely the road construction. And why is that?

California is so different than Michigan. I like the mountains. This is a good change for me. I like living out here on my own. Oh crap—and then I realize I'm about to miss my exit and it's four lanes away. Who decided to make four lane highways, anyway? Are they trying to kill us, in case we don't make it to our exit in time? This is total suicide!

I look out of my rear view window and hit the accelerator. I speed up to pass the cars in front of me and merge into the next lane over. I can hear the honking of cars coming from behind. I just ignore them and merge again into the next right lane.

"Hey, watch it lady!" A man cries out, throwing his left arm out the window.

I wave back at him but it looks more like a limp "hello from Michigan" rather than a, "sorry." He zooms up from behind and glares over at me. He spits out of the window, and then speeds up past me.

Did he notice I had Michigan plates? This is exactly why I hate driving on the California highways! What is wrong with these people? Just because I don't have California license plates, and I do plan on buying them . . . eventually, they assume Midwestern people can't drive, at least I'm assuming they assume this.

I merge into the far outside lane on the right, with sweeping grace, I might add. I smile out of my rear view mirror, since you see, Midwestern people are pleasant and friendly drivers. I catch a glimpse of the woman driving behind me. As she glares at me, I smile wide. Ha!

I finally swerve over just as my exit approaches. Thank goodness! Except I can't help feeling stressed. I've lived in Michigan all my life and I've never seen four lane highways. OK, wait, that's a lie, I think Detroit might have one or two. But, who's counting? Anyway, I just want to make it home without dying . . . or going to Jail.

Four

When I arrive back at the apartment, I find Adrian cooking stir fry in the kitchen. He looks cute, standing over the stove making dinner. I've been teaching him how to cook on the stove. When I first met him, he ate only fast food, yeah, I know, right?

So I changed him to a much healthier diet! Yay!

Although Adrian's not your average kind of guy, he doesn't wear designer clothes. He's not like a model or anything. He often wears black except I've been trying to get him into more colorful clothes, like the other day, I bought him a navy blue shirt and khaki shorts. He looked fantastic and I told him how handsome he was in that outfit.

I think he's adorable with his light brown hair, blue eyes and reddish beard, and he's willing to let me help him lose a few pounds. Either way, I've been trying to teach him how to live a healthy lifestyle. Since we met, he hasn't eaten fast food once!

"Hey, you're home early," Adrian says.

I rush up to him in the kitchen and give him a great big hug and kiss.

"I missed you today," he says.

I smell the peppers, onions and mushrooms cooking and say, "Hmm, delicious."

"I thought you would like this. I got everything from the Whole Foods store," he says, placing the spoon to the side and pulling me in for another great kiss.

We totally eat only organic food. I mean, who wants to eat antibodies that make you fat anyway? Actually, I'm not really sure if antibodies actually *do* make you fat, I just heard that from one of the passengers who sat next to me on my flight to California. She was from Australia and said the reason why Americans are fat is because they mainly eat foods with antibodies. Hmm, I should really look into that, I mean, what if it's true?

"What's that *smell?*" We turn around and find Jason coming into the kitchen with a can of beer in his hand. "It smells funny in here." Jason says.

"It's stir fry man, you want some?" Adrian asks, gesturing to the pot.

Jason gives him a confused look. "Wait," he says, and looks from me to Adrian. "Isn't Jenn making *you* dinner?"

I'm WHAT?

"I thought . . . I thought she . . . she makes . . . makes dinner for you," Jason says, grabbing a frozen burger out of the refrigerator.

"Nah, not today. I'm making stir fry for Jenn," Adrian says and winks over at me.

"Um . . . why?" Jason asks.

Honestly, how does Jason have the balls to ask these questions? I mean, I'm like *right here!*

Adrian just ignores Jason and keeps stirring the vegetables. He knows I can't put up with Jason, but he plays along.

I mean, Jason is like his best friend (unfortunately) and I'm like his girlfriend (fortunately). Although I should add that Adrian and I are tight, we're like best friends, not just your average infatuated couple.

"Is . . . is she . . . is she making . . . making dinner to-morrow?" Jason blurts out.

Can you believe this guy? Where did Adrian find this loser?

I'm starting to think this whole Asperger's Syndrome with Jason might be true! It's such a better excuse than claiming he's a "male chauvinist," right?

I decide to ignore Jason's rude remarks and proceed to set the table. I grab a few forks, plates and placemats.

"I'm . . . I'm going to . . . to make my own lunch," Jason finally says, throwing the frozen burger in the micro-wave.

I walk into the living room to set our plates down on the coffee table. Adrian and I have this ritual where we always watch TV and eat dinner or lunch together. Although, we've promised each other that when we're married, (yes, we've al-ready talked about marriage), we really are going to try to use the dining room table. For now, the dining room table is the place to throw boxes and backpacks.

We're not like the hoarders on TV or anything, and although I've watched that show several times, I will never let my house get that messy! I feel so bad for hoarders. I mean it's not their fault they suck at cleaning, right?

"Um . . . um . . . Jenn?"

Now what does he want?

"Is this . . . is this your cake?" Jason asks, holding up my delicious German chocolate cake I bought at the store yesterday.

Wait a second, did he just take that out of the fridge without my permission? That's my cake! Not his! I haven't even had a chance to open it and taste it!

"It's my cake. Why?" I ask, hoping he's not going to eat it. The last time I bought a cake, he ate half of it without asking me! Not again!

"Can I . . . can I eat a piece?" Jason asks.

No! "Um . . . " I'm not really sure what to say. He's leaning over the cake stuffing himself with a half frozen burger he nuked in the microwave. Gross. I can't help eyeing all his burger crumbs falling on the cake.

I know I shouldn't care how he eats, but why does he have to spoil my chocolate cake? Can he please sit down and eat like a normal person? And how can he buy such crap? I mean, bulk frozen burgers from a box at Costco and nuked in the microwave? It's like the box would almost taste better. I'm so organic, it's like disgusting! Except I'm not vegan! Ew! I could never do that to my body, I absolutely love Milk! Wait, do vegan's drink milk? Or is that vegetarians?

"So, um . . . I'm . . . I'm going to . . . going to take a piece of cake, OK?" Jason says.

NO!

I feel completely ignored.

"Stop!" I say as he starts slicing a piece of cake and putting it on his plate. No, Jason! Bad boy. If I treat him like a dog, do you think he would listen?

This is typical Jason. He will literally eat all the food he finds. That's the one drawback about having him as a roommate. If I say "no," he gets pissed and defensive and whines like a baby, which might or might not be the Asperger's, and then complains to Adrian, who complains to me, and the cycle continues.

Adrian hates being in the middle of my arguments with Jason and I don't blame him for it. But hey, if we're dealing with a male chauvinist here, which I believe we are, then Adrian has to be in the middle of everything! As far as I'm concerned, the words of a woman mean absolutely nothing to Jason.

"Jenn, food's done." Adrian calls out from the kitchen.

"OK, what do you want to watch? Supernatural or Nip/Tuck?" I ask, looking up at the DVD shelf where all our movies are stored.

"Anything you want. Your pick," Adrian says.

I grab the last season of Nip/Tuck and place the first disc in the DVD player. Just as I'm about to hit the play button, the doorbell rings.

That's odd. No one ever rings our doorbell, except . . . well, no one does, actually.

"I'll get it." I rush over to the front door and look through the peephole. I instantly recognize Brad, who's a good friend of both Jason and Adrian. "Hey Brad, come on in," I say as I open the door. Brad is a short, stocky Asian student studying business.

Brad looks at me and smiles, carrying two huge sacks. He looks over to Jason and then Adrian. "What's up guys?" He puts one sack on the dining room table and tosses the orange sack to Jason.

"What's this?" Jason asks, looking through the sack.

"It's all the video games I bought yesterday after my school exam," Brad says.

"So you're done with finals, then?" I ask, but Brad either ignores me or doesn't hear me. I leave Brad and Jason talking near the dining room table.

"Shit . . . Final Fantasy? Awesome." Jason holds up one of the video games from the orange sack.

"Are you giving those to us?" Adrian asks.

"No way, I just came over to show you the new games. By the way, I'm flunking all my classes except one." Brad announces taking a seat next to Jason at the dining room table. He whips out his new PSP.

"Shit, you got a PSP?" Jason asks, pulling the PSP out of Brad's hand.

"Wait, did you just say you're flunking all your classes?" Adrian asks, placing our food on the plastic plates.

"Yeah, I totally went out and celebrated and bought all these cool games. Isn't it awesome?" Brad says, grabbing the other sack from the floor and dumping out all his video games.

I wonder where this guy even gets his money. Adrian told me Brad still lives at his mom's and he doesn't even have a job, or a girlfriend. Isn't that sad?

Adrian walks over to the living room couch and hands me a plate of food.

"It looks delicious, Adrian. Thank you so much for making this," I say, blowing him a hug.

"Well Jenn, I hope you like it." Adrian says, taking a seat on the couch. He turns around toward Brad. "Hey, Brad, you mind if Jenn and I watch a DVD?"

"What are you going to watch?" Brad asks, taking a seat in an armchair.

"Hey man, why don't we play one of your games?" Jason asks Brad as he walks over to the living room carrying a few video games in his hand.

"Dude," Adrian looks over at Jason. "Jenn and I were about to eat dinner and watch some TV."

"Well, why can't you wait till we're done?" Jason asks.

Am I the only one who has noticed Jason hasn't stuttered one word? Isn't this suspicious?

"Jason, come on!" Adrian says, starting up Nip/Tuck.

"Let's just watch some of it, Jason." Brad says, turning his attention toward the TV.

"Well there's no room in here." Jason says, looking around the living room.

Jason jumps over the couch and takes the seat right between Adrian and me, which was the only empty spot on the couch, well that, or the floor, which I might add, has lots of space for him *and* his ego.

I'm seriously going to kill Jason.

He never "gets it" sometimes. I can't figure him out and this is why I always get pissed at the things he does. But Adrian keeps telling me it's an Asperger's Syndrome thing. Whatever. I think Jason enjoys being a jerk.

"Dude, you mind?" Adrian nudges Jason and gives him a disgusted look.

Jason grunts and gets up. "Fine." He turns to Brad. "Hey, Brad, you want to chill in my room for the time being?" Brad nods, and they both go to Jason's bedroom, slamming the door shut behind them.

Again, Jason just spoke an entire sentence without stuttering . . . I'm on to him!

"Thanks, Adrian. I was about to hurt him." I say half jokingly.

"Don't worry, Jenn. Let's just forget about it." Adrian says, massaging my back.

Adrian starts up one of the episodes and we both sit there enjoying our delicious stir fry meal and watching Nip/Tuck, without anyone bothering us, for the time being that is. I compliment Adrian on what a fine cook he's becoming.

Later that evening, Adrian and I do our own thing. I'm sitting in the living room reading one of my favorite books from the library while Adrian edits wrestling videos on his computer in the bedroom.

"Oh, no! Oh no!" Adrian calls from the bedroom.

I get up from lying down on the couch and fold my book facedown on the couch. "What's wrong?"

"Jenn, I have a turd coming!" Adrian calls out.

I laugh. He's so hysterical sometimes. Adrian races down the hallway and looks over at me holding his hands over his butt.

"Adrian, why are you doing that?" I ask.

"I really have to *poop* and Jason's in the bathroom." Adrian says.

I immediately erupt with laughter. That's when I hear the sound of running water and the shower being turned on. "Oh, sorry sweetie, looks like you'll have to wait until Jason's done," I snicker.

"Jenn, you don't understand. It's coming whether I'm on the toilet or not. I'm *prairie dogging!*" He says desperately.

"Adrian, I don't need to know that!" I say, clasping my hand over my mouth.

"Damn!" Adrian says and rushes back to the bedroom. He scrunches down hard in the chair at the computer trying to hold it in and says, "Come and watch my wrestling videos, then."

I follow Adrian into the bedroom and take a seat by the computer as he opens up the video program Final Cut Pro.

"Dude, when are you going to teach me this program?" I ask, knowing full well he's offered to teach me several times but I've just been too lazy to find the time.

"Check this out," he says, launching the QuickTime player from the desktop and opens one of his wrestling videos. "Tell me what you think of it."

I watch it for about two minutes until it starts to repeat itself.

He turns to me. "Well? What do you think?"

Adrian is a videographer, or a video expert on making wrestling videos. He films, edits, and burns copies for the wrestlers. Ever since we started dating about a year ago, he's asked for my help to make short text animations for wrestling videos. I've even taught him some basic Photoshop techniques.

"Jenn, you're not saying anything? So I guess that means the video sucks." He looks back to his computer screen and minimizes the video.

"No, it wasn't bad, Adrian. It was actually really good and I know you spent a lot of time on it."

He cuts me off. "You hate it, don't you?"

"Honestly, it just needs a bit more graphics, that's all. But the video stuff is really good, the angles are cool." I smile at him and lean over, giving him a big hug of reassurance. "Let me see the other videos."

"Really?" He looks at me with surprise.

"Sure." I say, wondering how many more video clips I can stand to watch of wrestlers slapping and knocking each other down.

Adrian opens twenty wrestling clips in rapid succession in QuickTime, and I realize we're going to be here a long time.

After thirty minutes of watching Adrian's wrestling clips and giving him feedback, I realize he's thrilled watching them again, even though they all look the same to me. But I told him they looked really good, which they did, for a person who likes watching wrestling.

Adrian's job filming began a couple of years back when he was hired by the local wrestling company to be their videographer. For the most part, I think he enjoys it but sometimes it can be stressful.

"Oh God," I say, bending over in the chair, placing my hand against my belly.

"Are you OK?" Adrian asks, looking down at me.

"My stomach . . . oh . . . God . . . it hurts." My stomach all of sudden just shot massive pains throughout my body. I feel nauseous. I think I'm going to be sick. "I need to use the bathroom. Take me to the bathroom, Adrian. Please," I say desperately trying to get up. "I think I have to *poop*."

"Uh, Jenn, I have some bad news." Adrian says, helping me up from the chair. "I still hear the shower running."

"You what?" I look up in horror at him, still bending over. "You mean to tell me, Jason's *still* in there? But it's been over a half hour!"

"I know, let me go knock on the door." Adrian says, letting go of my hand and rushing over to the bathroom door. Adrian pounds the door frantically. "Hey, Jason. You almost done?"

The shower keeps running but I don't hear Jason's voice.

"Jason, hey, you in there?" Adrian pounds again, this time even louder.

But I don't hear any response from Jason.

Adrian comes back into the bedroom. "Shit, he's not even answering."

"Why don't you just bang the door down, then! That'll get his attention!" I say.

"Because I don't want to go in there and see him naked!" Adrian says, rushing over and helping me lay down on the mattress.

"Ew, please do not give me visuals!" I moan, but I can't help asking myself, what *is* Jason doing in there? I don't want to think about it . . . I don't want to think about it . . . but come on, I don't even take a shower that long! I mean, there is only so much you can wash—

Wait, wait a second. Is he . . . ? Oh. Dear. God.

"ADRIAN!" I yell.

"I'm right here." Adrian says, lying next to me on the mattress. "What is it?"

"I think Jason's whacking off in the shower." I want to curl up and die at the thought.

"Well, so what?" Adrian shrugs.

I playfully hit Adrian on the arm. So what? SO WHAT? "Adrian." I look him in the eye. "Do you realize how creepy it is? I mean, think about it."

"Let me go knock one more time." Adrian gets up from the mattress and walks over to the bathroom door, pounding louder. "Hey Jason—"

"Yeah, I'm coming out." Jason says as he finally turns off the water.

Within a few minutes, Jason opens the door to the bathroom, with a towel draped around his waist. "I'm done," he says and strolls into his bedroom, slamming the door behind him.

"Thank God." I rush over to the bathroom and before I can poop, Adrian beats me to the toilet. "Oh, come on!" I whine.

"Hey, I've had to hold it for longer," Adrian says and closes the bathroom door.

"Father is calling. Father is calling." Oh no, there goes my ringtone. My cell phone! I race back to the bedroom, and grab my cell phone.

"Hello?" I ask.

"Hi, honey. I miss you." It's Dad. "When are you coming back home for a visit?"

Do we have to talk about this now? I really have to poop.

"Dad, can I call you back?"

"Oh Jenn, I'm hurt. After a long day at work, I thought I'd give you a call, and now you just want to get me off the phone? Honey, that's really not very nice."

"Dad—"

"I was going to ask when you were coming home Jennifer, but now . . . well, I guess you don't have time to talk to your Dad."

"Dad," my voice just got higher, that was weird. "Look, I really have to go, but I can totally call you back in like five—" I hear the toilet flush.

"Jenn! I'm done!" Adrian calls from the bathroom.

"Jennifer," my father says into the phone. "When are you going to meet Barbara? And have you heard from your mother—?"

I flip the phone shut and the call ends. I run over to the bathroom and slam the door shut. I hope Dad forgives me just this once for hanging up on him.

"Um . . . hello?" I hear a guy's voice outside the bathroom door.

You have to be kidding me. I just got in here.

The voice answers, "I . . . I need . . . I need to use the bathroom."

I know that voice and I hate that voice. I hear more knocking.

The voice asks again, "Are . . . are you done?"

"No! Go away!" I yell at the voice. Can't I have some piss and quiet? Peez?

"Are . . . are you . . . are you done yet?" The guy's voice yells over the hum of the bathroom fan.

I get up from the toilet, run over and open the bathroom door and I'm staring directly . . . at Adrian? "What the hell are you doing?"

"I thought I would mess with you." Adrian laughs.

"That was *you?*" I hit him playfully in the arm. "I thought you were Jason!"

Adrian laughs and darts away, running around the living room and I realize my pants are still down, and start chasing after him, around the couch and dining room table.

"Damn it, stay where you are, I'm so going to kill you!" I say tripping over my pants, but Adrian heads straight for the bedroom.

I race after him and finally catch him at the door and tackle him to the floor, pulling him near the mattress. I tickle him and he puts me in a wrestling hold that I can't get out of.

"Ha! Looks like I won," he says, cuffing my right leg in both his hands.

"Not for long!" I try weaseling my way out but can't.

"I've put you in a hold, stop trying to get out, you can't." He says and finally lets go of my leg. He wraps me around his body and starts kissing me.

I instantly grab his crotch and squeeze him tighter, pushing my tongue through his mouth. We start French kissing and it's wonderful, so romantic and exotic. I almost forgot we even left the door open!

"The door!" Adrian says. He quickly gets up, slams the bedroom door and jumps back on the mattress, grabbing my shirt and ripping it off. He pulls me in closer and kisses my neck as I peel off his clothes.

It just couldn't get any better than this.

Five

It's time for a visit to the DMV, the Department of Motor Vehicles. I've been dreading this moment for the past few months. I'm such a procrastinator. But honestly, after that "Survey Crew" incident and getting pulled over by the cop, I was so freaked out that now I really think I should get my California ID card.

I park in one of the few empty parking spots in front of the DMV and walk toward the front door.

On second thought, where is the front door? I look back and forth but I don't see a "DMV Welcome" sign. Hmm . . . is this the right place or not? I look around and find a black woman with tight purple pants and a red shirt chain smoking and leaning against a gray building. There are a few Mexican teenagers exchanging cigarette packs on the corner. Where am I?

"Pardon me," I say, walking up to the black woman smoking a left and right cigarette lodged in between missing front teeth.

She scans me top to bottom. "What up, girl?" She lisps.

"Do you know where I can find the DMV office?"

"Yeah. Look behind you," she says with bouncing cigarettes.

I turn around. It's just an empty parking lot. What is she talking about?

"Girl, turn around," she says and points toward a large gray building directly behind her.

"Sorry. I guess I didn't see a sign."

"That's because those fuckerth don't have signs. Thons of bitches. They kicked me outta there." She motions toward the DMV building. "That's right," she says, shaking her head, Those thons of bitches are mean animals. They can go straight to hell."

"Without collecting $200," I say. The woman gives me a really weird look. OK, so I guess the Monopoly joke doesn't work on everyone.

"What did you say?" The black woman asks with a confused look.

"Oh . . . oh, nothing." I say, blushing.

"Whatever." She looks away and resumes smoking.

I spot a thin, young man with straight black hair in a nice gray suit walking toward two sets of doors off to my left. I follow him down a small alleyway until he reaches a set of doors to his right. I follow him inside and eventually find myself in a large open room filled with over a hundred people.

The air is smelly and the noise is filled with children running around laughing and people coughing and blowing their noses.

In the middle of the room is a squared off section with small countertops placed every few feet from each other. Each countertop has a number placed next to it and there are at least three dozen chairs in exact rows on either side of the room.

Televisions mounted from the ceiling broadcast three digit numbers indicated in red and a one digit number listed next to it. I glance in front of me and find a line extending to one side of the room.

Oh great. Is that the line to get in for just getting a California ID? I look at my watch. I have two hours and that's it. The meeting at the high school starts at 2PM.

I get in line behind an overweight woman wearing tight, stretchy black pants and a blue top. As I stare at her hair, I notice a large snake tattooed on the back of her neck, and it seems to wind down her back.

"Next." I hear someone at the counter say.

I count the people ahead of me. I'm number twenty in line? Geez. This could take awhile.

Nearly thirty minutes later, I reach the counter. Finally!

"How can I help you?" A white haired woman asks from behind the counter.

"I'm here to get—"

"We're only taking applications right now for California driver licenses, ID's, license plates and tags."

"Great. I need—"

"Which one are you here for?" She interrupts.

Well, if she would just let me speak, I could tell her!

"I'm here to get—"

"Your California driver's license?" She asks.

"No—"

"Well?" She asks impatiently.

"I'm here to get my California ID!" I say.

"OK." The woman grabs an application from behind the counter and sticks it under a clipboard. "Here. Fill this out and wait for your number to be called." She hands me a pen and a number, imprinted on plastic with red lettering.

I glance around the room, looking for an empty seat anywhere. I walk over to the right and all the seats are taken. I walk around the other side of the room and I spot two empty seats in the corner. Perfect.

I rush over to one of the empty seats and put my purse on the ground. I start filling out the application, which only consists of two pages. This seems easy enough.

"Is that seat taken?" A middle age Mexican man asks.

I look up. "Oh, nope, I don't think so."

He smiles at me and takes the seat. "So, what's your name?" He inquires, leaning closer to me.

I really need to fill out this form. Why is he distracting me?

I look up at one of the television monitors dangling from a pole near my seat. I look at all the red numbers indicated on the screen. Unfortunately my number isn't listed yet. How long can it possibly take?

"So, are you a student at Fresno State University?" The man asks.

I look at him and he smiles . . . a bit too wide with some teeth missing.

"I'm Pablo. What's your name?" He asks.

I glance back at my application. I have to ignore him and finish this darn application before they call my number!

"I like your hair," he says.

OK, now he's just getting creepy.

"I have a son, he's about your age. You might like him."

OK, this guy is sooo creeping me out! Police! Help! An illegal Mexican is trying to lure me into his van and I bet he plans to force me to marry his son!

I grab my purse and get up from the seat and walk over to the other side of the room. I will not be seduced . . . in public with a middle aged man or his son.

I finally find an empty seat next to a young girl who looks around my age. She seems safe to sit next to. I take a seat next to her in the front row. I pull out the pen and finish the application.

When I'm finally done, I look up at the television monitor. Ah ha! I see my number across the screen. I get up from my seat.

Oh wait, what counter do I go to? I walk back over to the television and look across the screen to another number "6." Counter 6. I look at the countertops in front of me, "7 . . . 8 . . . " I'm not on this side. I walk over to the other side, "1 . . . 2 . . . 3 . . . " where is number 6?

"Ruben? Ruben Jennifer?" I hear my name being called. I see a man of about thirty wearing an Army uniform and dog tags. His head is shaved and his skin is lightly tanned and he has enormous muscles. He's standing behind one of the counters, waving his hand up in the air.

"I'm Jenn Ruben." I say as I walk up to the Army guy.

"You're Ruben, correct?" He asks.

"That's me." I smile politely.

He grabs the application out of my hand and scans it over.

"You're getting your California driver's license." He says as if it were a comment, not a question.

"Um . . . actually, no." I say.

He looks up at me. "What did you say?"

"No, I'm not. I'm getting my—"

He puts his hand up. "Stop right there."

Huh?

"Do you have a California driver's license?" He asks.

Isn't that why I'm here? "No." I say.

"Are you going to apply for one today?" He asks.

"No." I say again.

He shoves the application back in my face. "I can't process your application today. Come back another time," he says.

Huh?

"I'm sorry, maybe you didn't hear me. I said, come back another time," he says sternly, shooing me away.

Can he do this?

"Martinez, Eduardo." The Army guy yells out and a young man walks up to the counter and cuts in front of me.

"Excuse me," I say, pushing the young Mexican guy out of my way. "I would like to get my ID today please." I tell the Army guy.

"I said, 'No,'" he says impatiently.

Can he actually deny me my legal right to get an ID? "But I need one. Otherwise I'm going to get pulled over by the cops." I say.

"That's not my problem, lady," he says.

I slam my clipboard down on the countertop. "I filled out my application and I want my ID, *now.*" I demand.

He hesitates for a second. Then he grabs my application and rips it off the clipboard, almost tearing it in half. He looks really angry. "Fine. Wait here."

I look over at Eduardo and I smile lamely. He grunts and takes a seat back down in the corner. He can wait his turn. I was here first.

"Jennifer." The Army guy walks back toward the counter and throws, literally throws, a California driver's pamphlet at me.

"Thank you."

"You must read this." He flips open the pamphlet and points down at the page. "See this?" He asks.

I look over at what he's pointing at. Which paragraph is he talking about?

"Do you see this?" He asks, sounding upset. Is he getting angry with me?

"Sure," I say politely, trying not to make him angry.

He pulls out a yellow highlighter from a top drawer and circles one of the paragraphs in the pamphlet. "Read it."

I look up at him. "Now?"

"What?" He asks.

"Do you want me to read—"

He slams his finger down on the page. "Read it *now.*"

OK, now I'm feeling a little intimidated.

"Did you read it?" He asks even more impatiently.

I skim the paragraph quickly. It says something about getting a California driver's license after so many days of living in this state. I'll read the rest later.

"Do you know what it means?" He points down at the paragraph.

"Yes," I say.

"Do you know what it *means*?" He repeats himself.

Does he think I'm hard of hearing?

"Yes, I do," I say.

"What does it mean?" He asks.

Is he challenging me? At the DMV? I just want my ID card!

"It means that . . . " I glance down at the paragraph and start rereading through it again.

He slams the pamphlet shut in my face. "It means that after I process your California ID card, you have ten days to get a California driver's license."

"Sounds good," I say but my answer sounds a bit sarcastic.

He stares directly at me, looking very angry. Is he that tan or is that smoke pouring out of his ears?

"OK, thanks." I say, trying to grab the pamphlet out of his hand.

He throws the pamphlet at me. "So, after I process your ID card today, what are you going to do ten days from now?"

I feel like I'm the bad child and he's the parent.

"I said . . . what are you going to do ten days from now?" He persists.

Shit . . . I'm really scared of this guy. "I'm going to get a driver's license?"

"What kind of driver's license?" He tests me.

What *kind?* There's more than one? Is this a trick question?

"I don't know." I finally say.

"You don't know?" He asks angrily. "This is why you need to read the pamphlet."

Is this how all DMV employees treat people?

"You remind of all the college kids who come in here, asking for their ID cards. They apply to get a California ID card and then they never come back." He leans forward in my face menacingly and adds, "They never obtain their California driver's license. That's the kind of license you need to drive in California."

"Right," I say cautiously. I know that!

"Are you going to be that silly, college kid who gets pulled over for drinking or smoking crack?" He asks.

What?

"Are you going to be one of those college kids who's going to drive without a California driver's license? Are you—"

"No, sir. I'm not," I say, feeling my body shaking. He's scaring me. Really scaring me.

"You stupid college kids," he says, shaking his head.

"Actually, I'm not a college student. I'm a volunteer. I'm with AmeriCorps and I'm going to get my California driver's license as soon as possible. I promise." I say, trying to calm the situation.

He leans in further and looks me in the eye. "As soon as possible?"

"I mean . . ." I quickly change my words. "I'm going to get my driver's license ten days from now . . . or sooner!" I say.

He slams his fist on the pamphlet. "You will get your license in the next ten days," he orders. He signs the bottom of the application and slides it over to me. "Go to counter one. She'll take your picture." He says, pointing over to the other side of the room.

Finally!

"Next. Johnson, Sheila," he calls out another victim to interrogate.

I quickly grab my application and hurry over to counter one. I really want to get out of here.

After I finish with pictures, the lady behind the counter tells me I will receive my California ID in the mail in a few weeks. For now, I receive a temporary ID card from the DMV office, which is more like a piece of paper with my name and address typed on the front.

I walk out of the DMV. Wow. I have never in my life experienced such hostility. He's like the scariest DMV employee I've ever met. Actually he's the scariest California employee I've met so far. Is it because he's in the Army? Maybe he enjoys scaring the crap out of people. Or is he one of those Army guys who's trained to torture hostages? Either way, I never want to go back there!

After the DMV incident, I went back home to make a sandwich to calm my nerves. I finished up and drove to the Career Center for an orientation meeting.

So now I feel better and I think I'm prepped for the meeting with Jackie and all the tutors who are part of the Upward Bound Program.

Technically, tutoring is supposed to be scheduled for today. But since we're having a meeting, Jackie cancelled all the tutoring sessions. I'm a little excited and yet really nervous.

"Jennifer?" I look up and see Jackie sitting behind her desk.

"Hi!" I peek into her office.

"If you want, you can head into the conference room." She points to several rooms nearby. "They're down the hall and to your right. I'm having all the tutors meet in there."

"OK, sounds great." I grab my black shoulder bag, which looks more like a laptop bag, and I swing it over one shoulder and head straight for the conference room.

I walk past Susan the secretary and I smile at her, hoping she doesn't remember me. She just glares at me. I look away and decide not to let it trouble me. Maybe it's just the California way of saying, "Hello!"

"Excuse me, Miss." I hear someone say.

I stop and stare up at a giant of a girl about seven feet tall! Well, maybe that's a little bit of an exaggeration.

"Hello!" I show her a perky smile.

The giant girl looks down at me and asks, "Do you know where I could find Mrs. Hernandez? I'm a new student."

"You're a *student?*" I ask, trying not to look too surprised, but like wow, she's tall!

"I'm on the basketball team," she explains. "I haven't had time to stop in yet for tutoring. Do you know where I could find Mrs. Hernandez?"

"Definitely. She's in the Career Center." I point the giant girl in the right direction and she sprints off. Wow, a student asked me for help! I feel so . . . so special!

When I reach the conference room, I find five other tutors in there around my age. They're all sitting down and laughing. One girl has a scarf draped across her neck and earrings dangling down her shoulders.

The rest of the girls look really formal. Oh no, did I dress wrong? I look down at myself and I'm wearing jeans and a tie-dye sleeveless top. I look like a girl out of a 1980's movie. Oh well, it's not what's on the outside, it's what's on the inside that counts!

"Hi!" I say as I approach the table.

The girls are having private, idle conversations with one another and no one even looks up to notice me. I'm guessing no one heard me. "Hello!" I say a little louder and smile. I want them to know I'm super excited to meet them.

They stop talking and stare up at me. One of the girls glances my way and turns back to her friends and then before I know it, they're back to chatting again.

Fine! I decide to take a seat at the far end of the table, away from the group of girls. I pull up a chair next to a black girl, who is alone writing stuff down in a planner.

"Hello!" I say but she doesn't respond.

"Ladies!" Everyone looks up to find Jackie strolling in. They all get up and run over to Jackie, greeting her with a big hug like she's the center of attention.

Should I be doing that, too? I mean, I want to fit in, right?

I get up from my chair and wait until a Mexican girl gives her a hug and then I slide in after her.

"Hi Jackie!" I say and try to give her a hug but she pulls back.

I hear someone giggling in the back and I turn around to find the black girl, who was alone, laughing at me. I look around the room and the rest of the girls are staring back at me with surprised looks on their face. What?

There's total silence. This is so awkward.

"Let's sit down." Jackie finally says, breaking the awkward silence.

Everyone takes a seat at the table. I decide to take a seat at the opposite end of the table, away from the black girl who was laughing at me.

"Now," Jackie begins, pulling out itineraries from her folder. "We have a lot of things to go over, but first, I want to introduce a new tutor." She distributes the itineraries and then looks over at me and grins. "Let's all welcome Jenn."

A few of the girls look up but the rest are buried in the itineraries.

"Jackie!" One of the tutors interrupts, looking down at the itinerary. "We have to record the students' hours?"

"Yeah, I mean, this could take forever," another tutor adds.

"Girls, girls, please. The items on the itinerary are a direct order from my supervisor. Unfortunately we have to do as they ask." Jackie looks back over at me. "Before we begin, I want Jenn to introduce herself. She's from Michigan and she'll be staying with us through the end of the school year."

Immediately all the girls look over at me and their jaws just drop.

"You're from Michigan?" The black girl asks, as if it was near the North Pole.

"Um, like, isn't it cold there?" A tutor named Amy wearing a scarf adds.

Are they for real?

"Yeah, like of course it totally snows there! I would never go there!" A girl with shiny, blonde hair says to the group.

"Brrr." A Mexican girl named Maribel pretends to shiver. "You're courageous," she says.

Um, OK?

"So, Jenn, why don't you go ahead and introduce yourself," Jackie says.

"Um, right. Well, I'm from Michigan . . . " I hesitate for a few seconds. Oh, right! "I'm part of the AmeriCorps Program."

"The Ameri— what?" Amy asks.

"It's called 'AmeriCorps' and it's a one year volunteer program. It's kind of like the Peace Corps—"

"God, I'm so sorry," Amy says.

"I was thinking of doing AmeriCorps." A chubby black girl walks into the room carrying a tote bag. "Sorry, I'm late Jackie." She swings her bag across the table, grabs an empty seat, and glances over at me. "Oh, I'm Monique by the way."

"Hi Monique, I'm Jenn, nice to meet you," I say across the table.

"So what do you do in the volunteer program?" Amy
asks.

"Look," Monique says to Amy. "It's like this. Imagine
traveling to a different state and helping out poor people or
helping out students get a better education." She points to
me, "like she's doing."

"Right, well I got that," Amy says.

"You get paid less though," Monique says.

"Oh, how much less?" Maribel asks.

Monique looks over at me. "Well, I think you get a
choice. You can either take an award or a stipend. Is that
right *Jinn*?" Monique asks, pronouncing my name like "Gin."

"Um . . . " I hesitate for a moment trying to remember how it actually works. "I think the education award is like
$4,725, except this year they bumped up the award to $5,500
and the stipend is like $2,000 or something like that."

Monique says, "See? It's worth it. I'd take the award
over the stipend because it's more money and you can use it
toward your student loans."

"Wait, so like, I can't use $5,500 to go shopping? It
has to go toward my loans? That's stupid," Amy says, brushing her hair away from the scarf.

"Girl, it ain't stupid," Monique insists, "you're helping
people out."

"Whatever. Sounds too complicated," Amy says.

"So, anyway, girls," Jackie begins, "I'd like to move
on. OK?"

A few of the girls nod.

Jackie continues. "Next thing on our list is an activity
I have prepped for the kids. We're going to do—"

"Oh my God! We're going to do a ropes course! This
is *so exciting!*" The blonde hair girl interrupts.

"So what do you guys think? I thought it would be a
great team building exercise for the kids," Jackie continues.

"Sure, sounds fun," Maribel says.

"Jenn," Jackie looks over at me, "Would you mind taking pictures during the activity? As part of your duties as an AmeriCorps volunteer here, we've asked that you prepare a slideshow of photos from the ropes course. Does that sound OK to you?"

"Definitely!" Hey, as long as I don't have to actually *do* the ropes course, I'm totally fine with it! Who wants to climb ropes anyway?

"Where is it being held?" Amy asks.

"I've decided we'll take a bus over to Fresno State University. They have a ropes course there," Jackie announces.

Oh that's fantastic since I totally live right across the street from campus! Yay, I don't have to worry about parking! This couldn't get any better.

"So everyone's OK with the location then?" Jackie asks.

"I live right across campus. Do you want me to pick up a few students?" Maribel asks.

"Hey, so do I!" I blurt out. Everyone stops to look at me. I feel slightly embarrassed. There's an awkward pause as Jackie and the other tutors just look at me without saying anything.

I decide to rephrase my statement. "I mean, I live across campus, too," I say, looking over at Maribel. At this point, I expect them to nod and smile but they just keep staring at me, like I'm the village idiot. I continue, "Do you live in Ivory Park Apartments, too?" I ask her.

"Um . . . " Maribel looks lifeless.

I think I have totally freaked her out.

"Er . . . " Maribel mutters, trying to find the right words without insulting me.

Maribel's probably thinking I'm a stalker. I bet she doesn't want to tell me "Yes" or "No" since she thinks I'm going to stalk her place. I promise I won't! I'm actually really nice, and did I mention I'm from the Midwest? We, the people, are nice over there!

Maribel looks down and fidgets with her pen.

"Do you want to walk over together?" Shoot! I can't believe that just came out of my mouth! Why can't I just stop talking? I'm totally embarrassing myself!

"I don't know," Maribel says at last.

"OK, so next on the list . . . " Jackie trails off, pulling out a manila folder with our names scribbled on it.

I feel myself blushing. I can't concentrate. I feel humiliated and stupid.

For the rest of the meeting, which lasts approximately forty minutes, I just sit there in silence, too afraid to even open my mouth for fear of what might come out.

When the meeting ends, I toss my shoulder bag over my shoulder and race out of there. I sprint out of the administration building and head straight for my car. I just want to go home! I never want to come back here again. Ever!

When I get in my car, I immediately flip open my cell phone and dial Mom.

"Hello?"

"MOM!" I practically scream into the phone.

"Hi, how's my precious girl?" She genuinely asks.

"Mom, I hate this place."

"So come back home," she says.

"Mom, I really hate it here in California and—"

She cuts me off. "You won't believe this! They actually publicized me, they publicized my website!"

"Mom, what are you talking about? Who?"

"The movie, haven't you heard? My website is listed on the film's website. Here, write this down."

I look around my car and find a torn sheet of paper in the trash and pull it out. I grab a pen from my purse. "OK, go ahead."

"It's called '*The Fourth Kind*' and it's a new movie coming out. It's all about UFOs and aliens. And Jenn, they put my website as the number one source for alien research."

Mom's a UFO fanatic. In the 1990's, she created a website, www.abduct.com, and it's about UFOs and aliens. It's pretty cool. She gets a lot of readers and tons of people writing in to tell their stories. Sometimes she'll even share some of their stories with me, and when she does, they are super interesting.

"Well, did you watch the movie trailer?" She asks.

"Mom, I'm in my car. I'm not even home yet!"

"Well, watch it when you get home. I want to know what you think. Should we go see the movie? Oh Jenn, this is so exciting!" She continues. "Did you know last night I got over twenty thousand hits on my website? That's incredible I've never had that many in one night. It's all because of this movie. I can't believe they listed my website as number one."

"Wow, that's pretty cool," I say, not sure if she's listening to me.

"They got their research from my website. Isn't that cool?"

"I promise to check out this movie trailer when I get home, OK? And then I'll let you know," I say.

"OK, sounds good. I have to go. I love you," Mom says.

"Love you too, bye," I say slowly, wondering why she's saying goodbye if *I* called *her.*

Oh well.

I close my cell phone, turn on the car and pull out of the school parking lot.

I can't believe how cool this is. I mean, I know most people like my friends don't really believe in this kind of paranormal stuff, but what if it's real? What if the government really has aliens hiding away in some foreign or remote place? We would never know.

I kind of feel sorry for those little alien dudes. I mean, those poor creatures might be trapped somewhere in a giant volcano and here we are, just too distracted to care, playing with our iPads or brand new laptops!

Bzzzz. Bzzzz.

I look down in my lap and find my cell phone vibrating. I switch it open but keep it low so I don't get pulled over by the cops.

"Hello?" I ask.

"Jenn. What are you doing?"

"Hey Adrian. Oh, guess what? We have to watch this movie trailer about aliens when I get home. I'll tell you all about it when I get there."

"I'm coming home early so I'll see you soon," he says.

"OK, bye, love you," I say.

"Love you too, bye," he says.

He hangs up and I throw the cell phone in my purse.

I turn on my signal and merge onto the highway. I look up and spot a gray object floating at least a hundred yards away from me in the sky.

HONK.

I look behind me and see a slew of cars pouring onto the highway so I merge into the slow lane. I look back at the sky, the same spot where I saw the object, but it's gone.

Wow, that's weird. I try looking over my shoulder and I spot it. There! I blink a few times to get a closer look but it vanishes. How did it do that? Maybe I'm just seeing things?

HONK.

I look in my rear view window and one of the cars passes me. I dare not look out the window in case the driver decides to give me the middle finger.

HONK.

OK, OK. Enough already. These California drivers are really insane. I look over at my speedometer and I'm going like sixty miles an hour in the slow lane. Isn't that fast enough? I spot a sign up ahead that reads, "Speed Limit 65." Oh well, close enough. They can pass me, right?

I glance out the back window but I still don't see any sign of the weird object. In fact, I don't see anything up in the sky except floating cumulous clouds.

Hmm. Well, that was definitely not my imagination! I know I saw a round object that was like dark gray, and that's all I remember.

Hey, what if it was a UFO? Sweet Lord! I can't wait to tell Adrian about this one! I look out my back window to see if anyone is behind me, and then I merge into the far lane. I push a little harder on the gas pedal to speed up and head straight home to tell Adrian about my weird UFO experience!

"So what do you think?" I ask Adrian as we finish watching the movie trailer for 'The Fourth Kind' on his Mac desktop computer. I told him all about my UFO experience on the drive home.

"It seems interesting," he says.

"Which part?" I ask. "My story, or the movie?"

"Both." He looks up at me and pulls me close to him so that I'm practically resting my head on his shoulder. "I think the movie looks great. We should definitely see it some-time."

"Yeah, you think so?" I'm so excited he's thrilled. I didn't know what he would think of it. "So, do you think I was like dreaming or something when I saw that object in the sky, or what?"

"Well, if you think you saw it, then you probably did."

"So, you don't think it was like an airplane or weather balloon?" I ask.

He gazes at me, his soft blue eyes pouring deeply through me. "I think that whatever you saw was real. I be-lieve you."

"Oh!" I give him a big, squeezy hug. This is sooo ro-mantic! We're like the perfect couple! Honestly, I mean, how many couples would support each other through a UFO ex-perience? Then again, how many of them would actually *tell* their spouse or partner they even *had* a UFO sighting?

"Listen," he pulls me on his lap. "I believe you. I think UFOs could really be out there, too."

"Really?" I smile and kiss him on the lips. This is so amazing! I'm so lucky to have such a wonderful husband . . . I mean, boyfriend. I quickly add, "So, you're totally cool with seeing the movie then?"

"Of course!" He says.

"Oh thanks, sweetie." We hug each other one more time.

"Um, Adrian, I don't mean to . . . to interrupt you . . . but . . . but—"

Damn it, Jason!

We both look over and Jason's standing in our bedroom doorway. "Hey, is it . . . is it OK if . . . if I use the TV?"

"Yeah, sure but shut our bedroom door." Adrian says as Jason turns around and closes our door.

"Why does he always have to interrupt us, sweetie?" I ask, giving Adrian a kiss on the nose.

"Let's not worry about him. Jason's gone now. He'll be out there for hours." Adrian pulls me down on the mattress, slowly peeling off my shirt one button at a time . . . .

Six

A few days later, I'm outside the office in downtown Fresno, waiting to meet with my supervisor, Rosaline. She's the director for an organization called Reading and Beyond. It's a nonprofit group that works with volunteers from the community and AmeriCorps.

As I look around the parking lot, I glance out toward the distance and catch a glimpse of the mountains. That's one of the great things about the California scenery. The mountains totally surround the Central Valley. Anywhere you go, the mountains are staring back at you.

"Jenn?" I look over and see Rosaline, a heavyset woman wearing a large red dress, black heels and long brown hair fastened up in a ponytail.

"Hi Rosaline!" We shake hands and she escorts me to her office.

When we get to her office, I take a seat in one of the chairs behind her desk. She pulls out a thin packet of information.

"This is something you might find useful. We try to hand them out to all of our AmeriCorps volunteers." She says, handing me the packet of information.

I've come to the conclusion that AmeriCorps is basically divided up into three different categories of volunteers. First, you have the "AmeriCorps VISTA" volunteers, like me, who aren't allowed to take up a part time job while doing their volunteer service, and we mostly work under the direction of poverty or education.

Then you have the second group, the "AmeriCorps NCCC" volunteers, between the ages of 18—26 who work on team projects like Habitat for Humanity and stuff like that.

Then you have the last group, "AmeriCorps State and National" volunteers where anyone over the age of 17 can be a volunteer. The nice thing about their program is the volunteers can have a part time job while serving. This is the group I applied to, but didn't get any interviews.

Oh, and did I mention, I applied to like thirty something AmeriCorps jobs and I only got like four interviews! Isn't that ridiculous? I mean, I felt like my resume wasn't good enough or something! I was lucky to land the job in Fresno as an AmeriCorps VISTA volunteer, which is mainly why I took the job, and because of Adrian.

I knew Adrian lived in Fresno. We were internet buddies who met on YouTube. We became professional video penpals after he found my class video about past relationships. This was really random considering very few people viewed it. Anyway, so that's how we got to chatting. Two years later, I got this volunteer job near him in Fresno.

I'm glad I took the job with AmeriCorps. Otherwise, I'd still be living at home with Mom, without a job, without a boyfriend, and without friends for the summer. Rosaline's tapping interrupts my thoughts.

"Now if you take a look," Rosaline says, tapping the packet in my hand, "you'll find plenty of useful information such as food stamps and care packages."

"Oh, OK, thanks. I'm sure this will come in handy," I say as I flip through some of the information.

"Well if you turn to page three of your packet, you'll notice that there's some information regarding food stamps."

I look up at her. "You mean, I could apply for food stamps?" Now I'm paying attention. That totally rocks.

"Of course, you're eligible Jenn. Just make sure you receive at least $127 from food stamps. They sometimes get confused and think your biweekly living allowance is actual a paycheck," she explains.

It isn't?

"But what they don't realize is the money acts as a stipend for you to use for housing and that sort of thing."

Oh, gotcha.

"Are you familiar with food stamps?" She leans forward in her chair.

"Well . . . not really," I say.

"Basically, you sign up and attend an orientation, meet with a caseworker, and then they provide you with a debit card which will have your food stamp money on it."

So I'm not going to be carrying around paper food stamps or coupons? It's a credit card? Awesome.

I flip through another page and spot something in regards to the electric bill. I show Rosaline the page. "What's this all about?"

"Oh, that. Well, it's called the C.A.R.E. package and it's for California residents who are either unemployed or earn wages at or below the poverty line." She looks at me. "You qualify. Just go head and give them a call and they'll set you up with the discount." She looks off to the side. "I think it's like 10% off your electric bill every month."

Wow! This is fantastic! I had absolutely no idea I qualified for all this free stuff! I love being poor!

"So, do you have any questions so far?" She looks over at me.

"Hmm, not really. I think I'll just go through this when I get a chance," I say.

"Well you might want to contact food stamps right away. It will take a few weeks before they process all the paperwork," Rosaline says.

Oh darn. I was hoping to get free food as soon as I leave here today!

"Do you have a soup kitchen around here?" I blurt out.

"Oh, um, I think so. There's a church around Fresno State University which offers free meals every Friday," she says, "Do you want to volunteer there?"

"No thanks," I say. I just want a free meal!

This is totally awesome! I'm going to absolutely LOVE being poor! Free money, free food, free electricity. It couldn't be better! Why would you want to be rich when you could be poor?

"Can you work over at the high school until June?" She asks.

"Of course." My last AmeriCorps position ended a month or so ago, and it's already January, so I only have a few months left, well, more like six more months.

"Great," she says, smiling. "Oh, I almost forget to add." She pulls out something from her top drawer. "Here." She slides over a slip of paper. "This is the information we need from you regarding your TB test results."

My WHAT? "TB?" I ask, feeling stupid.

"TB is short for Tuberculosis. Every volunteer or staff member who works in a school has to obtain a TB test before they meet with students. It's school policy, unfortunately." She gives me a reluctant smile.

What if I find out that I have TB? Then what? Should I tell Adrian?

"So, is this test like *really* required?" I ask.

She looks at me strangely. "Um . . . Yes." She pauses. "We can't have anyone in the schools without testing results."

"Um, what if I *am* TB positive?"

"Well," Rosaline looks at me with confusion, "Why don't we just cross that bridge when we come to it. I think you'll be fine though," she smiles at me.

She seems to be reassuring me that I'll be fine. I guess I should trust her. She should know. She's hired a lot of volunteers. But, did all of them test negative for TB?

"So how do I *get* the test?" I ask.

"What do you mean?" She looks confused.

"Like, how?" I can't figure out how to phrase it.

"It's a shot," she interrupts. "They inject you with a needle. Is that what you mean?"

A SHOT? Oh my God, I'm going to die, I just know it!

"Yes, that's what I meant. Thank you," I smile back, trying to show her I understand and that I'm not scared at all about having a shot injected into my arm which might or might not kill me, depending on the person who is giving me the shot and if they're having a bad day, which I really hope they aren't and—

"If you want, I can call Urgent Care and schedule you an appointment for this afternoon," she says genuinely.

"Sure. Why not?" I smile at her. I should really think this through. Too late.

She dials the number on her phone and immediately gets through. "Hi, this is Rosaline Cruz from Reading and Beyond. Yes, Hi. I have an AmeriCorps volunteer here with me and I need to set her up with an appointment to get a TB test. Yes, that's right. Oh? Let me check." She cups one hand over the phone and looks over at me. "Can you be there right after our meeting?"

"Um, sure, OK," I say.

"Great." She smiles at me and puts the phone back to her ear. "Sure, that sounds good. Thank you. Bye." She hangs up the phone and looks over at me. "Well I just scheduled you for an appointment in a half hour. It's only about two blocks from here. When you get out of the parking lot, take an immediate left and then turn right and it should be right there."

"Thanks," I say.

"Oh, I almost forget," Rosaline says, getting up from her chair. "Did you receive you California driver's license yet?"

Um, what? Oh, right! You mean, did I get my California ID? Of course!

"Sure," I say, pulling the sheet of paper out of my purse.

"What's this?" She asks as I hand her the typed copy of my ID card.

"Oh, it's a temporary ID card. I haven't yet received mine in the mail."

She looks at me for a few moments. "So is this your driver's license or your California State ID?"

I sit there for a few seconds contemplating. Hmm. What should I *really* tell her?

"It's my state ID." I tell the truth.

"No problem. Sit right there and I'll be right back. I'm going to go make a copy." She walks off toward another room in the office.

Well I guess it's not so bad telling the truth after all. She didn't seem to care if it was a driver's license or ID card anyway.

I grab the cell phone out of my purse and check to see if I have any missed calls. Oh Adrian called! How sweet! But why didn't he leave a message?

"Jenn?"

I look up as Rosaline hands me back the piece of paper for my ID. "Thanks. I made two copies so Jackie can hand those off to the school."

"Great," I say cheerfully.

"And that's all I have for you. I just wanted to provide you with that information to help you out." Rosaline gets up from her desk and I follow her out of the room.

"Thank you so much," I say as we shake hands and I walk out of the office carrying a packet and the fear that I will die this afternoon after taking this TB shot.

I get in the car and head out. A few blocks later, I'm there. How can you miss it? There's a huge blue sign out in front that says, "Urgent Care. We want you dead." I shake my head and look again. "Urgent Care welcomes you." Ah, that's better.

I get out of the car and walk up to the entrance. I'm freaking out. This is extremely scary. The last time I ever got a shot was like when I was ten! That was way long ago. I don't even remember when I was ten!

"Are you going in?" A man with a Spanish accent asks me.

I look over and there's a Mexican man just staring at me.

"Yes, I'm going in." I pull the doors wide open and walk up to the counter.

"Hello, do you have an appointment?" The big bosomy lady in yellow and blue behind the counter asks.

Oh, I love her SpongeBob outfit.

"Hi, yes, I have an appointment. I'm an AmeriCorps volunteer—"

She cuts me off. "Jennifer?"

"Yes?" I ask.

"You're the one Mrs. Cruz called about, right? Have a seat. Someone will be with you shortly."

Great! Well, that went well.

I take a seat in the lobby and my knees start shaking. I try to stop them but my thumbs start wiggling. I need to control myself but I'm so nervous! This might be my last chance to ever see the light again. Oh, I know, I should probably text Adrian and say "Goodbye." I grab the cell phone out of my purse and start texting him.

"Jennifer?"

I look up and a nurse of about thirty is carrying a clipboard and wearing blue scrubs. She's looking right at me.

"I'm here." I wave at her like I'm being called for attendance.

"Right this way," she calls out.

I finish texting Adrian and I throw the phone back in my purse. I get up and follow the woman to a private room around the corner.

"Take a seat up here." She gestures for me to hop up on the chair.

Do I need to take off my clothes? You know like they do at the doctor's office? I really don't want my last outfit on Earth to be a green paper cloth.

"Go ahead and lift up your sleeve so I can swab it." She walks over to the counter and grabs a cotton ball.

So long, me. This is my last will and testament. Oh no! Wait! I can't get a shot. I never created a will! Wait! Wait!

"Now, Jennifer, just relax." The nurse says, turning around toward me. "This won't hurt much." She grabs the needle from the counter.

Screw this!

"Lean back and relax." She's gesturing me to sit and lean back against the wall. She squeezes the needle a little in the air so a few droplets of poison pour out.

I try to lean back but my mind won't get off the fact that I'm about to die and she's the last person I'll see.

"So what's your favorite music band, Jennifer?" She says, putting one hand on my arm while the other hand holds the needle.

My favorite music band . . . let's see, well, I love all of them! "Linkin Park is my favorite group. I really like the old school stuff like Goo Goo Dolls, Three Doors Down and Breaking Benjamin. I've been getting into 80's music lately—"

"That's it. Thank you," she says.

Huh?

I look down at my arm as she applies a Band-Aid to the spot.

"I'm done?" I look up at her in disbelief.

"Yep. Sometimes it helps to distract someone when we ask them questions. I gave you the shot when you were telling me about your favorite music groups."

Well, I'll be! She's good!

"Wow, that's terrific. So I'm not dead, then!" I say, smiling.

"I'm sorry?" She asks quizzically.

Oops. "Er, sorry, nevermind." I smile back at her.

"Well, if you want, go ahead and pull your sleeve down. Just go up to the counter and they'll get your paperwork processed."

"Thank you." I hop down and grab my purse and head toward the counter. "Hello," I say to the lady with the SpongeBob outfit.

"Here, I need you to sign." She slides a piece of paper across the counter and hands me a pen.

I look over the page and notice the dollar sign. "Excuse me," I glance at her, "what's this?" I point to the dollar amount.

"Oh, the test costs $26." She looks up at me. "Will you be paying by check or cash?"

Um, say what? "I think you're mistaken." I begin. "You see, I'm a volunteer. I don't think I have to pay—"

"Everyone pays." She glares at me.

All right, all right. I'll pay.

"How are you paying the $26?" She asks.

"Cash." I pull out $30 from my wallet and hand the money over. She gives me my change and prints a receipt.

"You need to come back in 48 hours so we can look at your arm. That's when we can tell you the results." She says.

"Oh OK. I'll see you in two days then?" I ask cheer-fully.

The woman doesn't look back. She returns to her fil-ing. I walk out of the office, get back in my car and pull out of the lot. Well that was fun. I feel a buzzing sound coming from my purse and I grab the cell phone.

I flip open the phone and find a text message waiting for me. It's from Adrian.

It reads, "What do you mean, you're going to DIE?" Oops.

I text him back, "Nevermind. I love you. Miss you." There, that should do it. I throw the phone back in my purse and put the car in reverse.

I hear my phone instantly buzzing back. I grab the phone out of my purse. A new text appears from Adrian. "OK. Love you."

Guys are so simple. You tell them "Nevermind" and they forget it ever happened! Thank goodness! I pull out of the parking lot and head out. I should probably call Rosaline to tell her about the money thing for the TB test.

I dial her number.

"Hello, Rosaline Cruz speaking."

I put her on speakerphone and hide the phone be-tween my legs.

"Hi Rosaline? This is Jenn. I just met with you a few minutes ago."

"Oh, hi, Jenn. How did the TB appointment go?" She inquires.

"Great! But—" I pause, "I had to pay $26 for the test."

"Oh," she seems surprised. "Well—" She pauses for a few seconds. "Um, try calling the AmeriCorps VISTA Mem-ber Support Unit and see if they'll reimburse you. If not, let me know, OK?" She asks.

"OK, sounds good."

"Thanks, bye." She clicks off and I set the phone aside.

I start dialing the number for the VISTA Member Support Unit except I remember they close at five and that's Eastern Standard Time and I'm in Pacific Time.

I look at the clock on my cell phone and notice it's almost five in the afternoon Eastern Standard Time. I better call them before they close for today.

I wait for the automated recording voice to come over the line, "Thank you for contacting the VISTA Member Support Unit. All technical support is currently on another call. Please wait patiently and we'll be with you shortly." Then I hear the music of Mozart, or one of those dead guys.

"Hello, VISTA Member Support Unit. How can I help you today?"

"Hi! I have a question regarding—"

"Hello?" The woman over the phone cuts me off.

"Hi! Hello? I'm here!" I'm say, screaming into the phone.

This is the problem with calling people on speaker-phone in California. You can't have it by your ear, otherwise you'll get pulled over by the police, and so you only have a few options. I could either buy one of those earpieces, but I'm poor, remember? I can't afford those things.

So I have the phone between my legs while I scream into the phone so the person on the other line can hear me. Although, I suppose there could be another option, which would be, "Don't call while driving?" But come on! Who really believes that crap?

As I merge onto the highway, I hear the woman come over the line. "Hello, how can I help you today?" She repeats.

"Hi! I just got a TB test and I want to know how I can get a reimbursement."

"I'm sorry, what test did you want to get a reimbursement for?" She asks.

I yell louder. "I got . . . a . . . TB . . . test . . . done and I want a reimbursement. How can I do that?"

HONK.

What? I look back and a driver flicks me off while passing me. What did I do? I look down at my speedometer and it reads, "fifty five." I immediately look behind me, making sure it's clear to cross over into the right lane and I merge into the slower lane.

"Ma'am? Hello?" The woman's voice comes over the line.

"YES! I'm here!" I screech into my lap.

"When did you get the TB test? You would need to send in the results." She says.

"Oh I won't know the results for two days." I say.

"What was that?" She repeats.

I yell again into the phone.

"I said, I won't . . . know . . . the . . . test results . . . for two days!" Ugh, I hate T-Mobile cell phones. The damn thing is so hard to hear even when I'm on speakerphone. It's like, you would assume that if you put someone on speakerphone that you would be able to hear them *better*!

"That's fine," the woman says. "When you get your results, go ahead and mail them in to us and we'll take care of it. Is there anything else?"

"No, that's it. Thanks." I hit the end button on my phone and flip it closed.

I'm finally near my exit and as I get closer, I merge onto the exit and head left toward the apartment complex.

Seven

I arrive at Urgent Care two days later for my follow-up appointment. As I approach the counter, the SpongeBob woman immediately recognizes me.

"Jennifer?" She looks up at me, this time wearing a new nursing outfit with Dora the Explorer printed on it.

"Yes?" I smile brightly.

"Let's take a look at your arm." She whisks around the counter and takes off the Band-Aid. "Oh, dear." She has a horrified look on her face.

Wait, what's wrong? What does she mean by, "Oh dear?"

"Juanita, can you look at this young woman's arm?" She calls to a young Mexican woman, wearing bright pink scrubs, who comes walking into the lobby swinging a water bottle in her hand.

"What?" Juanita says, looking up at the other woman.

"Look at her arm. OK?"

Juanita grabs my arm and lightly runs her finger over the tiny, red bruise on my arm. "Oh, no problem." She nods and looks up at me. "OK?" She nods her head again.

"I think so?" I ask.

Juanita signs a few pieces of paper and then hands them over to me. "Here. These are you results. This is your copy and this is for AmeriCorps."

I take both copies in my hand and look them over. "So, am I OK?"

"Do you have TB?" Juanita asks.

She's asking *me*? Wait, who's asking the questions here?

"You are OK," Juanita says.

So I *don't* have TB?

"Negative," she says, reassuring me.

"So," I trail off.

"You are fine," she says.

Terrific! I nod and walk out the door. I get in the car and head straight to the post office to mail my TB results to AmeriCorps. I can't wait until my reimbursement check comes in the mail!

After I leave the post office, I get back in my car and head straight over for my Food Stamp Orientation meeting. I'm supposed to meet up with Adrian at orientation this morning. He was so thrilled to hear about the free food that he wanted to tag along. So we're both meeting up there.

I pull off the road into a tiny parking lot that reads, "Parking for Employment and Temporary Assistance." I look down at my notes and scan the information provided by Rosaline. I verify this is definitely the right place.

I hear my phone ringing. I grab my purse and flip open the phone.

"Hey, you, where are you? I just got here." Adrian says, "I parked right next to you."

"Really?" I look over and sure enough, a white Jeep pulls up next to me. "Great. See you." I click off the phone and walk over to his Jeep.

"Hey, good timing," Adrian says as he gets out of the Jeep. He's wearing a blue sleeveless shirt and khakis and his tattoos are really apparent.

"Oh, I love your tattoos," I say, smoothing my fingers over the one on his left arm that's inscribed, "NAT," which is his nickname.

So yeah, he has tattoos, which may or may not work to his benefit when meeting new people. What's wrong with this culture? I mean, just because you see a guy with tattoos doesn't make him a "mean-green-fighting-machine." Adrian is like totally far from that. He's a snuggle bunny. He's soft, kind, friendly, loving, totally nothing you would expect.

"It's not like you haven't seen them before," Adrian says, taking my fingers and kissing them.

He's such a sweetheart.

"Let's go or we'll be late," I say, looking at my watch. Well, OK, it's not like anyone wears a watch these days. I still call my cell phone my "watch." It makes me sound more professional.

We walk toward the building and spot a small group of Mexicans leaning against the wall, smoking. There's a pregnant woman standing nearby wearing stacked heels and a red dress that bulges from her stomach and . . . is she smoking?

Adrian nudges at me to stop starring at the pregnant woman. I manage to look away as he opens the front door. I follow him inside. Wow. The walls are a bright white. I spot two police officers standing in the corner behind a brown desk and they're staring at me. Oh no!

I grab Adrian's hand and we walk into another room down the hall. The room is completely lit and I spot a ton of people sitting down in wooden chairs. A few Mexican kids play tag and run around the room and several babies cry out in their mothers' laps.

It smells pretty bad, with a roomful of people who haven't showered. We walk past a huge crowd of kids playing on the floor with their toys, and we stand in line at counter 1.

At the counter, a heavyset woman looks up at us with puffy red lips and green eye shadow. Wow, what a combo!

"Hi!" I say with an upbeat attitude. "We're here for our Food Stamp Orientation today. Where is it being held?"

The woman pauses and looks at me for a second and then scribbles something down. She hands me a slip of paper. "Give this to the woman at counter 5."

"Thank you," Adrian says.

Luckily we're the only ones in line so we just walk up to the counter and find an elderly black woman typing away at her computer.

"Hi," Adrian says, handing the slip of paper to the woman.

"Can I help you?" The woman looks over at him.

"We were told to give this to you," Adrian says.

I interrupt. "We're here for our Food Stamp Orientation."

"Then what are you doing over here? You're in the wrong building," she says, looking annoyed.

Wow, I totally feel like the biggest idiot ever. Maybe it would help if they actually put *signs* somewhere. I mean, the building didn't even have a sign on it!

"Where do we go?" I inquire.

"The next building over and give them this," she says, handing us a yellow slip of paper. She turns her back on us and walks over to another counter to talk with one of the ladies.

"Well," I look over at Adrian. "Come on, then." I grab his hand and we walk out of the building and try to find another building which might look like a Food Stamp Orientation building. Whatever that's supposed to look like.

After a few minutes, Adrian gets annoyed. "So where is this building? This is ridiculous. She didn't even give us any directions."

"Sweetie, don't worry, we'll figure it out," I say.

"Jenn, why don't we just ask those police officers we passed on the way in?" Adrian asks.

"OK, I'll wait out here." I say.

He looks at with confusion. "Wait, so you're not coming in with me?"

"California police scare me, remember?" What if they ask for my California driver's license and I show them my Michigan license? Won't they get suspicious? I really don't have time to go to Jail this year, remember? I have things to do and places to travel!

"Fine." Adrian rolls his eyes and walks back into the building.

"Hey you!" A young guy with a Spanish accent winks at me.

Oh. Dear. God.

Ew! I run back inside and find Adrian talking to one of the officers.

"So, right out there? Great. Thanks." He turns back to me. "I thought you said you didn't want to come in?"

"I changed my mind!" I say, holding him tightly.

I follow Adrian about twenty feet until we get to a small, white building with only two windows and a door.

I look over at him. "Is this it?"

"That's what they said." Adrian goes up to the front door but it's locked. "What the hell?" He starts pulling at the knob.

"What's wrong with the door?" I ask.

A woman suddenly opens the door and looks at both of us. "Excuse me, we're in session. What are you doing?" She snaps.

"We're here for our Food Stamp Orientation. Could you help us?" I beg her.

"You're late. Come on in." She doesn't look very pleased. She gestures us in the lobby area and closes the door. "Right this way."

We follow her down the hallway to a room and find a random desk positioned near the door.

"Grab a pencil from the desk and go ahead inside. They're about to start," she says.

"Thanks so much!" I say as she turns around and heads back toward the lobby.

We each grab a pencil and paper from the desk and walk in the tiny room. It's crammed with a ton of Mexicans and a few black people sitting at individual desks. Oh, look, there's one white person sitting in the back of the room. It looks like everyone's sitting in rows of five and I count at least thirty people!

"Jenn, come on," Adrian whispers and grabs my hand. I follow him to the back of the room and we take a seat at two empty desks.

"Hello, everyone!" We all look up and a white, heavy-set man, about five feet tall walks into the room. He's wearing gym shorts and a red polo shirt. Interesting choice of clothing combination. He's bald and wearing the most hideous 1980's eyeglasses I've ever seen.

Has he not been to the optometrist lately? Has he not checked out the new selection of upgraded Gucci and Vogue black and red eyeglasses?

I totally got my Vogue eyeglasses from Lens Crafters. They were awesome, except I had to get them in red. I really wanted to buy them in black except they were all sold out! I mean, how many brunettes do you see wearing bright red eyeglasses?

"So, who's excited about getting free money?" The heavyset white man says, throwing some papers in the air.

The papers come crashing down on the floor and a few Mexican guys in the front just laugh.

"What? You guys aren't excited? This is free government money. How cool is that?" He says.

Is this our orientation leader? Wow.

"I'm EXCITED!" It just got silent. Oh no, was that me? Did I say that aloud? I look over and everyone is staring at me. Yikes! I look over at Adrian and he cracks a smile.

"Shh," Adrian whispers to me.

"Sorry." I whisper back. I look over and try to manage a smile at everyone.

"So, let's get started!" The leader says like a motivational speaker. "Here are a few packets I need to pass out." He walks up and down the rows. "My name's Tom and I'm going to be your trainer for the next hour or so. Please take one of these and pass them along."

"I'm only here for food stamps, and it says on the packet that this is for Cash Aid only." I look over at a Mexican girl in tight jeans bursting out of a red tank top. "I'm in the right place, no?" She asks with a Spanish accent.

"You're in the right place!" Tom says with an upbeat attitude. "I want you guys to get EXCITED." He says, dancing around the room. "Do you realize you are eligible for food stamps and Cash Aid?" He chuckles at his own jokes. "Maybe you are not eligible for Cash Aid, but I know you're eligible for food stamps. And why shouldn't you be? You guys are AWESOME." He says robustly.

I have never seen someone so turned on by his own presentation. I feel like I'm watching Tony Robbins. I look over at Adrian and we exchange a few giggles.

"You there!" Tom turns around, pointing directly at me. "You're excited. How about your husband there?" Tom says, looking at Adrian.

Adrian blushes and I grab his hand underneath the table and stroke his fingers to hopefully calm his nerves.

"Sure, I'm excited I guess," Adrian says, looking over at me and grinning.

"And all of you can be just as excited as this really COOL couple!" Tom attempts a dance move in the middle of the room, swaying his hips from side to side.

I try to smile at Adrian but he just glares at me. "Sorry," I manage to whisper over to him.

"Yo, question!" A young, black, pregnant woman in her thirties raises her hands.

"Great! What's your question, lovely lady?" Tom hops over to her like he's dancing.

"I need food stamps and that uh, Cash Aid thing. And I need them by tomorrow fo' ma' kids, otherwise they ain't gittin' no food and no clothes. Now, how am I gonna' raise ma kids wit out the items they need? Hmm?" She glares at Tom.

"Have no fear!" Tom says, spinning in a circle. "Your kids will get what they deserve!" He gives her a smile. "Let's just fill these forms out and once you turn them into me, I can get you what you need, lovely lady!" Tom chuckles and the black woman just rolls her eyes.

"Now, for those of you who are here for food stamps, turn to page five and start filling out the basic information. It's pretty easy." He parades up to the front of the room humming to himself. "So most of this info is just your personal contact information and biweekly payment, nothing hard!" He laughs and flips through his copy of the packet.

I get Adrian's attention by poking his arm. "Hey, are we doing food stamps or Cash Aid?" I whisper.

"Food stamps, I thought," he says.

"Thanks," I say as I start filling out the form.

"Now, for those of you who are here for Cash Aid," Tom says, "keep in mind, Cash Aid is free money, meaning, you can use it anytime you want, isn't that cool? Yay!" Tom says, throwing his arms up in the air and twirling around.

Darn I wish I were getting free money. I guess I'm only getting free food. Wait, a second . . . .

"I have a question," I say, raising my hand.

Tom looks up. "Wonderful! And what's your question, darlin'?"

"How do you know if you qualify for Cash Aid?"

A few of the Mexican boys in the front turn around and giggle.

"Are you unemployed?" Tom asks me.

"Not at the moment, no." I say.

One of the Mexicans boys interrupts. "Not at the moment, she's not!" They burst out laughing.

"Excuse me boys, settle down now," Tom stares at them.

"OK." The boys turn around in their seats and go back to filling out their forms.

Adrian grabs my hand and gently kisses it, reassuring me.

"Thanks!" I whisper to him and he smiles.

"Well, here's what I've been told," Tom says, looking over at me. "You're usually eligible for Cash Aid if you're unemployed, if you're a veteran without work, if you have a disability or if you're a single mother. Are you any of those?"

Um . . . no, I guess not. Adrian hasn't knocked me up . . . yet.

I look up at Tom and shake my head, "No." And I don't think working for AmeriCorps counts, either. Oh well. At least I'll get free food, which is better than not getting anything at all, right?

"For those of you who are applying for Cash Aid," Tom sits down on the front desk and continues, "Turn to page one and you can begin filling out the forms. If you have any questions, let me know. I'll give you a few minutes to fill these forms out," he says, strolling out of the room.

"So, we just fill out page five or all the pages?" I turn to Adrian.

"I have no idea. I'm just filling out what I know." Adrian says, showing me his copy.

"Hmm . . . all right." I scan the forms and start filling out the basic information.

Several minutes later, Tom walks back in to the room. "Any questions?"

No one speaks and Adrian pokes me in the shoulder.

"Ouch," I say.

"Don't say anything this time to embarrass yourself, OK?" He grins.

"Yeah, yeah." I say jokingly.

"If you're done with your forms, please let me know so I can go ahead and take you to the next part of the orientation, which is even more exciting!" Tom says, twirling around in a circle. "Free food! Free money! It can't get any better!" He laughs at himself.

The room falls silent and everyone just watches him dance around the room for a few minutes.

Finally Tom says, "So, let's get you to your interview with your caseworker."

My caseworker? What's that?

"So, who's done with their forms?" Tom asks.

"Are you done?" I poke Adrian in his tattoo.

"Yeah," Adrian says, looking up and slides his packet over to me.

"My boyfriend and I are DONE!" I say waving my hand in the air. Oops. I look over and Adrian is glaring at me.

"Jenn!" Adrian says with frustration.

"Sorry!" I say, grinning back.

"Fantastic! You two!" Tom points over at us. "Please follow me." Tom gestures for us to follow him. "Bring your packets as well."

I grab my packet and we follow Tom out of the room down the hall.

"Now, are you two filing separately?" Tom asks.

"Yes," Adrian says immediately.

Wait, what? I pinch him in the side. "I thought we were doing this together, remember?" I whisper.

"Jenn, if we do it this way, we can each get our own money for food. More money, more food, got it?" He whispers.

Oh, he's good!

"This way, Ma'am, you're with Sophia Garcia," Tom says, indicating a cubicle around the corner. "Sir, follow me and I'll take you to your caseworker." Adrian follows Tom into another room.

I take a seat inside a blue cubicle where I spot several picture frames of kids.

"Hello!" I glance over and a perky woman in her mid-forties smiles down at me. "My name is Sophia Garcia and I'll be your caseworker while you're on food stamps," she says with a Spanish accent and takes a seat next to me.

"Hello, nice to meet you," I say, shaking her hand. "I was just filling this out." I hand her the packet from Food Stamp Orientation.

"Oh, wonderful. Let's take a look." She reads through the first page and then flips through a few more. "Now, Jennifer," she says, looking up at me, "have you ever applied for food stamps, before?"

"Actually, I've never even heard of them," I say.

"Really?" She gives me a surprised look. "But it says here, you're in AmeriCorps, is that right?"

"Yep," I say with a smile.

"So you are eligible for food stamps."

"Right, well my supervisor recently told me about food stamps. It's great. I never realized there were all these government programs."

She looks at me surprised, "Oh."

"Plus, I've been doing AmeriCorps for like six months and no one ever told me about this. It's so great!" I look down. "But I really wish someone would have told me about this sooner. Just think," I look back at her. "I could have received free food a long time ago and I wouldn't have to be spending my own money."

The caseworker just stares at me. OK, maybe I did take it a little too far.

"Let's just have a look and see how much you're eligible for next month, OK?" She grabs a calculator from her drawer and punches in a few numbers.

I watch as she keeps hitting the plus and minus signs on the calculator. Just hit the plus signs, I keep telling myself.

"Hmm." She rests her arms on the desk. "Well, the minimum amount you can get is $127 and it looks like you're eligible for that . . . " She trails off, reading through my packet of information.

"What's the maximum amount I can get?" I inquire.

"$200."

Oh, wow! What if I could get that in Cash Aid? Then I'd definitely be rich! Maybe not like *really* rich, but I could buy so many cool things! It would be a total shopping spree! It's not like I have to report any items I buy, right?

After all, I have been bugging Adrian to get a new TV since ours keeps going out! Who really wants to sit and watch Jennifer Gardner in '*13 Going on 30*' wearing a vomit-color dress instead of the bright red she's supposed to be wearing? Stupid color pigments!

"When you get your food stamps," Sophia says, interrupting my thoughts, "you need to make sure that you report any food you buy. We need a copy of all your receipts," Sophia says.

What?

WHY?

"Um . . . all of my receipts, or just a *few*?" I ask openly.

She looks at me with uncertainty. "*All* of your receipts, Jennifer," she says at last.

"Right, of course!" Obviously!

"So, do you live with any roommates?" She asks.

"Um—"

She interrupts. "Think about this," she trails off, grabbing a pen from her top drawer.

Huh?

"If you decide to room with someone, then we can't put you on two separate accounts, so you couldn't be filing for food stamps as two separate individuals. You would be sharing your food stamps."

Yikes! Didn't Adrian say *not* to do that?

"I'm actually living by myself," I say confidently.

"Perfect." She smiles at me and scribbles something on the form.

This is going so well!

"Now, all I need from you is a formal document on AmeriCorps letterhead showing proof of your term of service. Can you either fax or mail that to me in the next week?"

"Definitely. And if you want, I can even email it to you, too!" I say enthusiastically.

"That isn't necessary," she frowns. "We aren't allowed to receive emails from food stamp participants. It will have to either be faxed or mailed." She gives me a weak smile.

"Sure, no problem. Oh, I love your earrings," I say, trying to change the topic.

She blushes. "Oh, thank you." She starts playing with one of her earrings.

"So when can I have the free food, I mean, the food stamps?"

"Those usually take up to four weeks." She says, signing her name at the bottom of the last page of the packet.

Four weeks! That's like . . . a month!

"Please sign." She points to a line on the bottom of the page.

I take her pen and sign my name in black ink.

"I'll process the paperwork as soon as I can, once I receive your AmeriCorps letterhead," she smiles.

"That sounds great."

"Well, Jennifer, that's all I have. You're done." She gets up from her chair and shakes my hand. "Have a nice day." She says and walks down the hall.

I get up and walk over to a tiny room where I spot Adrian talking with an elderly man.

"Thank you, Adrian. Have a great day." The man says with a Spanish accent. They get up and shake hands.

I wait near the door until Adrian appears through the doorway. "So, how did it go?" I ask.

He almost jumps when he sees me.

"Damn, Jenn, you almost scared me!" He says.

"Sorry, I just got finished with my caseworker. Want to go for ice cream?"

It's not like I'll have to pay for ice cream in a month, anyway! So I should totally celebrate my last time ever paying for ice cream, right?

"Jenn, I don't know if I have time to go out. I have to get back and work on a paper."

I give him my puppy-dog look. "Please! I love you." I say, giving him a huge hug and kiss.

He rolls his eyes. "Well, all right."

I grab his hand and we make our way out to the parking lot.

"Let's just take one car, it'd be easier. Do you mind coming back later and picking up your car?"

"That works." I say, hopping into his Jeep.

He gets in and turns on the engine. As he pulls out of the parking lot, I hear a familiar sound.

"Father is calling. Father is calling," my ringtone chimes.

"God, you are so weird . . . " Adrian trails off, looking over at my purse. "You're the only person I know who records your own voice and then uses it as people's ringtones so you know who's calling." He shakes his head. "Why don't you just buy everyone a different ringtone?" He asks playfully.

"Because it's ridiculous to buy ringtones! Such a waste of money," I conclude. "We're poor, remember? We can't afford luxuries like that!" I say, slapping him playfully on the arm. I grab the cell phone out of my jeans pocket and flip it open. "Hi, Dad!" I say encouragingly.

"Hi honey, you never called me back," he says with disappointment.

"Right, sorry! I forgot!" I was having the most, amazing makeout session ever that night, with the most wonderful, loveable boyfriend in the entire universe!

Well, maybe not the *entire* universe, I mean, there's like more than one universe out there, isn't there? There's like a million (or more) and I mean, I did promise Adrian that I would *never* cheat on him.

However! *If*, and only if, I meet a Nordic alien, (they're the hot ones), I would "have" to fly away in his craft and leave Adrian behind! Who can resist a muscular toned man with blue eyes and long blonde hair?

When I told this to Adrian one day, let's just say he wasn't too keen on the idea of me flying off with an alien. But I mean, what are the chances I'll ever *see* an alien? I probably have a better chance of getting struck by lightning! Oh, wouldn't that be an awful thought?

"Jennifer?" My father cuts me off from my daydream.

"I'm here Dad," I say into the phone.

"I'm sad. I miss my family," he says.

Come again?

"Dad," I begin. "What are you talking about?"

"You know what I mean, Jennifer. Our family."

"Dad, we're not a family anymore. Remember?"

"Oh, Jennifer, You're being silly," he says, teasing me. I think my father is still in denial.

Is that even possible? Can a father who wanted a divorce really miss his family?

"So, how's work going?" I say, changing the subject.

"Have you talked to your mother, lately?" He persists.

"Are you still working late hours, Dad?" I ask, trying harder to really change the conversation.

"I haven't talked to your mother in over a week. How is she? Is she all right? Does she need me?" He goes on.

I don't believe this!

"Dad, I have to go." I'm not going to sit hear and listen to Dad grill me about Mom this way. It's too weird!

"Jennifer, don't go. Your brother will barely speak to me and besides, you hung up on me the other day."

Did he just guilt trip me?

"Yes, and I'm very sorry for that Dad. It was an accident," I try apologizing.

"If it was an accident, then why didn't you call me back right away?" He asks, challenging the logic.

I look over at Adrian and make a disgusted face and point to the phone.

"Just get off the phone, then," Adrian whispers.

I cover up the phone with my hand and look at Adrian. "Adrian, I can't just get off the phone with him. He's already mad that I hung up on him the other day!" I whisper.

"Give me the phone," Adrian says, holding out his hand.

"No!" I brush his hand away. I put my mouth over the phone. "Hey Dad, can we talk later?" I ask.

"Our family was very happy together. Did you know that?" My father continues.

Is he rewriting history?

"Dad, I'll call Mom later and tell her you said, 'Hi,' OK?"

"When will I hear from you again?" He asks.

"I'm not sure, Dad. I'll give you a call maybe this weekend," I say.

"Thanks honey, bye!"

I shut the phone and throw it in my purse.

"He's so persistent sometimes," I say to Adrian.

"Your Dad needs therapy," Adrian says rationally.

"But he's already a family therapist. He writes books on this stuff," I say.

"Maybe he should read his own books," Adrian says.

"My Dad calls and says he misses his family and he's the one who wanted the divorce. I'm so confused. What does he want? A family or not?"

Adrian pulls into to an empty lot and puts the car in park. He takes his seatbelt off and leans over and gives me a kiss.

I wrap my arms around him and hold him close. He rubs my back and I slowly feel tears running down the sides of my face. "I'm sorry."

Adrian lifts my chin up and kisses me. "Hey, it's OK." He wipes the tears from my eyes.

"Thank you," I smile and he gives me another kiss.

"How about a nice, hot fudge brownie sundae from Baskin Robbins?" He suggests.

"Sure," I smile as he grabs me under the arms and tickles me.

I laugh and we hold each other for a while until he puts his seatbelt back on and backs out of the lot. Baskin Robbins here we come!

Eight

Well, I received my California ID in the mail today. It's a cute little card with a yellow background and it says *California* at the top in blue lettering. I scan the card and notice my picture. Oh . . . my . . . God.

My hair is all messed up and the right side of my hair is blowing straight out. And look at my expression and why didn't I smile? I look like an ex-convict! Actually, the lady behind the camera didn't tell me to say *cheese*. She just took the picture and I didn't have time to prepare!

I study the ID card for a few more minutes. It has my name and address, including my height and weight . . . actually, come to think of it, it looks exactly like a driver's license! Hey, I bet I don't even need to worry about getting a California driver's license anymore! Who's going to know the difference? And it's not like I've been pulled over by the cops yet with a California ID!

Anyway, it's been a few days since I mailed off my TB tests to the AmeriCorps insurance office and I haven't received my reimbursement check yet. Then I mailed a letter to the Food Stamp caseworker with proof of my volunteer status with AmeriCorps.

I guess Adrian and I have to play the waiting game with the Food Stamps office, which is really hard considering how much food I want to buy with my free money! Four weeks is such a long time to wait! And they said it might take even longer than that! Ugh.

Why can't they just mail the food stamps card sooner? I mean, the paperwork's not that much to process since I only signed like three sheets of paper!

Well, I called PG&E, the Pacific Gas and Electric Company for the state of California and after I got off the phone, I raced over to the bedroom to find Adrian editing his wrestling videos.

"Hey, guess what?" I say.

Adrian looks over at me, still wearing his yellow, smiley face pajamas. "What's up?"

"They said they're going to change our bill."

"How?" He asks.

"Well, I talked with one of the PG&E reps and she said we qualify for the C.A.R.E. Program. Isn't that great?" I say enthusiastically. "That means we get like 10% off our electric bill every month!"

"Oh, SWEET!" He says.

The toilet flushes and Jason pokes his head out of the bathroom. "Adrian, what . . . what are you . . . you yelling about?"

I turn around to face Jason. "We aren't *yelling*."

"Yes . . . yes, you were! Yeah . . . yeah . . . you were yelling," he says defensively. "I could . . . could hear you . . . from the . . . the bathroom!" Jason says.

When can I dunk his head in the toilet?

"Dude, relax. We weren't yelling," Adrian calls out.

Jason walks into our room and looks over at Adrian. "Adrian, don't . . . don't I look relaxed?"

"We weren't yelling," Adrian says.

"Fine," Jason throws his hands in the air, "what . . . whatever. I'm just . . . just saying that . . . "

I cut him off, "Anyway so we get like 10% off our electric bill all because of me!" I say sarcastically to Jason.

Jason looks at me and rolls his eyes. He turns around and walks back into the bathroom, slamming the door.

"I guess he had to crap again," I say.

"Jenn!" Adrian hisses at me.

"What?" I shrug, "What did I do?"

"Don't piss him off," Adrian demands.

"Why not? What's he going to do?" I ask.

Hurt me? Not if I can help it!

"Jenn, if you keep pissing Jason off, he'll just get more and more defensive."

"Adrian," I say, raising my voice, "I want to stick the remote control up his ass."

"Fine. But stop talking so loudly. He'll hear you."

"How?" I point to the bathroom door, "The bathroom fan is running. He can't hear over the noise of the bathroom fan!" I exclaim.

I know this for a fact. One time when Jason was sleeping on the couch, Adrian and I went into the shower and made out for the longest time and I was moaning really loudly. Anyway, when we both came back out of the bathroom, Jason was still asleep on the couch!

"Jenn, can you just try to tolerate him for now? Please?" Adrian gets up from his chair and wraps his arms around me.

"I hate him," I say, looking down at my feet.

"Look," Adrian says, giving me a hug, "He doesn't have a place to live right now and I told him he could stay here for a few more months."

A few more WHAT? Like how many?

"He bugs the crap out of me!" I say.

"Jenn, why do you hate him so much?" Adrian asks.

He doesn't know?

I give Adrian a dirty look. "How can you not hate that stupid boy?"

"I told you, it's just his Asperger's," Adrian says.

So, now he's defending Jason?

"That's ridiculous, Adrian, and you know it!" I raise my voice again.

"Jenn, please, don't yell." He puts his arm around me and strokes my face.

"Your friend is an asshole and I hate him, and that's that, got it?" I look up at Adrian and he frowns.

"Jenn, he's going through a lot right now. And you know how his girlfriend gets. Plus his mom kicked him out and his dad—"

"I don't care!" I say, interrupting Adrian, "Jason's a jerk and he thinks women are only useful for buying groceries, or cleaning and refilling the toilet paper holder!"

"No, Jason really respects women," Adrian says.

"Really? Is that so? Then why does he keep asking me to refill the toilet paper holder?" Wait a second, why is Adrian even defending this chauvinist?

"No, he doesn't," Adrian says.

"Whatever!" I throw my arms up in the air and hear my phone ring, "Mom is calling. Mom is calling. Mom is calling."

"You really need new ringtones!" Adrian says, teasing me.

I run over to the living room and grab my phone from off the couch and flip it open. "Hi Mom!" I say, trying to sound cheery.

"Hi honey, I've missed you," she says softly.

We just spoke a few days ago but she's already forgotten. "Right, I miss you, too." I say nonchalantly.

"You do, really?" She asks with enthusiasm.

"Yes, Mom, you know I do!" I say, reassuringly.

"Well your brother never tells me he loves me," she says.

"That's because he's a *guy*, Mom," I remind her.

"Well, does Adrian tell you he loves you?" She asks.

"That's different, Mom. He's my boyfriend." I roll my eyes.

"Well, does Adrian tell his mom he loves her?" She asks.

Why does she keep pursuing this?

"Anyway, so what are you calling about?" I ask, trying to change the topic. This is like talking to Dad!

"Did you get a chance to watch the movie trailer?" My mom asks.

"'*The Fourth Kind*?' I liked it, Mom. It was really awesome and Adrian loved it, too. He said he'd be willing to see it with me when it comes out in the theater."

"I was hoping I could see it with my beautiful daughter," she says, talking to me like I'm ten years old.

"Mom, I'm out in California. By the time I come home, the movie will be out on DVD or free at the library."

"Well, what's wrong with that?" She inquires.

"Mom!" I say.

"All right, Jenn," she pauses and an awkward silence hangs over the conversation.

I hesitate for a moment. "Mom, I just spoke with Dad the other day. He says he misses our family."

"Your father is so unpredictable," she blurts out.

"Anything else?" Why do I bother asking?

"I hate this weather. It's awful," my mom cries out.

"Well what do you expect, Mom? You're living in a cold climate. If you don't like it, why don't you just move out of Michigan?" Her complaints about cold weather are getting on my nerves.

"Your father has a new life now," my mom says.

Yes, Mom, I think everyone knows that.

"Anyway . . . " I trail off, unsure of what to say next.

"I love you, Jennifer. Are you going to call me later?" She makes kissing sounds over the phone.

"Um . . . " how do I tell her "No" without sounding mean? "Sure, Mom. Bye."

"Wait!" She yells over the phone.

"What now, Mom?" I ask.

"You didn't say you love me."

Oh, right. "I love you, Mom."

"No, you don't." She says.

Not this again!

"Yes, I do." I say.

"Really? Oh you're such a sweetheart," my mom sounds happy now.

Honestly, Mom, I love you even if I forget to say it. Doesn't she realize that?

"So you're hanging up now?" She asks.

"Yes, I have to go. Bye Mom." I say and close the phone gently.

Adrian walks into the kitchen.

"How did that go?" He asks.

"It was all right. My mom just wanted to know I still loved her."

Adrian walks over to me and puts his arms around me.

We both stop and listen as Jason walks out of the bathroom and into the living room. "Hey . . . um . . . Adrian? Can . . . can I . . . can I use the TV?"

"Go for it," Adrian says.

"Thanks." Jason jumps over the couch, turns on the TV and grabs his video game controller.

I swear, Jason has no life.

"Let's go for a walk." I grab our jackets from the dining room chairs.

I need to get out of this apartment for a while.

Adrian grabs his keys from the kitchen counter and closes the front door behind us. We head out for our peaceful walk, away from Asperger's and chauvinistic boy, away from those stupid video games and away from Mom and Dad.

Later on in the night, I suddenly feel severe pains coming from my stomach. Oh, no! I think I'm going to explode! I throw the covers off the mattress and run to the bathroom.

When I'm done, I look around the bathroom for a hand towel to dry my hands. Where are all the shower towels?

Jason! He always takes things that aren't his! Stupid boy!

As I look through the bathroom cupboards, I hear a loud crash coming from the living room. It's the sound of a dining room table being thrown against the wall.

What was that? I immediately open the bathroom door. But I don't see any lights coming from the living room or the kitchen. There's no sign of Jason, and I know Adrian went to bed a few hours ago.

I slowly creep out of the bathroom. I want to know what that sound was, but I really don't want to get raped by the neighborhood burglar! I mean, assuming it's a burglar!

These apartments aren't the best. They don't have alarm systems, so a burglar could sneak around the corner and I wouldn't even know it! I think they were built in the 1970's and the walls are so thin you can hear the neighbors from downstairs! Wait, that's it!

What if the sound came from one of the neighbors below? Great! I've fixed the problem. Now I can go back to bed.

As I walk out of the bathroom, I see something in the corner of my eye. I freeze. There's a translucent object floating across the floor.

Oh God, oh God, oh God . . . .

I turn around to get a better look. It's floating across the living room and into the kitchen. What *was* that?

I walk slowly back to the bedroom, occasionally looking behind me down the other end of the hallway. In case it's a burglar, I'll let him steal Adrian's TV and that crappy DVD player that skips. Then when he gets to Jason's room, he can steal his computer and all his video games. Although once he reaches my bedroom, he's toast. Adrian will put him in a wrestling hold and then we'll call the police and—

There it is! I see it again out of the corner of my eye! I swirl around to get a better look. It's black, or brown, or is it gray? It's moving slowly out of the kitchen back into the living room.

I can't even see it's face. I mean, does it even have a face? What is that . . . thing? It stops. Right in the center, between the living room and the kitchen. Oh my God. Please don't look at me, please don't—

Where did it go? Did it just vanish?

I walk down the hallway toward the living room. I stop. Wait, what am I'm doing? What if it's like a ghost or something? Maybe it's a hologram. I mean, it *was* translucent. I could practically see right through it!

Oh, I know! It must be a new technology being tested by the NSA! That's it! And they just *had* to choose me to be the test subject? Come on! Why me? I get scared really easily, remember? Why not Jason? He's got nothing to lose. Scare him instead!

"Jenn?"

Huh? I jump up and turn around.

"Hey, what are you doing out here?" Adrian says, stumbling out the bedroom door with sleepy eyes.

"Hey, I, um . . . " I catch my breath, "you scared the crap out of me!" I say, running up to him and putting my hands against Adrian's chest.

"What are you doing up? It's 3AM," Adrian says, standing in the doorway wearing his boxers.

"Adrian, I just . . . I just . . . " I can't even get the words out. Now who's sounding like Jason? "Adrian, um . . . oh gosh!" I put my hands to my face and burst into tears. I don't want to start crying but I'm so scared, I'm shaking.

"What is it?" He asks, wrapping his arms around me.

Tears are trickling down my face.

"Let's go back to bed, OK?" Adrian gestures toward the bed.

When we get to the bedroom, I turn around and lock the door. Now I feel safe!

I get into bed and Adrian throws the covers over me. He gets in bed after me and throws his arm across my chest.

"Goodnight," he says, snuggling comfortably next to me.

A few seconds later, I hear Adrian snoring. How does he do that? I could never fall asleep that fast!

I lay my head against the pillow and try to close my eyes. It's not working. I force myself to dream. Still nothing. I can't sleep. I'm getting scared again.

I open my eyes and look in front of me. I'm staring at a white wall. This sucks. I really want to sleep. I just want to go back to bed and—

Wow. We really need some posters on this wall! It's too bare. Come to think of it, all the walls are empty. Who likes looking at a plain wall while lying in bed trying to sleep?

I mean, why are all apartment complexes white on the inside anyway? Can't they have like pink or blue walls? Like, what resident really wants to move in and spend their time painting bedroom walls? Isn't that a maintenance job? Hmm . . . I bet I could paint these walls green or yellow! Oh, now that would look—

Zzzzz.

Nine

The next day, I arrive at the high school and stroll into the Career Center hoping to find a few students with their tutors in session. But the room is empty. That's weird. Where is everyone?

I go on ahead and take a seat by one of the student computers. I feel weird. Should I turn on one of the computers? I'm the only one in here. Would they mind if I checked my email?

I guess it doesn't matter so I turn on the computer and wait for it to load.

I'm a little nervous about the meeting this morning with Jackie. It's going to be our first one-on-one meeting together!

I guess it could be fun though, I've never been a tutor before. Oh, I'm sure it will be like being a camp counselor! I've always wanted to work with students. Except I would never give them homework! I want to be a cool teacher and have all the students like me!

Hmm . . . although come to think of it, maybe that wouldn't be a good idea after all. If I tried to be their friend, then they might not think of me as their superior which

means they wouldn't respect me which means I'd end up being mistreated and I wouldn't be a good teacher after all!

"Hello?"

I look over my shoulder and a twenty something girl
walks in wearing a tight black top, slacks and bright red eyeglasses, just like mine! And is that a Coach handbag?

"So, are you Jenn?" She smiles over at me.

"Yes, hi!" I say with enthusiasm.

"I'm sorry I missed the meeting with you guys the
other day. I know Jackie really wanted all the tutors to be
there." She says, placing her handbag on the table and taking
a seat next to me.

"So, you're one of the tutors, then?" I ask brightly.

"Of course! I'm one of the best tutors this school offers! I love this job. It's amazing," she says and smiles at me.

"I haven't started yet," I explain.

"Well you are going to love this place! Jackie is like
the best supervisor ever!" She turns around and flips on a
computer, "Most of the time I'm just on these silly computers
checking my email. It sucks though because we can't access
Facebook *or* MySpace." She loads up Firefox on the desktop.

"Yeah, that does suck." Gosh, I feel stupid. I'm not
sure what else to say. I want her to like me.

I want to say, *Wow, you sound really nice and will you be my
friend? You smile at me and look almost exactly like me, and, are we
twins? Let's go bowling!* Except, maybe not bowling since no one
really likes bowling.

"So, do you have a boyfriend, Jenn?" She asks, looking over at me from behind the computer.

"Um, yeah. Do you?" I inquire.

She frowns. "Oh my God, that's so sad."

Wait, why?

"I'm sorry, Jenn," she says, "but hey—" She grabs a
notepad out of her handbag, "if you do ever break up, give

me a call." She writes her name and number down and hands it to me.

"Oh, great," I say, looking down at the paper. "Thanks." I smile back. I'm totally confused.

"Jenn!" I turn around and see Jackie walking into the Career Center wearing a gorgeous black outfit with a matching blue scarf. "Hi, how are you?"

"I'm doing great, thanks. How's your day going?" I ask.

"So far, so good!" Jackie replies. Her dark hair bounces up and down as she talks. Her hair is bleached on top and her face is completely plastered with foundation and maroon eye shadow. Somehow, Jackie manages to make herself look beautiful even with all that make-up.

Jackie reminds me of an old friend I once had in high school who painted herself with foundation and tons of mascara! I mean, if you touched her cheek, all this gunk would rub off. Either way, she still managed to make herself look so beautiful! I guess it worked out since a few years later, she won the "Miss India" contest. I was so jealous!

"I'm so glad you could make it!" Jackie says, her earrings dangling on her shoulders.

"Hi, Jackie. I got here as quickly as I could," I explain.

"Great. Come on in," she says, gesturing me into her office.

"Hey, Jenn, wait . . . " I hear that same girl call out to me, "I forgot to tell you, my name is Vanessa. It was great meeting you today," she smiles. "Call me anytime, OK?"

"Sure, it was nice meeting you, too," I say as Jackie closes the door behind us.

We step into Jackie's office and two desks are placed perpendicular to each other.

"Take a seat, Jenn," Jackie says, motioning me to sit in front of her desk.

The office is very tiny, about the size of my bedroom back home in Michigan. There are four gigantic filing cabinets

lining the walls on the opposite side and in the middle of the
room is a table with four "old school" wooden chairs.

"I can't wait to start tutoring," I say.

"Well, I'm glad. I wish we had you sooner, back in
September. Sometimes the students feel more comfortable
with someone they know from the start of the semester. But I
don't really think getting acquainted with the students will be
a problem for you."

"That's great because I'm really excited to meet all
the students!" I say.

"That's wonderful! But first I want to make sure you
understand the photo project I've given you. Remember, at
our orientation meeting, I asked if you could be the photographer for our Saturday activity? We're doing a rope climbing
exercise," she reminds me.

"Oh, of course!"

I tried to forget about that!

"Great!" She says. "So you'll need to bring a camera.
Do you have a camera?"

"Not a very good one," I say.

"That's all right. You can probably borrow my camera," she says.

"Would I need a camera chip, like a smart card?"

"Oh, no need. I have a few I could lend you," Jackie
says, brushing her hair away from her face. "Anyway, I just
need at least fifty photos of the students and tutors working
on team building exercises. Then I need them edited into a
photo slideshow. I want to show the parents and students. I
was thinking of doing a slideshow presentation with your
photos?"

"Sure, that sounds great." I say.

"Would you be willing to come in on a Saturday? We
have Saturday Academy every month."

"I can definitely be there," I say excitedly.

"Great. So, is that enough time to get the photos done, then?" Jackie asks.

"Oh, yeah, definitely." I've never had the best video editing skills. But when it comes to taking photos and putting them together as a slideshow, it's not so hard.

I had a project like this during my last AmeriCorps position. I got to use Adobe Premiere. But it was quite outdated, I think I was using Adobe Premiere 6.0! Which was *so* 2001!

"That's great. So, do you have any questions, then?" She asks.

"When do I begin tutoring?" I ask eagerly.

"Hopefully soon," Jackie says, pulling out a typed sheet of paper with names and phone numbers across the page. "Here." She slides the paper over to me. "These are all the contact numbers of the tutors. You might find this useful in case you ever need to get a hold of them."

I nod and smile over at her.

Jackie turns around and pulls out a few more typed papers from a small gray filing cabinet. "Here is a list of all the students I have assigned to you." She hands over the list.

"Oh, I can't wait," I say. How exciting!

"I even prepared this for you." Jackie reaches across her desk and grabs a bright, purple binder with tabs sticking out from the sides. "I divided the binder in several sections. Go ahead and look through it," she says.

I open the binder and flip through its pages.

"You'll notice I printed out all the student's contact information, their parent's information and their current transcripts from last semester." She leans over and points to one of the pages. "I also have their current school schedules. Are you familiar with block schedules?" She looks up at me.

I shake my head. "What is that, again?"

She smiles at me, skipping over block schedules, and points to one of the tabs in the back of the binder.

"Anyway, this is where you'll find all the information on scholarships, financial aid, FAFSA, everything you need to inform these students about. Now, I've assigned you seven seniors and you'll be working with them until the end of the school year," Jackie says.

Only seven? Wait, as in seven students? That's all? What about the thirty something students that each of the other tutors have?

"So, um, are these my *only* students, then?" I finally ask, looking at one of the pages in front of me.

"Yes, I've assigned you seven seniors. Those are all the seniors we have in the Upward Bound Program. Oh, and if anyone asks, your title is 'Upward Bound School Advisor.'"

"But I'm still a tutor?" I ask, looking confused.

"Not really," she says.

Oh?

"You're an advisor. So you aren't going to be tutoring students in the basics like math or science. You'll be going over college prep stuff. So for this week, I'd suggest you start your homework."

"Homework?"

Jackie looks puzzled. "Is that a comment or a question?"

AmeriCorps didn't tell me that homework was in the contract! I came out here to enjoy the *sunshine* and eat free food!

"Look, Jenn," she leans in, "I'm only asking for a little help here. I got you started on the binder but I need you to fill in the rest," she grins.

"Sure!" I manage a weak smile. "I'll definitely get started on this right away," I say, closing the binder, not sure where to begin.

Jackie leans over and grabs the binder from me and flips it to a blank page in the back entitled, *Scholarships.* "You see this page?" She says, pointing to the last section of the binder.

I nod my head.

"This page needs to be filled with a list of scholar-ships for the students." Jackie says.

"Oh, OK." I try to sound enthused.

"And this page," she flips back through the previous set of tabs, "this is where you need to print off information regarding financial aid, FAFSA, anything you find relevant regarding money for college." She plops the binder back down on the desk. "Does that make sense?"

"Absolutely," I say.

So this is my homework?

Argh.

"I was hoping you could meet with the seniors today. Can you do that?" Jackie asks.

"Of course."

"Great," Jackie says, smiling. "I'll call the students out of class and have them meet you here in the Career Center. Go ahead and take a seat at a table out there," she says, point-ing to a round table sitting in the middle of the room.

"Sounds great!" I say cheerfully, reaching out my hand to shake hers. But she looks at me, confused by the ges-ture.

I pull my hand back and blush. I feel so stupid. I turn around and head out of her office and take a seat at the round table.

A few minutes later, I spot a few students walking into the Career Center.

I wave them over. "Hi, are you guys the seniors?"

A boy walks over to me.

"Hi. Are you Jenn? Jackie sent me down here."

Wow. Who is he? He's smiling over at me with huge dimples and greasy blonde hair.

"Yes, I'm Jenn! Nice to meet you. What's your name?" I ask, pulling out the typed document with the stu-dents' names listed on the top.

"Zack, Zachary Stone," the greasy blonde says.

I look down the page and find a "Zack Stone" listed near the bottom of the list.

"These are the other seniors, too," he says, gesturing toward a few more students staggering into the room. "Guys, yo, over here," he calls out to them. "This is *her.*" He says, pointing right at my face.

Gosh, how rude! Didn't they ever learn not to *point* in people's faces?

"Are you Jenn?" A black guy with a small Afro walks over to me and pulls out his hand.

"Yes, hi. What's your name?" I ask.

"I'm Gregory Clawson." He shakes my hand and takes a seat at the table.

"Dude, you're so stupid sometimes," Zack says, taking a seat next to me. "I told you it was her. Don't you listen?"

"So?" Greg looks over and gives Zack a look of who cares.

"Excuse me, Jenn?"

I look up and a short, pudgy girl with dark brown hair stares at me. "I'm Alejandra, Alejandra Garcia," she says with a Spanish accent, "um, just so you know, I can't stay long. I have like . . . this thing to do."

"OK. What thing?" I ask.

Alejandra looks up at the digital clock hanging on the wall. "I have like two minutes and that's it," she says, looking back at me. "So, why am I here?"

If Alejandra has to go, I clearly don't want to make her late.

"Do you have a doctor's appointment or something?" I ask curiously.

"Yes! How did you know?" Alejandra says, agreeing too quickly.

I smile at her. "Well Jackie called you guys over here because I'm supposed to be tutoring you this week."

"Great, so we'll be seeing more of each other later on," Alejandra says and prances out the door.

Wait!

"Well, hey," Zack says, combing his fingers through his hair, "I don't have time for tutoring either," he says, getting up from his chair. "My grandma's in the hospital. I have to go back to my house and take care of her now."

Wait, huh? "So your grandma's at the hospital but you're taking care of her at your house?" I inquire.

"Yes . . . I mean, no . . . no, she's um . . . she's at the hospital, remember? I have to go to the hospital, bye." Zack immediately runs out of the room.

I didn't even have time to stop him! Well, I probably would have looked like an idiot chasing after him calling out, *"Zack, come back, come back! I need you."* It might look a bit wrong, especially on school property. And just think, what would Jackie think of me? And the teachers? I would be known as the volunteer pedophile. Ew!

"Zack ain't comin' back now," Greg informs me.

What? Wait, why?

"He ain't comin' back ever. He tries to avoid Jackie cuz he hates this whole program," Greg says.

I want to ask, "Then why does he bother coming in at all?" Jackie led me to believe the students wanted to be here. Why are the students suddenly disappearing?

"Sorry I'm late, Jennifer!" A girl strolls in, sweating profusely and carrying a gym bag. "I ran as fast as I could."

Wow. She smells like dirty gym towels. Of course I won't tell *her* that. "Hey, can I get your name?" I ask her politely.

"Sure," she smiles at me, "I'm Arianna Arslanian. I'm Armenian," she says proudly.

I hope she doesn't ask me to repeat all that!

"Hi! We're here!" I hear two girls call out as they walk through the door. "I'm Sonia and this is Kavita," Sonia announces.

I check and find their names listed on the page.

"Are you Jenn?" Sonia asks with a Bengali accent.

I know it's Bengali since my neighbors back home were from India and their dad used to speak Bengali all the time.

"Hey, thank you guys for coming to the Career Center today," I say.

"So, why are we here?" They ask politely.

"I'm going to be one of your tutors this year until you guys graduate," I explain.

"Another tutor? Cool," Arianna says.

Oh, I love this Arianna girl already!

"Actually, I'm not really going to be a tutor, maybe more like an advisor," I tell them.

"Huh, say what?" Greg says.

"Well," I begin, "I'll be helping you guys out with—"

"Sorry, I'm late. I'm Priscilla." I hear a girl calling out in a Spanish accent.

"Hi, nice to meet you." I look over and find a short Mexican girl walking over to me. "Well I was just telling everyone that I'm here as your advisor for the school year." I continue, "I'll be helping you out with scholarships and finding money for college—"

"Free money is always nice," Greg says.

"Absolutely! And that's why I really want to help you guys look for scholarships, grants and sign you up for FAFSA!"

"Cool. Well when do we start?" Sonia asks.

I love their enthusiasm!

"If you guys can meet this week, that would be great," I say.

"Yo, that works!" Greg blurts out.

"OK, so are you going to call us?" Arianna asks, "because I have softball practice so I can't meet after school. Did you want to meet during lunch, instead?"

"Sure, I guess."

"Cool," Arianna pulls out a pen and pad of paper from the front pocket of her backpack, "I'll give you my cell phone number. You can text too, if you want. It doesn't cost me anything."

"Yo, Jenn," Greg asks. "Can I have that?" He asks, pointing to the typed sheet with all the students' names on it. "I was gonna write my cell number on it."

"Here." I hand it over to him and give him my pen. What a great idea!

For the next few minutes, they hand off the paper to one another and put their cell phone number next to their name. Only, I have everyone's name and number except Zack and Alejandra's. But at least this way it's very convenient. This is so thoughtful of them! I didn't even have to ask! Gosh, this meeting is going so well, I wonder what our sessions will be like.

Greg grabs the sheet from Priscilla. "You done?" He asks.

"Yep." She hands him back the pen. "So, are we done, now?" Priscilla asks, looking at me.

"Yep. I'll give you guys a call or text you this week to set up an appointment," I say.

"Great, thanks Jennifer." Arianna says and walks out of the door.

"See ya." Greg smiles and walk out.

"Nice meeting you." The Indian girls wave and walk out.

I turn toward Priscilla. "Nice meeting you Priscilla."

She gives me a weak smile and leaves the room.

"Jenn, can I see you in my office, please?" I hear Jackie calling my name.

I walk over to her desk and take a seat. "You wanted to see me?"

"Do you have a laptop?" Jackie asks.

"No, not yet. Do I need to buy one?"

"Gosh, no! We would never make you buy one." She says.

Thank goodness.

"I actually just got off the phone with Rosaline and she suggested you check out one of their laptops. They have a Mac. Are you familiar with how to use a Mac?" She asks.

Oh, I love Mac laptops! They're like the best! And you never have to worry about viruses!

"Yeah, I've used a Mac before." Well, a few times. Adrian owns one.

"Great, well, I told her you would stop by to pick one up. She also said she wanted to speak to you regarding your previous AmeriCorps position."

Shoot! What does she want to know? I don't like telling people about my last job . . . well, volunteer "job."

"Does she want me there now?" I ask.

"Is that OK?" Jackie asks eagerly.

"No problem." I get out of the chair and start to head toward the door.

"Oh Jenn, did you see Priscilla today?" She leans forward in her chair.

"Yeah, she came by just now."

"Shoot, I really wanted to speak with her. Next time you see her, please let her know I need to see her, OK?"

"Sounds good. I'll let her know when I see her this week."

"Great, thanks Jenn." Jackie smiles.

"Thanks." I sprint out of the room and head toward my car. I can't wait, my first Mac laptop! How cool! Adrian will be so jealous! He's always telling me how much he wants a Mac laptop for his video editing, in addition to his Mac desktop computer.

A few minutes later, I pull into one of the parking stalls and head toward the office of "Reading and Beyond." I walk in the office and find people working in cubicles with computers and phones. I head to the first counter and a young girl with braided hair looks up at me.

"Hello, can I help you?" She asks politely.

"Hi," I say to her. "I'm here to see Rosaline."

"She's in her office. Go ahead." She points down the hall toward the back of the office.

I head down the hallway and find Rosaline sitting behind her desk, reading a pamphlet.

"Hi Rosaline."

Rosaline looks up and smiles, "Hi, I'm so glad you could make it. Jackie said you might stop by. Have a seat," she gestures toward one of the chairs in her office.

Wow, it's hot in here! It's like steaming in this office. I'm wearing a fleece sweater on top of one of my cutest tanks. But I had to dress a little professionally for today, so it's not like I can take off my sweater.

"Are you cold at all? Sometimes it can get a bit cold in the back of the office. All the hot air rushes to the front." She laughs.

Is she serious?

"No, I'm fine." I can't possibly tell her I'm *hot*, then ask her to turn on the cold air and I'm sure she doesn't want to increase the electric bill.

"So, there are just a few things I wanted to talk to you about. Jackie did mention that you need a computer, too, so we'll get to that before you leave today."

Awesome! Actually, do you think I could have it now?

"So, Jenn, tell me," she leans across her desk, "Why did you leave your previous AmeriCorps VISTA job?"

"Well, I'm not sure where to begin." Hmm, should I tell her about the strange white people or the nice Mexicans?

"I guess I'm wondering," she leans back in her chair, "why you left? If you enjoyed being with the people there, why did you leave?"

Um, well, I have too many answers to that question and I'm not sure which to pick. Hmm . . . should I begin by talking about the Mormon family I lived with and the weird people who came over for dinner? Or how about the nice Mexicans who never spoke English? What about the bat incident where I almost got killed? Does she want to hear about that? How personal does she want me to be?

"Well, there's a lot to think about, I guess." I finally say.

"What about the job? Tell me about your last job and the people you worked with." Rosaline leans closer to me from across the desk. "Jenn, if you don't want to talk about it, I understand. I don't want there to be any pressure. I was just curious why you chose to switch positions," she smiles.

"It's not a problem." Is it? "It would be nice to tell someone about my experience." Actually I've been meaning to call the VISTA Member Support Unit and bitch them out about it!

"So, would you like to begin by telling me about your last supervisor? Would that make it easier?"

"Sure, well my last supervisor was mean." There, I said it.

"How so? If you don't mind me asking." She says.

"Of course not," I begin. "Well, you see, when I first started, I had one supervisor. He was this old guy and he made a lot of corny jokes." Actually he was super duper nice and he never made me come to work on Friday! Yay and I still got paid!

"That's great, Jenn." She says.

"Unfortunately, a few weeks later, he retired from his job and they had no one to replace him. They didn't know he was retiring I guess, otherwise they would never have opted for an AmeriCorps volunteer in their town."

Mind you, I worked in a town of about 12,000 people, and half were prisoners or mental patients. Although if you ask anyone there, they will tell you this, "We have a large city, one of the largest towns in the Central Valley of California, roughly about 12,000 people live here." Little did I know that 6,000 people, or half the town, made up two prisons and a psychiatric hospital.

"Why did he retire?" Rosaline asks.

"I don't know, exactly, but I was sad to see him leave. That's when it got bad. I had two supervisors looking after me at the time. I was assigned to the City Hall Director and the City Hall Marketing Specialist. I had to report to them on a daily basis. They made sure I was busy all the time. But that only lasted for a month until they finally found a replacement for the old guy."

Up to this point, my whole AmeriCorps VISTA job was going OK, not bad, but not good. This only got worse when the replacement came.

"What department did you work for, Jenn?" Rosaline asks.

"Well I worked for City Hall, under the direction of the Economic Director and Marketing Specialist," I explain.

"Did you report back to someone in Fresno?" She asks.

"Well, we worked a lot with the Economic Development Department of Fresno County and I met a few of the guys who worked there, like Adam."

"Oh, of course, I've met Adam. He's a wonderful person." She says.

"I like to think so," I say.

"And you said you worked for two people?" She asks. She really does ask a lot of good questions.

"Well, when the replacement came, they finally assigned me to just one supervisor, which was the Economic Director. Anyway, she was nice at first but then she didn't like the way I did things."

"What do you mean?" Rosaline asks, smiling at me, "is it OK if I ask these questions?"

"Sure. It's not a problem." I kind of like that she asks questions about my experience. This starts to feel like a therapy session.

"I guess I'm just wondering what kind of projects you did for City Hall?" She asks.

"Well the new supervisor's name was Candy. She made me do these marketing projects. Like, I had to put together pamphlets, brochures, stuff like that. I learned to use software programs like Illustrator. But she was really picky, not like the old guy, James, who was really laid back."

"So, Candy laid more ground rules, that kind of thing?" Rosaline asks.

"Yeah, kind of. Except Candy was really rude about it. I could never take breaks." Like OK, every time I left the office, she would peek out of her office and watch me. It was kind of creepy. "Oh and I forgot to mention, when she got hired to replace James, she made me move my stuff into City Hall."

"Where were you working before?" Rosaline asks.

"Actually, they had me assigned to this really small office which was around the corner. But I only worked there for a few months before Candy become the new supervisor."

"Was she new to the marketing department?" Rosaline asks.

"Yes. We never got along. Candy really had no prior experience in running a department and—" and on top of that, she was a complete witch! She was too young to run an office! She was only three years older than me and she was telling *me* what to do!

Candy was way too blonde for her job! She was making $35,000 a year, and showing it off with her new shoes and her fancy bag and her fancy ways and ugh! Did she have to flirt with *every* guy in City Hall?

Even the Mayor winked at Candy as she passed him in the hallway, and this guy was like in his sixties. And why did she always make me her slave? I'm not her secretary!

They pay the secretary, an elderly lady, to do that sort of thing! Except the secretary was really very nice. Even so, I felt my services were being taken advantage of and I didn't like it one bit.

"It sounds like things didn't go well," Rosaline replies softly.

"I know it sounds bad but I couldn't keep up with Candy. She wanted all these projects done in a short period of time and she never gave me advance notice! I just couldn't work for someone like that." I say, looking down at my feet.

Ugh. I can't find a way to express how awful this experience was with Candy without going into too much detail. I hated her, absolutely hated her!

"Did you ever talk to a California State Supervisor?" Rosaline asks.

She must be referring to one of the State Supervisors, like Nancy Reed. Nancy deals with AmeriCorps VISTA problems, VISTA volunteer issues, troubles with your supervisor, that kind of thing. I learned about this in training.

I found Nancy's name and contact information on the AmeriCorps website. She never returned any of my calls or emails. And to this day, I still don't have any idea if Nancy knows about my situation back in that small town or what!

"I did call Nancy Reed."

"Well, hopefully Nancy got back to you," Rosaline reassures me.

Um . . . I don't think so. I called her like, oh, two months ago.

"Well if it makes you feel any better," Rosaline begins, attempting a smile, "Jackie is a wonderful person and very laid back. I'm sure you two will hit it off well."

"I'm sure we will. She seems very nice," I say.

"Good, so if you want," Rosaline says, grabbing a form off her desk, "we can go ahead and sign you out with a computer."

"Oooh, that would be great!" I'm so excited. Let's do this! I really need cheering up! This is almost as good as shopping!

"Kong can help you with the computers. He's in the cubicle to your right when you walk out of my office and down the hall," Rosaline motions.

"Thank you so much." I say.

"Oh, no problem, Jenn. And thank you for sharing your experience. I'm really glad you did," Rosaline says, handing me the form.

"Definitely," I say.

"Enjoy the rest of your day," Rosaline says, smiling at me.

I walk out of Rosaline's office and down the hall. I spot Kong, a Hmong looking man of about forty, dressed in a short sleeve shirt, slacks and a baseball cap. He's sitting and talking across the room to a woman in another cubicle. They each have their own green cubicles! How cute!

I decide to wait for his conversation with the woman to end. But I just stand there, holding the form in my hand, feeling stupid.

"Hi, are you Kong?" I ask, deciding not to wait any longer, and walk up to his cubicle.

"Hello," he looks over at me. "Yep, you found me. You're Jenn?"

"Yes, Rosaline gave me this form to fill out." I hand him the form and he snatches it out of my hand.

"Right. OK. Follow me and we'll get you set up with a laptop," he says.

I follow him down the hall to a storage room with a large cabinet and shelves along the wall. There are tons of computers and I spot two boxes of Mac laptops.

"So, here's one," he grabs one of the Mac laptops from the bottom shelf.

Would it be a crime to take two instead of one, one for me and one for Adrian?

No? Just kidding . . .

"Here you go," he hands over the computer still in its original box.

"It's new!" I exclaim.

"So, you're going to take care of this, right?" Kong asks in a serious tone.

"Yeah, totally."

"No scratches on the laptop or else it's on you," he says.

"Right. Of course!" I say, trying to lighten the conversation.

"OK, so you have until the end of your volunteer service and then you have to bring it back," Kong says.

"Do you by chance, have a laptop computer bag I could put this in?" I ask, holding up the computer box.

"Um, that *is* the laptop bag," Kong says, pointing to the cardboard box with its plastic handle and colorful pictures.

"That box," I ask, pointing to the box, "is supposed to be the computer bag?"

"You're good to go," he says, ignoring my question.

Haven't they noticed people carry laptops in bags and not boxes?

"OK, no problem," I say, agreeing to his peculiar logic. I really don't want to carry a laptop everyday inside its original box. I mean, it says "Mac laptop" in bold letters on all sides and there's a picture of it for those who can't read! Why would anyone carry a laptop in a *mug me* box with a billboard on its side?

"So if I get mugged carrying around this computer box, is it my responsibility to replace it?" I ask, realizing I'm an open target for crime.

"You're all set. Just sign here," Kong gives me a pen and points to a space at the bottom of the page for my signature. Once more he ignores my question.

I sign where he indicates and thank him.

As I get closer to the car, I pull the box closer to me, making sure no one's watching or about to rob me. I took self-defense, so if all else fails, I'll gouge out their eyes!

I hear conversation and turn around to spot a few Mexican men smoking by a grocery store over on the far left side. They ignore me and my *mug me* box. Good!

I look back toward my car and almost bump into a boy. I nearly drop the box as the boy runs right past me. Then I hear a woman yelling in the distance.

"Jorge! Enough! Come back!" The woman calls out to the boy a few cars over.

I hurry toward my car before the boy circles back. Maybe now she's upset her son wasn't able to snatch the computer box out of my hand! What if it was all a set up for her boy to steal my *mug me* box?

Ah!

I heard the French government hires kids to go up to tourists and pick-pocket them, and afterward, pays them a reward. I think I heard that on the History Channel, or was it the Discovery Channel? No, I definitely heard it on the local news! No, wait . . . Jason told me! Damn it Jason! Why do I believe anything you say? Stupid boy!

I decide to get in my car and hurry home to show Adrian my brand new Mac laptop! OK, so it's not exactly *mine*, but it is for the next few months! Oh, Adrian's going to be so jealous!

It's really too bad they don't let the volunteers keep these things. I mean, why can't they be all nice and friendly and be like, "Welcome aboard! Here's your very own laptop!" Whoo hoo! After all, I *am* volunteering my own time, when I could be relaxing at home in my own bed, reading or watching TV and eating M&M's. I mean, I'm living on less than nothing here! Can't they afford to at least *buy me* my very own laptop?

Ten

Later that evening, I get a call from Seven Corners, the insurance company for AmeriCorps volunteers. They tell me they finally received my TB test results from the VISTA Member Support Unit. However, Seven Corners says they can't issue me a reimbursement.

"But, why?" I ask the woman on the phone.

"I'm sorry, Ma'am, but you're on your mother's insurance, not Seven Corners, and the Seven Corners Insurance guarantees reimbursements."

"What does that have to do with anything?" I ask, confused by her explanation.

"You see Ma'am," the woman continues with a nasal voice, "If you're on your parent's insurance, we can't issue a reimbursement check because you're on another insurance plan. You should have *them* pay for it. Not us."

"What do you think I should do, then?" I'm very desperate to get my reimburse check. It was like $26! That could pay for half a tank of gas! Every poor person would be fighting this!

"Well, I suggest you call your parent's insurance and mail or fax your TB results to them so they can pay for it. Then they can reimburse you, instead of us." She says.

"How do I do that? Just call them up? That's all?" I ask desperately.

"Yes, and then call us back," she says.

I hang up and dial the number for my mother's insurance. Thank goodness I have it programmed in my phone. I knew it would come in handy . . . one day.

I wait for someone to answer.

"Hello, PHP, this is Rebecca speaking."

"Hi, I need your help. I'm an AmeriCorps volunteer and—"

She interrupts. "I'm sorry, what did you say?"

Oh good God. I do *not* want to go through this again with someone else!

"I said I'm in *AmeriCorps*." I slowly say again.

"Never heard of it. What is that?" She asks.

"It's like the Peace Corps," I just *had* to bring that up again. "It's volunteering and I do it for a year and I don't have to pay my student loans . . . "

She cuts me off, "OK, and what was your question?"

"Basically, as part of my AmeriCorps volunteer service, I had to pay to get a TB test done and I need a reimbursement," I explain.

"Let me look up your information. Are you on your parent's insurance?" She asks.

"Yes," I say.

"Your last name, please."

I give her my name and she clicks a few buttons on the keyboard.

"Linda? Is that your mother's name?" She asks a few seconds later.

"Yes, that's her."

"And you are Jennifer?" She inquires.

"Yes, I am."

"Jennifer, it says here, you were taken off your mother's insurance about two months ago when you turned twenty four."

"So, I'm not on my mom's insurance?" Then why did AmeriCorps tell me I was?

"Nope. You're no longer on her insurance. Did you want to set up one for yourself?" She offers.

Yeah right, I'm in AmeriCorps, does it look like I have money growing out of my ears?

"So you can't give me a reimbursement, then?" I ask desperately.

"No, I'm sorry, we can't," she says, sounding genuinely sorry.

"Thank you anyway." I close the cell phone and lean back on the couch. This totally sucks. I feel like I'm just going back and forth. I feel useless. Why can't anyone help me out here?

I decide to call Seven Corners back and tell them they were wrong and demand to get my money back. I scroll through my phone numbers and dial their number again.

"Hello, Seven Corners Support, this is Tina. How can I help you?"

"Hi, I just called like two minutes ago and I want my money." I think I might have sounded just a bit over the top.

I really don't want to be aggressive, but it's like, that's my only option here! I'm really in need of that cash. After all, I could totally buy like the whole last season of "The Office" DVD with that money!

"Let me check. Please hold." She puts me on hold and I'm listening to Bach or Mozart or what was that deaf guy's name?

Ugh.

"Jennifer?" She says as I hear her pick up the phone.

"Yes?"

"I'm reading through your history and it says you obtained a TB test and you would like a reimbursement for $26. Is that correct?" She explains.

I knew they would come around!

"Right!" I say.

"Unfortunately—"

Shit.

"We cannot send you a reimbursement check for $26 because you are not entitled to a reimbursement," she says.

WHAT?

"Since you're on your mother's insurance—"

And let me stop you right there. "Actually, Ma'am, I just called my mother's insurance and they verified I'm *not* on her insurance anymore."

"Were you on her insurance when you started your AmeriCorps term of service? I believe that was," she pauses, "almost 6 months ago, is that correct?"

I count backwards. Argh. "Yes, that's correct."

"That's probably the reason why. If you were on your mother's insurance when you started your AmeriCorps term, then we're unable to change our computer systems to allow you to get a reimbursement check."

Huh?

Wait!

"But I'm no longer on my mom's insurance *now!*" I insist.

"I realize that. But at the time you signed up for AmeriCorps, you were on her insurance. We cannot change insurance plans during your term of service."

Wait, that makes absolutely no sense. She has a computer and can make corrections. Is she messing with me?

"Are you for real?" I say half seriously.

"I'm sorry, but unfortunately there's nothing we can do. Have you tried contacting your mother's insurance company?"

Is she deaf? Didn't I just tell her I was on the phone with them a few minutes ago?

"So, I really cannot get my money back?" I ask again.

"I'm sorry, unfortunately, you can't." She says for a second time.

"So what can I do?" I ask.

"Unfortunately, I'm not sure," she says.

Could you maybe stop using the word, "unfortunately?"

Grrr.

"So, you can't give me any money back? Not even like $10?" I ask, willing to barter.

"Unfortunately, not," she says.

Argh! I slam my cell phone against the wall and smash my head into the couch.

"Jenn?" Adrian rushes out of the bedroom, "What was all that noise?" He kneels down beside the couch.

I look up at him and tears are spilling out of my eyes. "This totally sucks."

"What's wrong?" He gently brushes my face with his hands.

"AmeriCorps is stupid and I hate them!" I say, attacking the couch pillow.

He sits on the couch and places my head in his lap.

"I'm sorry, Adrian," I say.

"What was all that noise? I thought you were hurt."

"I was so mad I threw the cell phone at the wall."

"Figures," he says.

I look up as he rolls his eyes. I sit up, my legs straddling the couch.

"Is your phone broken?" He asks, looking at the phone on the floor.

"Probably not," I say as Adrian tickles my belly, trying to cheer me up. I jump up and tickle him back and he wraps his arms around me and kisses me, tongue and everything! He always knows how to make me feel better.

"So how about those condoms?" He asks, pulling me away from his face for a moment.

"What?" I ask in shock.

He laughs, "I'm joking."

"Hey you better watch it," I say, tickling him under the arms.

"I'm not ticklish there, remember?" He laughs.

I grab his feet and tickle him.

"Hey!" He throws me over his back, holding my wrists, and carries me to the bedroom. He closes the door and throws me on the mattress.

I undress and then I help him peel off his clothes. I grab his belt and throw it across the room.

He jumps on the mattress, grabs my waist and kisses my neck. This is what heaven *must* feel like, I'm sure of it!

Eleven

It's my first day of tutoring with Upward Bound! I'm so excited. I'm practically ripping my clothes off the hangers trying to decide what to wear for today!

"Jenn, I'm leaving. I'll see you when I get home," I hear Adrian calling from the bedroom doorway.

I rush out of the walk-in closet and dash out the bedroom to say goodbye. "Hey, have fun at class."

He rolls his eyes playfully. "Thanks, I guess." He gives me a kiss and then heads out the door.

I race back to the closet and throw on a pair of 1970's flare jeans, a dark red shirt, and sneakers I found at the thrift store.

Now that I'm poor and everything, I practically live at thrift stores! I never realized all the cool stuff you could buy there. Did you know you can buy greeting cards at a thrift store? They're like 50 cents each! Deal breaker!

I grab my keys from a cardboard box serving as an end table. We don't have the money yet to afford a real dresser, nightstand, or even a real bed for that matter.

I look at the clock and realize I'm going to be late if I don't leave now. I sprint down the hallway and—

Holy shit! What's that smell? It smells like mold . . . and is that mildew?

I hurry over to the kitchen and open the refrigerator door. I grab the milk and look at the expiration date. Nope. Still good. I turn around and decide to check the pantry for moldy bread. I grab both loaves and flip them over but I don't see any sign of mold on either loaf. Hmm. I'm about to check the living room when I hear the sound of zombies and gunshots.

Ah ha! I peer around the corner of the kitchen and there, sitting in the living room is Jason with a Capri Sun drink in one hand and a game controller in the other. I slowly walk up behind him near the couch and—

Gag! Instantly I get a whiff of the most disgusting stench in the world! It's Jason's armpit sweat!

How can someone who takes 40 minute showers smell that horrible? Jason's wearing nothing but boxers and playing a stupid zombie game! Doesn't he have a class to go to?

Come to think of that, I don't think I've ever seen Jason heading to class before 3PM, or even going to class at all? Which is really odd since Adrian told me Jason was taking sixteen credits of classes, which is like, what, five classes? None of which are online I might add!

I look at the clock on the Comcast cable box. It's five minutes past noon. Except I can't leave. I really need to clear out this sweaty odor!

While holding my breath, I race over to the balcony door and swing it open. I'm still holding my breath as I turn around and race out of the apartment as fast as I can.

Once I'm outside, I exhale it all out! Finally. Good, clean, quality air. Wait a second, didn't they say Los Angeles was known for having smog and bad air? Shoot, does that mean Fresno is polluted, too? Sometimes I really do miss the clean air of the Midwest.

When I arrive at the high school, I find an empty seat at one of the computers located in the front of the Career Center. A few other students are seated around the room, working on homework or projects for class. I hear giggling coming from the back of the room and a few teenage girls with pink hair and nose rings are eating candy and watching a video online.

"Good Morning, *Jinn*." Monique says, pronouncing my name like "Gin." She walks in wearing five inch heels, a bright green cami, and tight black pants one size under. Her boobs push out like they're trying to escape.

"Hey, how's it going?" I ask politely.

"Pretty good. Oh, I forgot to tell you," Monique says, taking a seat next to me and turning on a computer. "Priscilla's making up a test today, so she can't meet with you."

Priscilla was supposed to be my first student of the day. I had contacted my students yesterday and arranged for them to stop by for tutoring this week. This now leaves a two hour gap.

"Did she say why?" I ask.

"Nope. I guess you just have to call her," Monique says, opening Firefox on the computer.

"I don't actually have another student for two hours. Do you have any suggestions on how to kill time?" I ask eagerly.

"Well," Monique looks over at me, "I'd suggest checking your email."

Right, well, that should only take like five minutes.

"Oh, and just warning you," Monique says, opening Hotmail.com, "We don't get Facebook *or* MySpace."

Right, well, there goes like two hours of my time!

"Did you bring a book?" Monique asks, pulling out a *Cosmo* magazine. "I always carry these babies with me. You never know when you'll need them."

"No, but I guess I could bring one next time," I offer.

A voice from behind says, "Hello!"

Monique and I turn around to find one of the tutors walking in wearing cowboy boots and carrying a huge, designer handbag.

Oh no! That's the Mexican girl from the orientation meeting! I have to hide! She probably remembers me and how much I embarrassed myself in front of everyone. She probably still thinks I'm going to stalk her at our apartment complex!

"Hello? Jenn, right?" She says, taking a seat next to Monique.

"Yep," I say.

Don't act weird . . . don't act weird.

"Hi. I'm sorry I didn't get to introduce myself the other day. I'm Maribel," she says.

Hey, she said "Hi" and she's talking to me! Yay! She likes me!

"Hi, it's nice to meet you, again," I say politely.

"Hey Maribel, what up, girl?" Monique asks.

"Oh, Monique, have you seen my new cowboy boots?" Maribel says, throwing a leg up on the table.

Monique surveys the boot. "Girl, why are you buying those things? I thought you said you had to save money for a plane ticket to see your dad in Mexico," Monique says.

"I do, but look," Maribel slides off the boot and points to a logo underneath it. "See? They're handmade. Go ahead, try them on!" She says, bragging.

Monique grabs the boots and attempts to put them on. "Damn! They don't fit me. Your feet are too small Maribel."

"The boots cost $200," Maribel brags.

What? WHAT? That's over a week's pay!

"Maribel!" Monique says, tugging the cowboy boots off her feet, "Girl, I don't know about this. Where do you get the money to buy all these things? We barely get paid $10 an hour."

"I know, but I'm looking for another job," Maribel says.

I decide to leave them to their conversation. I go online and research a few scholarships for my students. After all, Jackie did say I needed to create a list of scholarships for my tutoring sessions. I open up Microsoft Word and Firefox, and start hunting for scholarships on the internet.

After two straight hours, my eyes are really straining and I think I have a migraine. Is this what it feels like to stare at the internet for so long?

As I'm about to close my eyes for a brief second, I hear the school bell. Great, in just under a few minutes, I hear a ton of students walking through the Career Center laughing and giggling. I look over and at least twenty students come in carrying backpacks. They grab empty seats at any computer they can find.

"Monique, did you hear? Priscilla's getting married. Can you believe it?" Maribel asks.

What? Priscilla? As in *my* Priscilla? As in, the girl who couldn't come to tutoring today because she had to make up a test? But isn't she like seventeen?

"Yep. Jackie told me a few days ago," Monique says nonchalantly while shopping online at Macy's.

"I can't believe it, she's so young, you know? What do her parents think?" Maribel asks.

"It was her idea, I guess. So I'm' sure they're very happy with their daughter," Monique says.

Whoa.

"Jenn!" I hear Jackie calling me from inside her office.

"Hi!" I call back.

"Come in my office for a second," Jackie calls back.

I get up and walk over toward her office.

"Hey, do you think you could fax these forms over to west campus for me?" Jackie asks, handing me several documents. "Here's the phone number." She hands me a slip of paper with a number written on it.

"Sure," but I have absolutely no idea how to use a fax machine. Why use a fax when you could just email? What's the point?

I walk out of Jackie's office and as I'm about to leave the Career Center, I realize I have no idea where the fax machine is in this school! I can't very well go back and ask Jackie. She'll think I'm not doing my job and plus, I think maybe she thinks I ask too many questions.

Hmm . . . Oh, I know! I could ask one of the students. I walk back into the Career Center and politely nudge one of the students closest to the door.

"Excuse me?" I ask.

He looks at me with disgust as I interrupt his phone texting. "What?"

"Do you know where the fax machine is?" I ask.

"The *what?*"

Has this kid never heard of a fax machine?

"What are you talking about?" He repeats.

"Nevermind. Thanks anyway," I say.

I decide to leave the Career Center. I walk toward Susan, the secretary at the front counter, even though I don't really like her but I don't have any other options, do I?

"Hello?" I ask as I approach her.

Susan looks up at me and frowns, "Yes?"

"Where could I find the fax machine? Jackie Hernandez from the Career Center sent me over here to fax some documents."

"Down the hall and to your right. It's room 222." Susan says and gestures with her hand.

"Thank you," I smile and walk down the hall.

When I get to the room, I find a set of chairs and tables lining a beige wall and there's a small refrigerator and toaster oven resting on the counter near the table. I spot the fax machine immediately to the right of the toaster oven and walk over.

Now, let's see, how do I actually send a fax?

I push a few buttons and instantly hear a buzzing noise. Is that a good buzz or a bad buzz? Hmm . . .

"Need help?" A soft voice comes from the hallway.

I look up and an elderly woman with a crinkly face and pleasant smile walks in.

"Sometimes this fax machine can be a little tricky. Here, allow me," she says, taking the documents out of my hand.

She pushes a few more buttons on the machine and slowly slides the papers in one at a time. When she finishes with the last page, she hands me back the forms.

"There, piece of cake," she smiles.

"Thanks so much. I really appreciate it." I say.

"Oh, no problem. Have a good day," she says as she walks out of the room.

I head back to the Career Center.

"Here you go," I say, handing over the forms to Jackie.

She looks up and smiles, "Great! Thanks Jenn."

I go back to my seat and open up Firefox again. I check my email one last time, even though I've already checked it now like six times. I look back over at the doorway. Still no sign of Greg. He was next after Priscilla. I pull out my planner from my bag and verify Greg's name for this afternoon's appointment. Where is he?

After about twenty minutes, Greg finally shows up. He's tall and thin with an Afro and wearing a sport's jersey.

"Yo, sorry I'm late," he says, plopping into the seat next to me. "So, what're we doin' today?"

"Well," I say, pulling out the binder Jackie had given me. "I was thinking we could go over FAFSA."

"Oh right. Um, I already did that," he says.

"What do you mean?" I thought he was supposed to do it with me?

"My mom did it for me." He says.

Oh, that's convenient, isn't it?

"So what else?" Greg asks, shaking his leg impatiently under the table.

Um . . . I look through the purple binder Jackie provided me. Well, we could talk about going to college. I scroll through the binder and notice a few pages on UC and CSU. What is that? I scan the page. Oh. "UC" is short for University of California and "CSU" is California State University. I scan a page showing at least twenty different branches of these schools. Wow, that's a lot of schools.

"What's that?" Greg asks, looking over my shoulder.

I glance up, "Have you heard of UC or CSU?"

"Yeah, I already know about those schools. But I ain't goin'." He says.

What? He has to go! Jackie said the students have to go to college!

"Why aren't you going?" I ask.

"I'm going into the Army." Greg says.

You're *what?*

Jackie didn't say anything about this! Is this allowed? I mean, shouldn't someone make him go to college?

"Are you going to college at all?" I ask.

He shakes his head, "Nope. Just the Army."

Well, so much for applying to college scholarships!

"Is that it?" He asks.

"Why did you apply for FAFSA if you aren't going to college?" I ask.

"My mom filled it out before I decided to go into the Army," he says.

Great, so now what?

"So . . . " he begins.

"So . . . " I hesitate for a few seconds, "Well, I guess that's it then."

"Cool. Well, it was nice meeting you, Jenn." He shakes my hand and grabs his bag and walks out of the room.

Well that went well, I think.

As I leave the school for the day, I glance at the clock in my car and it reads, "5PM." I pull out of the parking lot and before I merge onto the highway, I glance at my side view mirror and I see it! A UFO!

I look ahead and merge onto the highway and make my way over to the slow lane. I glance again at my side view mirror and it's gone! Hey, where did it go?

I look behind me to make sure I'm not being tailgated and I check my speedometer. Well, fifty five mph isn't bad for the slow lane. But the traffic is pretty hectic for getting off work.

As I look out my side window, I check again for the UFO. I swear I saw something flying out of the corner of my eye. I look back to the front of the window and there's a yellow, roundish object in the sky.

It's bright yellow, actually. And it's not moving. Hmm. It's not flying . . . anymore. It's just floating there, in the sky. Can anyone else see this? I look over at the person driving to my left but she's on her cell phone. Great. She's totally breaking the law. I guess this isn't news in California.

I look back and the object is still there, except this time it's getting bigger. I squint and it looks like it's getting closer. Or is it my eyes?

I stop squinting and stare directly at the object. It looks like it's coming to get me!

I look through my rear view mirror and continue driving at a steady rate without getting run over by cars behind me. I glance back up at the top of my front window and the UFO is slowly moving toward my left. It's at least 200 feet away from me.

Now it's a really bright yellow. I can't make out anything else. I don't see any other lights . . . or windows . . . or doors and it's definitely not a plane or a jet or any of those military aircrafts! Or is it?

I look behind me for oncoming traffic and I have to move over to the middle lane to allow the merging cars onto the highway. Unlike most California drivers who won't pull

over for oncoming traffic, I try to leave room for other drivers to merge.

I merge into the middle lane and look back toward
the side of my front window and suddenly, the UFO is gone.
Where did it go? I look out my rear view mirror but nothing.
I look out my side view mirror but I don't see anything.
Darn! I wish I had taken a picture of it with my cell phone
while driving, mind you. Maybe next time. If there is a next
time.

I finally approach my exit and merge off the highway.
I drive past my apartment complex on the right hand side and
head off toward the 7-Eleven store to grab some Ben and
Jerry's ice cream. After all, I did have a paranormal experience
of "The First Kind."

Twelve

The next morning, I walk up the stairs to our apartment, carrying two huge bags of toilet paper. Apparently, we ran out yesterday. Actually, Jason used the last roll of toilet paper. It was a funny story.

Last night, when I got up to pee, I had nothing to wipe myself with, except my hand! I was really upset and when I told Adrian, he suggested buying more toilet paper. That was his suggestion! I have a better one: Tell Jason to buy his own toilet paper. Who says we have to share toilet paper?

So, while the two guys sleep in until 11AM, I'm out buying packages of toilet paper rolls at the cheapest place I can think of . . . Big Lots. You can't beat $5 for 12 toilet paper rolls! Or can you? On second thought, I could have gone to the Dollar Store. But is the quality decent?

"Hey? People?" I call out as I enter the apartment. I throw down the bags of toilet paper on the dining room table and rush over to the bedroom. I swing open the door and find Adrian getting dressed. Well, at least he's up.

"Hey!" I say almost jumping on him.

He catches me in his arms. "I'm sorry I couldn't go with you."

"It's OK. I know you needed your beauty sleep after last night." I give him a kiss on the cheek.

Last night, Adrian got home really late from working. He was filming a wrestling show and the venue was four hours away so he didn't get in until 2AM. At least *Adrian* has an excuse to sleep in.

What's Jason's excuse? Oh, wait, let me guess . . . he was up until 3AM playing video games? Am I right? It doesn't take a genius to figure out Jason's schedule: sleep, breakfast, video game, lunch, video game, dinner. Didn't he have class today?

"I love you," Adrian says, wrapping his arms around my waist.

"And I love you too," I remind him, snuggling up to his warm body and giving him a hug.

"So, how much do I owe you?" He asks, kissing me on the forehead.

"Oh right! I'll go check." I rush out of the room and grab the receipt from the toilet paper bag. I scroll down the bottom of the receipt and divide the total amount into thirds. I start counting in my head. "I got it," I call out, "$3 a person."

Adrian walks out of the bedroom down the hall. "$3?" He sounds surprised.

I look over at him. "Yeah. Is that OK?"

"Are you sure?" He takes the receipt out of my hand. "Then what kind of toilet paper did we buy last time? Jason charged us $10 a person."

"Well I went to Big Lots. I guess I know how to thrift shop and Jason doesn't. I'm better, ha!" I say, hitting Adrian playfully on the arm.

"Hang on," Adrian walks down the hall toward Jason's room.

I walk into the kitchen and pull out the eggs from the refrigerator. I think I'm going to make an omelet for breakfast. I glance at the clock. On second thought, it's already lunch.

"Jason, hey, you awake in there?" I hear Adrian knocking on Jason's bedroom door.

"Yeah, I'm . . . I'm awake. What's . . . what's up?" Jason calls out as he opens the door.

"Hey. So Jenn went out and bought us toilet paper this morning," Adrian says.

"OK." Jason says.

"Yeah and we ran out last night because of you!" Adrian says jokingly.

"So, . . . so now . . . so now it's . . . it's my fault?" Jason says defensively. "Are you . . . are you blaming . . . "

Adrian cuts him off, "No, I'm not blaming you, I'm just— Oh forget it."

"OK?" Jason asks with confusion.

Adrian continues, "So we owe Jenn money."

"Why?" Jason asks still confused.

I realize Jason has a hard time grasping basic roommate concepts. Or did he just "forget" to go to class one day because the zombies were out?

"We owe her three bucks," Adrian says.

"Wait, how much?" I hear Jason gasp.

"Three bucks," Adrian says as he walks over to me in the kitchen.

"Hey, I'm making an omelet, sweetie. Do you want some?" I say, cracking a few eggs in the pan and throwing the shells in the trash.

"Sure," Adrian smiles at me. "Hey, Jason, you want some breakfast?"

We both watch Jason approach the kitchen. He takes a look inside the pan.

"No!" He shakes his head furiously, "Ew. I don't want that nasty shit!" Jason says, pointing at the pan of eggs.

Well, good. I wasn't making it for *you.*

"Um . . . Adrian?" Jason asks.

"What?" Adrian turns around to face Jason.

"How . . . how much . . . how much do I owe you?"
He repeats himself.

You don't *owe* Adrian. You *owe* me, you jerk!

"It's three dollars a person," I say, turning on the
stove and heating the pan. Oh, I almost forgot! I have to
spray the pan with Pam. Or, wait, should I use butter? Hmm,
is it too late? I already put the eggs in the pan!

"Hey, Adrian," Jason says, "Can you . . . can you
cover . . . can you cover me this time?"

I exchange glances with Adrian. How does Jason *not*
have three dollars? Come on, it's not that much money! Even
a five-year-old kid has three dollars! And what happened to
Jason's student loans? What does he do with all his money?
Oh wait, that's a rhetorical question.

Although when I had loan money, I had money left-
over to pay for rent, gas and food, before I had food stamps.
Plus, at least I had money for toilet paper! Gosh!

"Adrian . . . " Jason walks over to the living room and
sits on the couch. "I just . . . I just bought . . . bought a new
game. So . . . can you . . . can you cut me some slack here?"

Say that again?

He did *not* just admit to buying a new video game, did
he?

"Dude," Adrian walks over to the living room, "I
don't have the extra money to keep covering your expenses."

I really want to yell over at Jason, "Jason, you jerk-a-
saur-us! How can you sit there and tell us you don't have
three dollars? Somehow you had the money to buy a $30
video game . . . ? Um, am I missing something here?"

Exactly.

"Adrian, can you come in the kitchen and help me?" I
ask.

"Dude, what's her problem?" I hear Jason mutter under his breath.

Ex squeeze me?

"Dude, forget about it," Adrian whispers.

"Why is she always making you do everything?" I hear Jason whisper.

"Jason . . . " Adrian says.

"I can't stand to be around her," Jason mutters.

Um . . . *hello!* I'm right here you moron! I can hear you!

"Jason, just pay her the money, OK?" Adrian asks Jason.

"I don't have it," Jason says.

You bought a $30 video game! If you can afford $30, trust me, you can afford $3!

Argh!

I want to hurt Jason . . . very badly!

"Adrian . . . are you . . . are you planning . . . you planning on staying . . . staying with *her*?" Jason whispers.

Like I said, I can *hear* you, Jason!

"What kind of question is that?" Adrian asks defensively.

"Are you . . . are you serious? Look . . . look at her!" Jason whispers, giving Adrian a what's wrong with you stare.

That's it! I've had it!

Like the Clue game: The murder was done by Mrs. Peacock, in the living room, with the kitchen spatula. Victim's name: Jason. Occupation: Chauvinistic asshole. Reason for murder: Being a jerk-a-saur-us!

"Hey, Jenn, do you need help in there?" Adrian calls out the living room.

Go away!

"Jenn?" Adrian calls out again.

"WHAT?" I yell from the kitchen, slamming the spatula on the counter.

I turn off the stove, and throw the pan in the sink. I walk out of the kitchen toward the bedroom and slam the door. I collapse on the mattress, face down, and lie there, tears pouring out of my eyes. I can't do this! I can't live like this. I can't live with Jason. He makes me absolutely crazy!

"Jenn?" I hear Adrian open the bedroom door, "Hey, what's wrong?"

He has to ask?

"Jenn?" Adrian asks again. He closes the bedroom door, gets down on the mattress and lies next to me. He rests his head on my back.

"What?" I ask rudely.

"Hey, look, I'm sorry about Jason. He's been my friend since high school." He says.

I turn over, looking Adrian in the eye. "Are you seriously joking? The guy's a jerk-a-saur-us, Adrian. How can you not see that?"

"I know he can be a jerk, sometimes," he says.

"*Some* times*?*" I sit up.

"Don't worry. I'll talk to him," Adrian says.

"You say that every time, and look what happens when you do? Jason gets more upset every time." Which is true, he's like a baby, always whining, always getting his way until Adrian finally gives in and eventually says to Jason, "OK, do whatever you want. You don't have to pay me back." He lets the Asperger-male-chauvinist get away with stuff! Ugh.

"Jenn, I told you, Jason has the Asperger's Syndrome thing," Adrian reminds me.

"Whatever," I roll my eyes. "Yeah, right. It's probably Jason's excuse for being annoying."

"He's going through a lot," Adrian reassures me.

"Whatever," I say.

"Jenn, he's having problems with Lisa," Adrian says.

Lisa is Jason's girlfriend. She's a petite tomboy with a seriously bad temper. They have been dating for a year.

"Jason's always having problems with Lisa." I say.

How can this chauvinistic Jason actually get a girlfriend? I find that hard to believe.

"This time, Lisa's being a real pain in the butt. We should give Jason some space," Adrian says.

This, coming from the guy who always forgives Jason. I think it gives Jason an excuse to get out of doing things, like not paying his share of electricity or toilet paper. I still haven't forgotten . . . where's my $3?

I mean, if Lisa's so crazy, why not dump her? Which is exactly why I find it hard to believe that Jason is actually still dating her. I don't get it. He's a complete prick to me, and yet, when it comes to Lisa, he lets her be the boss. She runs all over him. So why does he treat Lisa better?

"Jason told me Lisa threw her cell phone at him on campus yesterday." Adrian says.

"Really?" I ask. "Is this for real? She actually threw a cell phone at him?"

Go girl!

"I'm serious. It really did happen," Adrian says, grabbing my hands and kissing them.

"Look," I say, "I'll let Jason deal with his own issues, OK? I really don't want to talk about him now."

"Hey, I'll give you $6, how's that?" Adrian replies.

"So, you're going to pay for Jason's share, too?" I ask.

"Jenn . . . " he trails off.

I cut Adrian off. "You can't keep paying for him, Adrian. It's like he's getting away with a crime."

"No one's getting away with anything. Just let me take care of it, OK?" He looks at me and frowns. "Please?" He begs.

"I want Jason gone," I say.

"What do you mean?" Adrian asks.

"I mean exactly what I say."

"You want him to *move out*?" He asks.

"Yes, I want him out of this apartment! Now!" I demand.

After all, I was the one who found this place anyway! Adrian and I had a wonderful time here before Jason moved in. So it's not like it's *Jason's* apartment. Besides, who does all the cleaning and shopping around here?

Exactly.

Who changes the toilet paper holder when it's empty?

Exactly.

Who wipes up the male piss on the floor in the bathroom?

Exactly.

Who takes out the trash with clumps of pubic hair in the bathroom wastebasket?

Exactly.

"Please, Adrian?" I beg.

"I'll talk to him," Adrian holds me close and gives me a warm hug.

"When?" I ask.

"Tomorrow," he says.

Thirteen

The next morning I get up early, around eleven, and head for the high school. It's my second day "on the job!" I know the first session didn't go well since Priscilla couldn't show up, but I enjoyed hanging out with Greg even though he *is* going into the Army. So I'm excited. Today I'll be meeting with Arianna!

As I make my way into the school, I hear the cell phone vibrating at the bottom of my purse.

I flip it open and press it to my ear.

"Hello?"

"Hey, Jenn. It's me," Adrian says.

"Oh hi! I miss you!"

"I miss you, too," he says genuinely. "I'm calling to let you know about Jason."

"You kicked him out already?" I ask hopefully.

That was fast!

"Not quite," he says.

WHAT? "Why not?" I ask.

"Listen," Adrian pauses, "I'm about to meet up with him. Is there anything else you want me to tell him?"

Yay! Today is the big day! Finally the Autistic-chauvinistic-jerk-a-saur-us is getting out of the apartment!

champagne for everyone! Speaking of which, should I pick some up after work today? Oh, I know! How about some sparkling apple cider? Adrian would like that. It's non-alcoholic, tasty *and* organic. Well, not quite organic.

"Jenn, you still there?" Adrian asks into the phone.

"Yes. Tell Jason I'm giving him one day to move his stuff out!" I smile, I'm so happy!

"How about a week?" Adrian asks.

Are we really negotiating this? I mean, Jason actually had the nerve to stand near me and ask Adrian what he thinks of me! There is absolutely *no* negotiating this.

"Adrian, go and talk to him! Good luck!" I say into the phone.

"Thanks Ill need it. Call you later," he says and hangs up.

I walk into the administration building and smile over at Susan, the secretary, trying to be friendly. She greets me with a grin, or was that a fake smile? Either way, it was a smile! Today is happy! Today is a good day and nothing is going to go wrong!

I walk into the Career Center and take a seat at the front table. I turn on the monitor. Oh good, the computer's already on. Perfect! I knew this day was going well!

I check my email as I wait for Arianna, my new student, to show up. As I begin typing my username and password into my email account, Arianna walks in, looking extremely exhausted in her T-shirt and shorts. She's carrying a gym bag and backpack which keep sliding off her shoulder.

"Hi, Jennifer, sorry I'm late," she says, dropping both bags on the floor with a thud.

"Hey! How's your day going?" I ask.

"So, I already applied for a few scholarships. Is that OK?" Arianna asks.

"Of course," I smile at her, closing my email window.

Any student who wishes to apply for scholarships outside our session is definitely number one on my list! It shows they are very persistent!

"So, what kind of scholarships did you already apply for?" I ask.

She pulls up a chair—holy cow! Someone get the Febreze! She really *is* sweating up a storm!

"Here, I'll show you what I applied for," she says, taking the mouse from my hand and loading Firefox from the desktop. "Have you ever heard of Zinch.com?" She looks over at me.

"Is that a scholarship website?" I ask.

"Yeah, it's a really cool website." Arianna types at the keyboard and a new window pops up.

"Um . . . what about FAFSA?" I ask. I really need to make sure these students fill out their online FAFSA applications. Otherwise, Jackie might get upset and I really want to make a good impression!

"What about FAFSA?" Arianna asks, typing in her username into the website.

"We really need to apply," I say.

"Oh, I already did," she says.

"Oh?"

"Yep. My dad did it for me," she says.

Really? Is this like a parent job? Oh well. I guess it saves me time so maybe I *should* be thankful!

"Here," she says, turning the monitor toward me, "We can login under my name." She types her password into the box and the window opens a new page.

"Oh, wow." I scan the list of scholarships. There must be at least a hundred scholarships listed here! I've never seen so many! I don't remember seeing this when I was in high school . . . wait, did we even *have* computers when I was in high school? Oh, right . . . I'm not *that* old!

"So, you've never heard of Zinch.com before?" She gives me a puzzled look.

"Not really." I say.

"Oh, I'm surprised. I thought you said you knew all about scholarships and stuff," she says.

I did?

"Oh . . . um," I begin hesitantly.

"So . . . you *are* the volunteer advisor, *right?*" She asks doubtfully.

"Of course!" I say reassuringly. This isn't right. My students aren't supposed to question me on these things, right?

"Just checking," Arianna says.

"So, let's work on some of the scholarships," I say, taking the mouse from Arianna and clicking on the first link listed, "Fraser Institute Essay Contest."

"Oh, I already did that one," she exclaims.

"OK," I say, clicking on the next one entitled, "Safety Scholars Video Contest." I look over at Arianna, "How about this one?"

She stares at the screen for a second and gives me a look of disgust. "Isn't that a video contest?"

"I think so." I say.

"Because I don't do video contests," she says.

"Why not?" I ask her.

"They're like, not cool, you know? Plus, you never really win a lot of money making a video anyway, so what's the point?" She gives me a disapproving look.

"Right," as if I knew that already. I scroll down the page and click on the very last scholarship listed. "This one looks interesting," I say, "It's a 'Calm-A-Sutra Competition.'"

"The what?" She asks, her eyes widening, "Are you crazy, Jennifer?"

What's the problem? You would have thought I asked her to apply for a *Cum* a Sutra scholarship.

"Huh?" I say.

"That's really inappropriate, Jennifer." She shoots me *another* disapproving look.

"It's not what you think, Arianna," I say hesitantly, at least I don't think so.

I move the cursor over the link and click on the scholarship.

"What are you *doing*, Jennifer?" She stares at me in horror.

I wait for the website to load.

"Why did you just click on it?" Arianna continues to just stare at me.

I wait for the page to quickly load. "Hey, look," I point at images of tea bags and tea kettles displayed on the left hand side, "it's all about tea!" I point out the images of cute, little pink tea kettles surrounding the page. And there's even an image showing different varieties of tea bags! "Hey, isn't this cute?" I ask, smiling at Arianna.

She looks paranoid. "Jennifer, I think we should go back to the other page."

"Are you sure?" I ask impatiently.

"Jennifer—" she snaps.

I let out a heavy sigh. "Well, all right." I click on the "back" button in the browser and wait for the page of scholarships to load.

"Hey, I have an idea," Arianna insists. "Why don't I just pick which scholarships I want, OK?" She grabs the mouse from me and scrolls down the page.

There's silence—and I can almost feel Arianna getting impatient.

"Listen, Arianna, I'm sorry . . . I didn't mean—"

"It's fine, Jennifer. I'm going to find the scholarships from now on, OK?" She says without flinching.

"Fine." I nod and attempt a weak smile.

Is this how my students are going to talk to me? Argh. I feel cheated. Why can't I work with the mentally handicapped or physically challenged? They wouldn't talk back to me or give me a hard time! Hmm . . . is it too late to change jobs?

Today didn't go well with Arianna. For the rest of the session, Arianna basically read through a couple of scholarships and then we called it quits, or rather, *she* called it quits.

I hurry out of the building and out to my car. I can't wait to get away from the Career Center. Oh well. At least now I can have some fun back at the apartment without Jason! I can't wait to have the TV all to myself! I'm so excited! It almost has that feeling of my birthday!

I can't even remember the last time I used the TV since Jason's been living with us! And since he's always in the living room playing his stupid video games, I never get the TV anyway. Now all that changes today! He's gone! I'm free! We're free! Adrian and I can finally have the apartment back. Yay!

I pull into the parking stall at our complex and get out of my car. I quickly scan the parking lot. No sign of Jason's truck. So far, so good. I head up the stairs to the front door.

I'm so excited I just want to jump up and down. Except, I don't think I should since there's a bunch of old Mexican guys looking at me across the complex. They're eating their lunch and sitting on the grass. A few of them are looking up and smiling. Ew! That should be like totally illegal! I spot a few cans of paint and supplies near them. They must be the apartment maintenance crew. Oh, right, of course, they must be painting.

I get the keys out of my purse and unlock the front door. There is a note on the door which I tear off and throw away. I swing open the door and there's an awkward silence.

No one is watching TV, no one is playing video games, and no one is in the kitchen. The room doesn't even smell like Jason which is a surprise. In fact, there seems to be absolutely no sign of Jason! Hallelujah! The Lord truly has heard me! Finally!

"Hey, you're home early," Adrian says, opening our bedroom door. "Why do you look so surprised?"

"Why do you think?" I ask, smiling and running over to him. I give him a great big hug, "I love you so much," I say over and over again.

"I love you, too, Jenn," Adrian says, putting his arms around my waist. He French kisses me.

I feel good . . . yes, *damn* good.

"It's so quiet in here," he says.

"I know, it's because Jason's gone!" I say and leap up and down. "Jason's gone! Jason's gone!" I say, clapping and singing at the top of my lungs.

"He's gone for now," Adrian says cautiously.

"Jason's gone, Jason's gone . . . " I sing over and over while jumping up and down.

"He'll be back soon," Adrian says.

"Jason's gone, Jason's gone . . . " I'm so excited I can't stop jumping up and down!

"He'll be back in two weeks, Jenn."

"Jason's gone, Jason's—WHAT?" I stop singing and freeze. "What did you just say?"

"He's gone for two weeks and then he's coming back." Adrian swallows hard.

"WHAT?" I scream, "What are you talking about?"

"He said he didn't have the money to move anywhere else and he couldn't go back home because his parents live too far away," Adrian frowns.

"WHAT?" Please repeat. I believe my ears have deafened. I *know* I didn't hear him correctly.

"Jenn, please don't be mad," Adrian says, trying to calm me down.

I take a deep breath. "Is he gone?"

"No, Jenn." He shakes his head.

WHAT

THE

F—ARGH!

"Jenn?" Adrian asks suddenly.

"WHAT ADRIAN?" I yell, feeling my face grow hot.

"Please don't be mad. I tried to get him to move out but he wouldn't budge," he says, gazing down at his feet.

"You were supposed to *make* him go! You aren't supposed to *give* him a choice!" I race over and leap down on the mattress. I feel tears pouring out my eyes.

"Jenn, I'm sorry," Adrian says, hurrying over to the bedroom after me. "I really tried to get him to leave."

"He was supposed to be gone when I came home," I remind him.

"Jason's gone . . . for now," Adrian hesitates.

"He is *not* gone." I say, throwing a pillow across the room at Adrian, who ducks.

"I'm sorry, Jenn." Adrian kneels down by the mattress and caresses my cheek.

I fling his hand away from my face and bury my head in one of the pillows.

"Jenn, I'm so sorry." He says, sounding genuinely sad.

Tears pour down my cheeks and all I can hear is the sound of my own thoughts. Why is Jason staying? *Why*? Why won't he leave?

"I'm so sorry," Adrian repeats apologetically.

I can barely hear him talking to me. I grab another pillow from the mattress and hold it close. I feel the tears stream down my face and the next thing I know, my thoughts go blank.

Fourteen

Adrian and I made up . . . we had sex. Amazing sex. We sat
on the mattress and talked everything out. Now Adrian thinks
Jason *might* be a jerk. He's not totally convinced yet, but he's
making progress, which is fine by me.

So we got to talking about our feelings for each other,
and then the cutest thing happened! Adrian started crying and
it was adorable. He curled up next to me and his head was on
my shoulder and tears were strolling down his face. He held
my hand and kissed it and then I started crying, again, and
then we were both holding each other and crying together. It
was so touching.

It was like in the movies, except way better! Then he
looked up at me and whispered, "I love you." Just like that.

I kissed him on the forehead and whispered back, "I
love you more." Then we giggled and did some French kissing and then from there, well, that's when we did the
dirty . . . all night!

Oh, which reminds me, we have to buy more condoms today.

"Jenn, I got the mail," I hear Adrian closing the front
door and calling from the hallway.

"I'm coming." I get up from the mattress feeling like I need to go somewhere, or do something, but what?

"We've got some bills," Adrian says.

"I missed you," I say, greeting him at the door. I give him a big hug and kiss.

"Well, I missed you too, Jenn," he smiles.

"I see the PG&E electric bill there," I say.

Adrian tears open the envelope with "PG&E" labeled on the front.

"How much do you think it is?" I ask.

"Let's find out," Adrian says.

I grab the envelope from him and pull out a few pages of the bill.

"Where is it? I can't find it," I say, trying to locate the dollar amount in the massive pile of PG&E forms.

"What are you looking for?" Adrian asks.

"The part that shows the amount," I say.

Adrian grabs the forms out of my hand and flips it over. "Here," he says, handing me the bill.

I quickly read it over. "$30?" Really?

"Let me see that." He grabs the bill from my hands.

"Is that really the total? I mean, I had no idea electricity was so cheap. I was thinking it would cost like $100 or something." I say.

"Holy crap. Look," he says, indicating the C.A.R.E. discount.

"Sweet!" I say.

I love being eligible for the C.A.R.E. Program. We both scan the other pages indicating the discount given by the C.A.R.E. Program. It cut our electric bill by almost twenty bucks. This is great! Sometimes I really love life, and this is one of them!

"Great. We only owe $10 each!" I say.

Adrian starts pulling out his wallet as I notice another letter in the stack of mail.

I flip it over and it reads, "Regal Loans." I rip it open and pull out a huge packet of information.

"What is that?" He asks.

"It's the student loan forbearance request they asked me to fill out," I say.

"I thought you did that already," Adrian says.

"Not yet. I was waiting for them to mail this to me," I say, flipping through the packet.

"Why couldn't they email it to you instead?"

I look over at him. "That's exactly what I asked them, too!"

Adrian shakes his head and we laugh.

"Do you have a pen? I want to fill this out now and mail it back," I say.

Adrian goes to the kitchen and grabs a pen from the counter.

"Here," he says, handing me a pen. "I'll be in the bedroom if you need me."

"Stay here with me and help me fill this out." I look up him and whimper, "Please?"

Adrian rolls his eyes and takes the packet from my hands. "OK." He scrolls down the page and squints at the bottom of the page. "It says you're supposed to attach proof."

I grab the packet out of his hand, almost ripping the page. "Where?"

"Here," he points to the bottom of the page where tiny words are encrypted in Greek.

"Shit." I say.

"What's wrong?" He asks.

I look up at him in horror, "I don't have proof."

"What do you mean you don't have proof?" He asks.

"When I talked to my student loan company the other day, they said they would send a form for me to fill out. But that was it. They didn't say I needed *proof*." I pull out a chair from the dining room and take a seat.

"Jenn, you look pale," Adrian says.

Oh no! I think they *did* tell me I needed proof.

"I think I just remembered something." I try to smile.

"What is it, Jenn? Tell me." He says.

"Oh, nothing." I grab the packet and rush to the bedroom. "I'm using your computer."

"Why can't you use that new Mac laptop they gave you?" Adrian asks, catching up to me.

"Because . . . " I race over and sit down at his Mac computer. I move the mouse and instantly the desktop turns on.

"What are you doing?" He asks, grabbing the extra chair by the mattress.

"Do you still have that Adobe Reader Program I installed for you?" I ask. "The one where you can edit PDF's?"

"Why?" He raises his brow, "what are you planning?"

I close his mouth, "It's a surprise."

"Are you about to do something illegal?" He grins.

I snap my head, "Adrian, editing PDF's is not illegal." How could he possibly think I would do such a thing? I'm as innocent as a butterfly!

I open up Firefox and type in, "Peace Corps icon." I wait for the page to load and then click "images" at the top of the bar. Immediately, several images load on the page displaying various Peace Corps icons and logos.

Perfect! I save one of the images to the desktop and open up Adobe Photoshop.

"Adobe Reader is in the applications folder," he points out.

"I know, I know," shooing his hand away from the computer. I find Adobe Reader and open it up.

I open the Peace Corps logo in Photoshop and "erase" the background to create a transparent background.

"Why, do you have a logo that says, 'Peace Corps?'" He asks with curiosity.

"Because . . . " I trail off and save the image as a new file. I click the "back" button on Google and type in, "AmeriCorps." I wait for the page to load and then I login to the website.

"Jenn . . . " Adrian begins.

"Adrian, quiet!" I say, "I'm concentrating." I open up my "service letter" which is a PDF file saved to the Ameri-Corps server and wait for it to open in Adobe Reader.

"Can I say something?" He asks.

"No," I say and click on "File-Open" and select my Peace Corps image.

"But you're not in the Peace Corps," he reminds me.

I roll my eyes. "You're not a very fast learner, are you?"

I have to provide proof that I'm in the Peace Corps. Here's the thing—I'm not actually *in* the Peace Corps. I'm in AmeriCorps, same difference. But they don't know that, do they?

"I don't like this," Adrian says.

"Check this out," I point to the top of the packet, "It says here that I *am* in the Peace Corps."

He looks at me with confusion. "But I thought you said it was called, 'AmeriCorps?'"

I kiss him on the forehead. "Sweetie, I love you, but sometimes you're slow," I say playfully.

"Hey!" He says, tickling my stomach.

"Stop! I'm trying to focus. I need to work diligently."

"I know what you're doing Jenn and I'm not letting you get away with it," Adrian says.

"Why?" I inquire.

"Because you can't create a fake letterhead from an organization you don't even *work* for," he says.

"You mean, an organization I *volunteer* for."

Adrian rolls his eyes. "Whatever." He gets up from the chair and walks out of the room.

And how did he even know what I was doing? "Where are you going?" I call out after him.

"It's not going to work, Jenn," Adrian calls back.

"Oh yeah, how do you know?" I call back. I try opening up the image in Adobe Reader but it won't open. Come on! Why won't it work for me?

Adrian peers around the corner of the doorway. "See, I told you it won't work."

"How did you know?" I ask.

"Because you can only edit the text," he says.

"How do you know all this?" I ask.

"Jason told me," he says playfully.

Oh, for crissakes!

"I'm getting something to eat from the fridge. You want something?" He asks.

"Fine. You win," I say, closing the programs and sprinting out of the room after him.

I pick up the packet from the student loan company and it has a check mark next to the box that says, "Peace Corps volunteer." Below that, it reads, "Must show proof." Ugh.

So, I did what anyone else would do in this situation. I told the truth. I printed off a copy of my AmeriCorps formal letterhead and mailed it back to the student loan company.

Fifteen

The next day I head out and it's gorgeous outside. I'm wearing a T-shirt and long flare jeans.

I really wish my mom would visit me out here. We could shop at the thrift stores and the antique shops and she would love the weather! It's great. It feels like seventy degrees.

I mean, it's not as cold as Michigan and that's a good thing! Plus it definitely has a ton of shops and things to do.

Of course, I do miss all the locally owned Michigan shops like the hobby stores and game stores and the cute little restaurants and places like that.

When I think about it, I really do miss Michigan. I miss the people. They're all so friendly, except if you're in Detroit. Oh well. Here I am in Fresno!

I get in my car and pull out of the parking stall and head toward the school. I'm ready to meet a few more students!

Today I'm meeting with the Indian girls, Kavita and Sonia, which is really cool since they're both from India and I know a lot of Indians.

I can almost speak the language, that is, one of the languages. Why does that country have so many darn languages? Why not just have the one? Then I could speak more than a word here and there.

I remember when I was little, we used to have these neighbors who were Indian and they were our best friends. They spoke a ton of Bengali at home and I learned practically the whole alphabet.

OK, so, I never actually *learned* the language (or the alphabet) but I would love to! I mean, doesn't that count for something?

I'm sure Sonia or Kavita could teach me! We could have Bengali class! How fun!

I arrive at the Career Center and walk in to find a few students checking their email or goofing around with friends. I take a seat at the front table or the "tutor" table.

A few minutes later, a couple of tutors arrive and take a seat near me at the tutor table. They chit chat with one another.

Even though they haven't said "Hello," they're still sitting next to me! How cool! They must think I'm awesome or something. I mean, why else would they be here, right? I feel like I'm finally fitting in!

Wait a minute. Is that laughing and giggling? I feel so left out.

Why are the tutors clustered at the far end of the table away from me? If this table were a boat, their end would sink.

"Jenn?" A girl's voice calls out

"Hey!" I look over and it's Vanessa!

She's walking through the doorway with bright red lipstick and purple earrings and her hair is braided so elegantly.

"Hey you, how are you?" Vanessa asks, walking over and putting her hand on my shoulder.

"I'm doing good, what's up? I haven't seen you in awhile," I say, trying to sound cheerful.

"So guess what? I went to an interview the other day for this rich charter school and they hired me on the spot! Isn't that great? I can't wait. I start next month," Vanessa says.

"Oh—"

Vanessa cuts me off. "So I won't be working here much longer, but it was nice meeting you," she smiles at me and walks over to Jackie's office.

I hear Jackie greet Vanessa as she walks into Jackie's office.

"Hey Jackie, sorry I'm late . . . " Vanessa's voice trails off.

I feel my body tense up. The one person who actually thinks I'm cool enough to talk to, is leaving! This is *so* unfair!

"Um, Jennifer?" I hear a girl's soft voice mutter.

I look over and Sonia and Kavita are standing behind me. They're both wearing matching tops and blue jeans with glitter. Their high heels make them stand so much taller, a California fashion trend. They almost look like twins!

"Hi!" Sonia says, taking a seat next to me, "I was wondering, can Kavita and I have our tutoring session at the same time?" Sonia asks, smiling hopefully.

"Sure, why not!" I say, then pause wondering if doubling up like this would be OK with Jackie.

"So, here's what I need to learn," Kavita says, throwing her binder on the table at me.

"Oh, I'm not actually a tutor," I say.

"I thought you said you were going to be our after school tutor," Kavita interrupts.

"Oh, well . . . um . . . " I trail off. Not again. I *hate* explaining my job!

"Kavita's just confused," Sonia jumps in. "You're our advisor, *not* our tutor," she says, looking at Kavita. "It means like she helps with college prep stuff, right?" Sonia asks, looking back at me.

I love it when my students understand what I do! It makes my job so much easier, doesn't it?

"Jenn doesn't help with homework, duh," Sonia says to Kavita.

"Exactly," I smile enthusiastically.

"So, can I go first?" Kavita asks, sitting on the other side of me.

"What are you doing Kavita?" Sonia asks. "I just asked Jennifer if we could go together."

"I don't want to be tutored with *you* Sonia. I had a hard day at school, all right?" Kavita says with an attitude.

Note to self: Stay on Kavita's good side today.

"OK, so what should we do first?" Kavita asks.

"Have it your way," Sonia says, walking over and sitting at one of the computers in the back of the room.

"So, I was thinking we could start with FAFSA," I say to Kavita.

"I already did that," Kavita says.

Did all of these students finish their FAFSA? Wow, I absolutely *love* their parents!

"I did it with my parents over the weekend," Kavita says.

Well, *obviously*. Who didn't?

"So what do you want to do then?" Kavita asks.

"How about scholarships? I heard there's a great website—"

"Sure," she says, interrupting me with a yawn.

"Great," I smile at her and open up Firefox. I'm trying to remember what Arianna showed me. Oh . . . right. I go to Zinch.com and click on the login page. "So have you heard of this site? One of my other students—"

"Sure," Kavita says, yawning again.

Is she listening to me? "Anyway, it's a great website for looking up scholarships. Here. Create a login and a password, if you want." I say, handing her the computer mouse. I move my chair away to give her space at the computer.

Kavita pulls her chair closer and lets out another yawn. She takes the keyboard and types in random letters and numbers and then a password.

"Are you going to remember your username and password?" I ask, squinting at the password, "aGtV1234."

Is she really going to remember this?

I quickly grab my shoulder bag and pull out a pencil and a pad of paper. I write down the username and password, in case she forgets the next time we have tutoring.

"So, what happens next?" She asks, running her fingers through her long, brown hair.

I look up and stare back at the screen. "Click 'OK' and then it should load another page and then we'll get to see all these scholarships you can apply for," I say confidently.

"Here," Kavita says, tossing me the computer mouse. "I don't mind watching," she smiles.

I take the mouse from her as she scoots her chair back. I pull up to the computer and wait for the page to load.

When it finally loads, I'm staring at only . . . ten scholarships. What about the hundreds of scholarships Arianna had on her page?

I scroll down the website and start clicking on a few scholarship links. I'm directed to another page with text that describes the scholarship and an image or logo of the person or organization sponsoring the scholarship.

"What now?" Kavita asks.

"If you want, we can do the fun part and apply for scholarships," I say, staring at the computer screen. "So, I think we should start from the top and work our way down the page. What do you think?" I ask.

There' s silence—

Kavita?

I turn around and Kavita's head is lying back on her left shoulder. Her eyes are closed and she's breathing heavily.

Oh, my, God! Is she asleep?

"Kavita?" I almost yell.

"Huh? What?" She jumps out of her seat as her eyes pop open.

"Hey?" I ask, waving my hand across her face.

"Oh, sorry about that. I'm a little tired," she says.

"Do you need a nap?" I ask her. Wait, when? During tutoring?

"Go ahead. I'm listening. I promise," she says.

"Well . . . OK." I say and she shoots me a weak smile.

I turn back to the screen and click on the first scholarship. These are definitely not the same ones as Arianna's. Maybe they change depending on what type of student you are. Except, Kavita never filled out a profile—a profile, that's it!

"Hey, Kavita, did you fill out a profile?" I stare at the computer screen like I'm waiting for an answer.

There's another awkward pause.

"Kavita?" I ask, turning around in my chair.

Her eyes are closed again and her head has dropped to the other side.

"Kavita?" I ask louder.

"Huh?" She jumps up, her eyes pop wide open. "What happened?"

OK, she *really* needs to get some sleep. Maybe I should send her home?

"Do you want to go home?" *After* you fill out the Zinch.com profile?

"Sorry about that. Keep going, I'm really listening," she reassures me.

"Well I need you to fill out a profile," I say.

"For what?" Kavita asks with confusion.

"See," I point to the screen where it says, *Student Profile* page. "So if you could fill it out, that would be great. Then we could—"

I stop. It got silent, again.

"Kavita?" I turn around and find her staring at the computer screen like it's sucking her in.

Earth to Kavita?

This girl is extremely exhausted.

"Oh, sorry!" She says, looking over at me, "I'm sorry. I'm really tired. I've had a really bad day."

"Why are you so tired?" I ask.

She looks at me and frowns, "Did I tell you, I pulled an all-nighter last night?"

On second thought, she doesn't look like the type of student who parties all night. I'm sure she's genuinely tired. She seems innocent enough.

"Can we do this another time?" She asks and frowns.

"Sure," I try to smile. I really want her to like me.

"Thanks," she grabs her bag from the floor and gets up out of her chair.

"Can I call you next week to set up another time?" I ask.

"Just text me. It's so much faster," she says.

Right, of course, I'll just send her a text message! I'm going to be the coolest tutor yet!

"See ya." Kavita walks past the table and out the door.

I look around the room and find Sonia talking to another student at the back table. I wave over at her, but a few of the students look up from their computers and give me a raised eyebrow. Whatever.

I look back at Sonia and I see her walking toward me.

"Hey, is it my turn already?" She calls.

"Yeah, are you ready?" I ask

"Sure," she glances around the room for her friend. "What happened to Kavita?"

"I think she left," I say.

"WHAT?" Sonia says with astonishment. "She didn't even say goodbye? What's with that girl?"

"She was tired, I guess." I shrug my shoulders.

"Kavita's always tired after tennis practice," Sonia says.

Well that explains it! I knew it wasn't a party!

"Right," I say knowingly. "So, are you ready to get started?"

"Sure," Sonia says, flashing me a smile. She takes a seat next to me.

"Did you finish your FAFSA, too?" I ask, already knowing the answer.

"Yeah. Kavita and I did that with my parents over the weekend," she says.

Figures. "Anyway," I begin, "I'm trying to get everyone set up with Zinch.com. Have you heard of it?" I ask.

"Yeah, I'm already on there. I have a username and everything."

"Oh, great," I say. Thank God!

Sonia takes the keyboard and types in her username and password and hits the "enter" button.

Immediately a thousand scholarships pop up. I've never seen so many. Arianna didn't even have this many! Maybe she can let Kavita borrow some?

"Hey, how did you get so many scholarships?" I ask with sudden interest.

"What do you mean?" Sonia raises her eyebrows.

I point out the page on the screen. "There're so many of them."

"Oh, that," she says with dignity. "They base it on your profile and stuff, like your grades, your test scores, that sort of thing. It's all based on how smart you are."

"Do you need my help with any of this?" I ask.

Sonia clicks on one of the scholarships in the middle of the page. "Sure, but I already applied to quite a few of these scholarships."

Immediately a new page loads and an application starts downloading to the desktop.

"Kavita's really stupid, actually," Sonia says.

"Huh?" I'm surprised by Sonia's remark about her friend.

"Well, like, Kavita hasn't applied to *any* scholarships or grants and she hasn't applied for student loans." She says.

Oh, so that's why Kavita had a small list of scholarships on Zinch!

"You look confused," Sonia points out.

I hesitate, "Oh, I was just thinking."

"Jennifer?" I hear a girl's voice calling me, "You're Jennifer, right?"

I turn around and there's a girl walking up to me. "Yeah?" I recognize her right away. It's Priscilla. What's *she* doing here?

"So, can we meet now?" Priscilla asks.

Huh?

Priscilla looks over at the clock and then back at me. "I have to go to dance practice soon." She stands over me wearing a purple, spandex top and a short mini dance skirt.

"Um, well . . . "I look over at Sonia and she's busy checking her email.

"I'm running out of valuable time standing here, Jennifer," Priscilla demands.

I'm sorry? "Listen Priscilla—" I begin.

She interrupts. "Listen, Jennifer," she says with an attitude, "Are you going to tutor me now or not?"

"Well, the thing is . . . " I'm friggin' scared of Priscilla right now. I'm afraid to piss her off, except I think she's already pissed off. She looks pissed anyway. "The thing is," I begin, "our session was a few days ago, and you missed it."

"I didn't miss it," Priscilla says, throwing her hands on her hips. "What are you talking about?" She says dramatically.

I manage to smile. "We don't have a tutoring session today. It was a few days ago. I'm sorry—"

"Whatever," Priscilla says and rolls her eyes in disbelief. "Do we need to talk to Jackie?"

Seriously?

"No, of course not," I say, trying not to get upset.

"Good. I didn't think so because I know Jackie wouldn't like it if she lost a tutor."

Is Priscilla threatening me?

"Anyway, I have ten minutes. What do you need me to do?" She asks impatiently.

"I'm sorry, Priscilla. I can't meet with you today, How about next week? I could call you?" I ramble on, trying to sound like I'm willing to compromise.

"Whatever!" She says and storms out of the room.

"So, as I was saying, I think Kavita really needs your help," Sonia continues, ignoring Priscilla. Sonia closes out of her email account.

Stop a minute. Should Priscilla be talking to me like that? And what if she reports me to Jackie? I might never get my job back! Why is Priscilla even treating me this way? What did I ever do to her?

"Kavita doesn't really do her homework so her grades are really low," Sonia says, trying to fill me in.

"Well I'd be glad to help Kavita," I say, if she could stay awake.

Sonia grabs her bag and pulls out a loose sheet of paper with typed lettering.

"What's that?" I ask curiously.

"This is Kavita's transcript from last semester. I stole it from one of the cabinets in Jackie's office."

You WHAT? Where do the students find time to do things like this?

"Are you going to tell Jackie?" Sonia asks guardedly.

"Of course not," I say, silently wishing I had not made such a promise.

"Here," Sonia says, ceremoniously placing it in my hand. "Take a look."

"Wow," I say, seeing D's and F's listed beside most of the courses.

"You can keep it," Sonia says, "Do you want to help me fill out this scholarship or do you just want me to do it at home?" She asks, changing the topic.

Only I can't put Kavita's transcript down. I'm too transfixed by the letter grades.

Do Kavita's parents know how bad she's doing at school? I mean, I think Jackie mentioned this to me once or twice, but who's counting? Oh, this isn't good!

"Um. Jenn?" Sonia catches me off guard.

I look up at Sonia. "What?"

"So, what do you think I should do? Fill out the scholarship here or at home?" She asks.

"It's up to you," I say quickly.

"Then, I'd rather do it at home, since I can get more stuff done there. It's too distracting here."

Yeah, no kidding. "Right. So make sure you remember which scholarships you apply for and which ones you haven't done yet." I say.

"So, can I go home, now?" Sonia stares at me.

Why do the students ask to go home before their session ends?

Sonia keeps staring at me. "Is that all? Or do we have something else to do?" She asks without hesitation.

I shake my head. "No, that's it for today."

"Great," she says, getting up from her seat. "Well, it was really nice hanging out with you, Jenn."

"Yeah, you too." I hadn't realized "hanging out" meant having a session together.

"Bye." Sonia grabs her bag and walks out of the room.

Wait! I forgot to schedule her next week for tutoring. Shoot!

"Help it's my loan lender! Help it's my loan—"

I left my ringtone on full blast which wasn't a smart idea. Some of the students can hear the cell phone calling me and are looking at me puzzled.

I grab my shoulder bag and feeling around at the bottom for my cell phone but I can't seem to find it. Where is that darn phone?

"Help it's my loan lender! Help—"

The ringtone's getting louder and louder. Shoot! Where is it?

Yikes! This is *sooo* embarrassing. Now everyone in the room is staring at me. Even the tutors have stopped their session just to watch me!

I dump out all the contents of my shoulder bag and I still don't see my phone. I feel my face growing hotter.

Oh, wait, I left it in my jacket pocket! I put my hand into the pocket and pull out the cell phone.

I flip it open. "Hello?" I ask.

"Hi, is this Jennifer?" A man asks on the other line.

"This is she," I whisper into the phone.

"Hi, this is John from Regal Loans. I wanted to call and let you know that your forbearance request on your student loans have been declined."

Declined? This means I'll have to start paying back my student loans right away.

"Unfortunately, we cannot grant your request at this time, so if you could, please send your first payment as soon as possible," he says.

"My first payment?" WHAT?

"It was due last month," he points out.

"But you said it was due next month!" I protest and then I realize a few students keep looking over at me.

"No, that would have been last month," he corrects me.

No, that would have been this month. Huh? This man is starting to irritate me.

"I'm sorry, Jennifer. Please mail the payments as—"

"Listen here bucko, I don't have any money, OK?" I whisper into the phone. "I'm a volunteer living out in California with no money and you're going to tell me—"

"Excuse me?" He asks.

"Sorry, I'm just having a bad day," I explain.

"Are you in AmeriCorps?" He asks.

How the heck did he know?

"Jennifer?"

"Yes! I'm here!" I say, almost choking on my words. I mean, how did he *know*?

"Have you filled out the forbearance request form at the AmeriCorps website? It will postpone your payments while you're in AmeriCorps." He asks.

Come again?

"Do you know how to log onto the AmeriCorps website, Jennifer?" He inquires.

"Yes, should I go there now?" I ask, still whispering into the phone.

"That depends. Would you like me to follow you through the steps on applying for the request?"

"That would be great!" I load Firefox and type in the AmeriCorps website. I wait for the page to load and type in my username and password.

"Please tell me when you login so I know when to begin," he says patiently.

I absolutely *love* this man! OK, so he didn't deserve to be called *Bucko*. "I'm in," I say over the phone.

"OK, once you login, click on the tab marked, 'My Education Award.' It's located to the right of the screen."

I click my mouse over the tab and a new page loads.

"Now, underneath 'My Education Award,' there should be a few more tabs. Click on the one that says, 'Create Forbearance Request,'" he says.

"OK. A form just appeared on the screen. Is that right?" I ask.

"That's correct. You want to make sure you completely fill out that form. Click on 'Search for Lenders' and select 'Regal Loans.'" As he explains this over the phone, I follow him step by step.

A few minutes later, I'm thanking him for his generosity. I feel like jumping up and down. As I hang up the phone, I fill out the rest of the form and hit the "submit" button. I can't believe it, I did it! Now why didn't they just tell me this earlier?

Sixteen

I head out the next morning. My shoulder bag swings as I lock the front door. As I grab the swinging bag, my arm brushes against the door and a huge smear of white paint appear across my arm.

Argh!

Where did this paint come from?

Jason?

No . . . wait . . . on second thought, it couldn't be Jason. It was that darn apartment maintenance crew! So why didn't they leave a note about 'wet paint'?

So maybe *that's* what that note was that I threw away!

Grrr. These Mexican workers really get on my nerves. Why couldn't they leave *two* notes, like one note that reminds you to read the other note?

As I drive out of the parking stall, I almost hit some guy riding a bicycle. When I get to the highway, I almost get hit by a semi-truck! Geez!

I pull into an empty spot in the back of the high school parking lot. I grab my things and walk into the administration building. As I walk into the Career Center, I throw my shoulder bag on the floor and turn on one of the computers.

A few students arrive early before lunch, eating and typing at their computers. Are they allowed to eat at the computers?

"Hey, excuse me?" Comes a booming voice from behind.

I look over and a skinny black girl walks in wearing a black and white striped shirt and black silk pants. "Are we allowed to use these computers if we aren't in Upward Bound?" She asks, gazing around the room.

"Of course," I say, but I really have no clue.

"Great," she says, strolling past me, flopping down on a seat in the back of the room.

I turn back toward the computer and wait for the green light to turn on indicating the monitor is on.

Except the light isn't green . . . and the monitor isn't turning on. Hmm . . .

I click a few buttons on the keyboard and move the mouse a few times. Except that doesn't seem to do anything either. I get up and jiggle the cords behind the monitor. There! That should do it! I sit back down and watch.

Nothing happens.

I stare at the black screen for five minutes. Well, OK, not really five minutes but long enough.

Ugh. Why isn't this stupid monitor turning on? The black screen just stares back at me.

Grrr!

This day isn't getting any better! Why can't bad things happen in the morning and then stop in the afternoon? Why does it keep going? It's like, if one bad thing happens, then more bad things happen all day long! This is annoying!

I kneel down by the computer, which consists of going under the table to find the computer cords. I find the monitor cord from the back of the computer and jiggle it a few times. Well it's definitely plugged in.

I get up and look back at the computer screen and it's turned on. I don't believe it!

I have no idea what happened, but I don't care, at least it finally turned on. Stupid computers! Adrian never has this problem with his Mac computer. Maybe this only happens to PC's! Schools should only allow Mac computers from now on. That way I could download free music without getting viruses. Wait, what?

"Jenn? Are you out there?" I hear Jackie calling from her office.

"Yeah, I'm here," I say.

"Can you come here?" She asks.

"Sure," I get up from my chair and walk over to her office. "What's up?" I lean against the doorway.

"When did you get here this morning?" She hisses, and looks up from her computer screen.

"Um . . . " I look helplessly around the room. "A few minutes ago?" I finally say at last.

"That's what I thought." She says.

OK?

"So I need something from you . . . " she trails off, looking from the computer to me. "I need you to check in with me when you arrive everyday."

"Oh! I'm here!" I say, bursting in with a smile.

"No, not for today. *Every* day," she snaps.

"Oh! Of course!" I reply eagerly.

"And you missed our meeting." She glares up at me. "Were you aware of that?"

Oops.

"I'm sending Rosaline an email and I will let her know." Jackie shakes her head and looks back at the computer.

I want to scream, *Wait, don't talk to Rosaline! What are you going to say to her?* Rosaline is the only friendly person I've met in Fresno. What if Jackie is saying something bad about me? I can't have that! I have to stop her from sending this email!

"Look, Jackie . . . " My voice trembles.

She snaps a look at me. "What, Jenn?"

"I don't think you should send that email . . . " I break off into silence.

I really want to keep my job!

"I'm very disappointed in you," Jackie says, glaring at me. "You need to take responsibility and be here when we have meetings." Jackie shakes her head. "What you did was unacceptable and *very* unprofessional."

"I'm sorry . . . " I trail off, looking down at myself.

"Did you know we were supposed to meet with one of the Upward Bound Directors at the other high school? Well, you didn't show up." She shoots me a look of disgust.

"I . . . "

"You have to attend meetings, Jenn. You can't skip them," she says with a disapproving stare. "So, where were you?" She snaps.

I knew I forgot *something* that day! I kept telling myself I had something to do but I couldn't think of it! And, well, it was amazing since Adrian and I were having a ton of sex. It was all this French kissing and making out—

"Jenn!" She snaps.

Oh, this is bad, this is very bad.

Am I going to lose my job over having sex with Adrian?

Jackie interrupts my thoughts. "I'm writing you up—"

"Wait, I can explain," I interrupt.

She keeps glaring at me and it's making me really uncomfortable.

"Yes?" She leans forward.

Argh!

Um . . .

If I lose my job, I'll have to move back to Michigan and tell my parents what happened to me in California. Then I'll really be jobless and homeless!

Note to self: Dear God, if you love me, will you help me? I know I haven't believed in you, um, ever, but still, help me out here, Dude! And if you don't want to help me, could you send Jesus? Where are you Jesus when I need you? Except I'm Jewish so you probably don't know me or even like me. I don't even celebrate Christmas!

"Jenn, did you want to tell me something?" Jackie interrupts my prayer.

"Um . . . " I whisper hesitantly.

"What are you saying? I can't hear you," she retorts.

"I ate something bad and I got the stomach flu and I was rushed to the hospital and I went into cardiac arrest and I was put into the emergency room and I almost died—"

"Do you have a bill?" Jackie interrupts.

What?

"Do you have a hospital bill?" She asks abruptly.

Oh, they give those out?

Hey, wait a minute! She's asking for a bill and I told her I almost died in the emergency room?

"Jenn?" She stares at me.

"No, I don't." I begin. "AmeriCorps refused to cover my emergency bill. They said their budget doesn't cover volunteers with serious illnesses."

"Really?" She asks suddenly.

"Of course," I nod, spinning my story out of control. "Isn't it tragic?"

"Gosh, I'm so sorry, Jenn." She warms up instantly, giving me a genuine smile.

"I think I still might have it, though," I say.

"I'm calling Rosaline," Jackie says, about to grab the phone.

Wait!

"I want to explain this to her. She'll have a fit with AmeriCorps." Jackie grabs the phone.

"I already spoke to her." I did?

"Oh . . . " Jackie pauses. "Did you want me to call her, again? I'm sure we can pull some money together to pay for your bill."

Oh, fantastic!

Aren't these people wonderful?

"But we'll need to see a hospital bill, first," she says.

I retract the last statement.

"Gosh," she frowns. "I can't believe you had major surgery."

"I know!" I agree. "Can you believe how horrifying it was for me?" I slap my hands across my cheeks. "There I was, lying on my back, naked, my feet spread across the countertop. Needles poking in me—" I continue.

"Oh Jenn!" She interrupts, looking horrified.

"It has been very detrimental to my health," I can't help but add.

Jackie gets up from her chair and opens a small filing cabinet to her right. "This must have been awful for you." She grabs a brochure from one of the files and hands it to me. "Here. It's a counseling crisis hotline."

"Uh—"

Huh?

She leans across her desk and points to a 1-800 number on the bottom of the brochure. "Call them if you need to speak to someone. They deal with these kinds of issues."

I flip through the brochure, scanning an image of a woman on the phone and another sitting on a couch, their arms folded in half, frowning. I turn over the backside and notice a bold text reading, "Rape Victim Hotline call 1-800-Victims."

What the . . .?

"What do you think?" She looks genuinely pleased.

It's a Rape Hotline. Not a Stomach Flu hotline!

"Um, it's great," I manage to say.

"I'll meet with the principal this afternoon and see if they can get you an early vacation," Jackie says.

Really? Will I still get paid?

I mean . . . I did have major surgery that was detrimental to my health, right?

"Don't worry, I'll take care of this Jenn," she says, smiling.

"What about . . . " I point to her computer screen. What about that email she was going to send Rosaline?

"Oh, that," Jackie says. "I'm so sorry, Jenn. I don't know what I was thinking. Forgive me. I'll just erase that." She selects the text and hits the "delete" button and everything goes blank.

This is great! I get to keep my job after all! I love being sick, *pretending* to be sick.

"Do you want to talk about it?" She looks back up at me.

"Talk about what?" I ask with confusion.

"Your surgery?" She asks.

My what? Oh, that . . .

I meet her gaze. "Oh . . . that's all right. I'm fine now."

"Are you sure?" She asks. "My friends tell me that I'm a really good listener."

Goodness, if anything, I deserve a two-week vacation for my Oscar-winning performance!

"Why don't you go home for the day? How about two weeks? Is that enough time?" She asks.

Wow, how did she know what I was thinking? Two weeks of free vacation!

"That's really kind of you—" I brush it off like it's nothing.

"Go home and rest, OK?" She smiles.

"Thank you," I say eagerly walking out of her office.

"Oh, Jenn!" She calls back.

Oh, no!

"Yeah?" I say, turning around toward her office.

"I have a favor to ask of you," she says.

Figures. Nothing is ever free in life.

"Sure," I say, popping my face back into her office.

"The ropes course is coming up soon. We still need someone to take good photos of the students." She says. "I know it's a lot to ask of you and if you don't feel up to it, I completely understand." She looks at me and waits for an answer.

"I'll be there!" I exclaim all too eager.

"Really?" Jackie looks surprised.

"Of course!" I say.

"That's great. It'll start at 7AM."

7AM?

Grrr!

"I know you'll take fantastic photos of everyone and then you can show off your talent at Saturday Academy the week after." Jackie looks out the window. "Um . . . that's another favor I would like to ask of you."

"I'll be there." That's if I don't forget again. Right?

"So you can come? You can take photos and be a part of Saturday Academy?" Jackie sounds very pleased.

"Of course," I smile.

Would they notice if I arrived at like, oh, I don't know . . . say, one in the afternoon?

"Oh, that's great. I'm so glad you can come. Thank you, Jenn."

"When is Saturday Academy?" I exclaim.

And, *what* is Saturday Academy?

"It'll be the Saturday after the ropes course." She turns her back to me to open the filing cabinet by her desk. "Here." Jackie pulls out a colorful orange flyer. "This has all the information on it."

I take the flyer and scan it over.

7AM - 10AM. Breakfast served.

Well, at least there's one good thing about getting up early. Free breakfast!

"Will this work for you?" Jackie gives me a pleasant smile.

"Absolutely!" I say with enthusiasm.

"Great! I'll see you there!" She perks up.

"OK. Bye!" I say, walking out of Jackie's office.

Gosh, I never realized that I could get a free paid vacation. This is the nicest Jackie has ever been toward me. I better take full advantage of lounging in the living room and watching TV! This is going to be the best two weeks ever!

Seventeen

This is the worst two weeks of my life! What was I thinking? This is awful. My wonderful vacation is totally backfiring. And to make it worse, guess who's back? Jason! Grrr.

Jason came back earlier than expected. I barely had time to catch up on my TV shows before he showed up at the front door, carrying a beer in one hand and a laundry bag in the other. Figures.

When am I going to finish my TV shows? And of course, now that he's back, he's playing video games again in the living room *and* the apartment smells of mildew and a dead corpse, except, well, I've never *actually* smelled a dead corpse before, not yet anyway, but I'm sure this is exactly what it smells like! And on top of that, I've tried everything to get rid of the smell—incense, candles, Lysol spray, nothing works. Argh.

Maybe someone should just spray Jason with a hose? I wonder . . . hey, I could always ask the maintenance crew!

Well I can't stay here. I can't live here with Jason. I want Adrian to come home from school and kiss me and tell me it's going to be fine and I want some M&M's, and . . . and I want to go back to work! What? Wait, did I actually just say that?

I'm in my room reading one of my favorite chick lit books except I keep having to reread each page. Stupid background noise. The sound of zombies and gunshots is getting on my nerves. Why does Jason have the TV on so loud? Is he that deaf?

And why am I asking rhetorical questions?

"Jason! Can you turn it down?" I yell from inside my bedroom.

I know he's playing that stupid Xbox zombie game again. It's the only thing he ever plays. Hasn't he won that game yet? Ha! I wonder . . . if I cut his Xbox cable, would he notice?

"Jason!" I call out again.

He isn't responding. Ugh. Do I have to do everything around here?

I get up from my cozy bed. Oh, I love reading in bed, even if it is a mattress on the floor, except it makes me tired and I end up taking two or three naps a day, which probably isn't good for my health to begin with.

I swing open the bedroom door and yell down the hall. "Jason! Can you please turn down that noise?"

Is he deaf or ignoring me?

This means war.

I sprint down the hallway, head for the living room and dash toward the TV. I stand dead center in the middle of the living room with Jason directly across from me. He sits on the couch holding the Xbox controller and wearing a silly spaceman headset. He looks ridiculous.

I stare down at him, waiting for a reaction. Nothing. Geez. You think my presence would make him squirm! He doesn't hesitate.

Jason keeps focusing on the television. I don't think he even sees me. Fine. I wave my hands trying to flag his attention. His eyes remain fixated on his video game.

"Jason!" I almost scream.

He keeps staring at the television mesmerized by zombies.

How loud do I have to be? By now the neighbors would have heard me. I'm going to hurt him . . . badly. Argh!

"Jason!" I scream one last time.

Nothing.

OK, fine, that's it!

I walk over and stand in front of the television. This is exactly what I was trying to prevent.

He suddenly looks up.

Finally! Jesus Christ! Oh hi, Jesus, did you ever get the message I sent you earlier? Remember the one about helping me out? It was sent through God and I was hoping he passed it along to you?

"Get . . . get out of the way," Jason insists, whooshing his hand at me.

"Can you please turn down the TV volume? I'm trying to read in my room," I say.

"Well . . . well close your door," he says matter-of-factly.

I did you stupid head!

"Please, Jason. The TV is really loud," I say.

He shakes his head. "Did . . . did Adrian tell you . . . tell you I should turn it down?" Jason asks.

No! Why do I need Adrian's approval? This is my apartment, too!

"I'm . . . I'm not . . . I'm not going to . . . to turn it down," Jason says.

I put my hands firmly on my hips.

"Please! I'm asking you *very* nicely." I'm also asking you to turn it down to prevent you from being stabbed. See the incentive in this? I do!

Jason shakes his head. "No . . . no."

Oh. My. God.

Adrian!!!!!!

"Move . . . move out . . . move out of my way, Jenn." Jason says, trying to push me away from the TV.

No. I'm not budging! This is war, remember?

"Are you . . . are you going . . . going to move?" Jason's voice gets louder. "Move Jenn!"

"Please?" Say please, you butthead!

"Fine!" Jason throws the Xbox controller on the floor, gets up from the couch and sprints down the hallway, slamming the bedroom door behind him.

Good boy!

Remember Jason, a woman always gets what she wants!

"Yeah, OK," I hear Jason talking loudly to himself from his bedroom. "Well, she . . . she wants me to . . . to turn down the TV—"

Oh, you have to be kidding me! Is he complaining about me?

"OK, . . . well, I know that Mom . . . " Jason says.

MOM?

WHAT? His mother? Jason called his mother to complain about me and she lives like three hours away? How can you consult someone who doesn't even live here?

Note to CSI staff: Murderer enters bathroom . . . gets razor . . . stabs annoying roommate . . . shoves body over balcony. Garbage pickup comes Tuesday.

"OK. Hang on," Jason says, walking forcefully into the living room and shoves the phone at me. "My mom . . . my mom wants to talk . . . to talk to you."

I push the phone away.

"Jason. This is between you and me. Not you, me and your mother," I say, in disbelief.

Jason takes the phone back. "She doesn't . . . she doesn't want to talk to you, Mom." He says into the phone.

He nods his head back and forth as if listening to the wisdom of his mother on this issue.

Argh. Why does he have to be such a little baby about this? Why can't he talk it out with me? I mean, it's not like I'm calling up my mother, who lives like 2,700 miles away!

He pulls the phone away from his ear. "My mom says . . . she says I can use the TV."

I roll my eyes. This is ridiculous. "Whatever." I walk off down the hall toward my bedroom.

Jason calls out after me. "My mom says . . . she says I can . . . I can keep the TV volume—"

I slam my bedroom door shut before he finishes his last word.

I grab my cell phone to distract myself and check for any new voice messages. Apparently I missed a call from Rosaline. She left a message telling me that a meeting will be scheduled next month with a California State Supervisor. It's going to be a mandatory meeting for all the AmeriCorps VISTA volunteers of Fresno County. Oh well, that's not for a while . . . .

So I pout a few more times over Jason and not being able to use the TV. Suddenly I get a really grand idea. When all else fails, go shopping! I get dressed and walk out of the bedroom.

As I pass Jason in the living room, he turns around to look at me.

"What?" I ask.

"What?" He repeats.

I shake my head.

"Did . . . did you want . . . want to use . . . use the TV?" He asks.

Yeah, I did, Jason. I wanted to use it like, oh, I don't know, yesterday? And the day before that, and the day before that! Argh! He's lucky he still wakes up each morning. I haven't yet found a plan to get rid of him and *not* go to Jail.

"I'm leaving," I say, grabbing my purse, a notepad and a pencil from the kitchen.

"Whatever," Jason says, turning back toward the TV.

I bet a hundred bucks he's going to be on that TV for the next twelve hours, even after I've gone to bed.

I swing open the front door and head out for a fun afternoon of shopping at the thrift stores! I haven't shopped at a real mall filled with brand name stores since I came out to Fresno. I mean, why pay more when you could pay less for something that almost looks brand new?

Eighteen

This morning, I had to get up at 7AM for Saturday Academy. Today is the day the students do the ropes course activity at Fresno State University. The sprawling campus is directly across from my apartment complex so the walk shouldn't take long.

Well, OK, here I am in the middle of the campus. But I'm lost. I can't find the right building. Students can find their way around. How hard can it be?

I've been walking in circles for twenty minutes now. I mean, it's a campus after all. Do I need to bring a campus map with me next time?

"Watch it!" I hear a male's voice call.

Huh?

"WATCH OUT."

Suddenly out of nowhere I see a bicyclist coming straight toward me. I jump to the curb just as he whooshes past me. Good grief. I almost got knocked down! Maybe he ought to watch where he's going!

But it's so foggy. You can't see much ahead of you. It's not like Michigan fog. Fresno fog is ten times worse. The fog is dense like a solid wall.

I guess the Central Valley is known for dense fog. It's worse in early mornings and late evenings. Grrr. Maybe Jackie ought to have considered that before deciding to meet at 7AM. The fog feels thick. I can't see any of the buildings in front of me until I almost run into them.

I pull out my cell phone and call Jackie. She picks up on the third ring.

"Hey, Jackie. I'm lost. Can you give me directions?" I explain where I think I'm at on campus. She tells me to follow the sidewalk I'm already on and keep going, and eventually I'll get there.

She gives me the name of the building, which I forget as soon as I hang up the phone. I keep walking on the same sidewalk like she said until I see a ton of lights pouring out a building toward my right.

Oh, that must be the library. Does this mean I'm getting closer?

"Ouch. What the hell?" I hear a girl's voice call out.

I almost jump up. OK, I did jump. I look down at my feet. Except I can't see my feet!

"Hello?" I hear that same voice again.

Oh my God! Who's there? I hear a voice talking to me through the fog. That's when I jump up again. This is so freaky!

"Who's there?" I hear the girl's voice getting louder.

Oh. My. God. Who's calling me? God? Jesus? Is it really you? Did you send Mary?

Or, maybe it was an angel? I mean I've never believed in angels before and if they really do exist—

"Hey, get off me!" The voice says again.

It's an angel and I stepped on her feet or her wings!

"Hey, you! Did you just run into me?" She calls again.

Oh no. She doesn't sound angelic at all. She must be human. I nearly jump up again scared to death.

I look down at my feet again except I can't see my feet because of the fog, I hope they're still on me. And that's when I decide to run, with, or without my feet. Gosh, I really hope they're there.

I run and I keep running without looking behind me.

Honestly, unless she was an elf, how can you knock someone over walking three miles an hour? I mean, can you go to Jail for something like that?

After running what seemed like a triathlon, my feet were hurting. I finally manage to find the building Jackie described.

At last, I arrive. Wow, I finally make it after almost getting hit by a bike and knocking over an elf. I know, right? So anyway, here I am.

I see lights coming from a nearby parking lot to the right of the building. Is that a bus?

I walk over to the bus and find myself immersed with students pouring out a dozen at a time. I didn't even know we had that many kids in the Upward Bound Program!

Eventually, the students all file out and that's when I spot Jackie, getting off the bus, last of all.

"Everyone, follow me," she says, gathering all the students in lines behind her. The students line up obediently and start walking. We walk over together toward the ropes course.

When we arrive at the gate, the fog starts to lift quite a bit. I can now see what Jackie meant by "ropes course." I look up and I spot fifty foot wood stakes spread out over the course.

Ugh.

The rope bridges are laced onto the stakes. It looks flimsy to me. Besides, I have a fear of heights. Nobody could pay me to climb that. Have I mentioned I'm just the photographer?

Two unfamiliar Fresno State University students arrive at the gate near us. They introduce themselves as ropes course instructors. The student instructors swiftly divide the students in two groups, with twenty students in each group.

The student instructors then lead everyone over to the gate. Where are my seniors?

The activity begins with students switching off later. One group puts on harnesses and climbs up fifty feet while the other group plays team games in the field with one of the student instructors. I stay by the ropes course taking photos of both activities.

I can't believe how high the students can climb. I could never put on a harness and climb fifty feet in the air. I would freak out. But the students enjoy it.

At one point, when the students reach the top, they walk across a ten-foot wide wood plank to get to the other side and climb back down. Another girl swings on these loose ropes, dangling from the top across a wooden pole. She's at least thirty feet in the air. I can't believe how relaxed she is. Doesn't she know how dangerous this is?

I take about a hundred photos of all the students climbing the elaborate ropes course. The event lasts a few hours, but I'm beat!

Jackie announces she's taking the students and tutors bowling next. There is a loud cheer from the crowd.

She turns to me and says, "But Jenn, you're all done for the day. Thanks for taking the pictures."

I stand there not knowing what to say. She's taking everyone but me to go bowling. All I can think to do is to wave bye, and walk away.

When I arrive back at the apartment, I'm so hurt by not being included. What a day! And it's only noon.

I unlock the door to the apartment and throw myself face down on the couch.

"Hey, you're back earlier than I thought," Adrian says, turning my face over and giving me a soft kiss.

"I missed you," I say, choking back the tears.

"What's wrong?" He asks.

"Everything went fine until the end when Jackie invited everyone but me to go bowling.

"Why didn't she invite you?" He asks.

"I thought she was starting to like me, but now I'm not so sure," I say.

"So, how was the ropes course?" Adrian asks, sitting down next to me.

"Well, I took about a hundred pictures. Now I have to make a photo slideshow of the ropes course for next week." I say.

"Can I help?" He asks.

"Thanks, I'll need it."

Adrian gives me another kiss. "Do you want me to make it for you on my Mac using Final Cut Pro?"

That would really help me out. Final Cut Pro is one of the best video programs in the world. Apparently, most of Hollywood uses this program.

"If you show me how, then I could make it myself."

"OK, when do you want to work on it?" Adrian asks.

"Let me eat some lunch and then we can start on it. OK?" I say and reach over and give him a hug.

A few glasses of Pomegranate Juice and four chocolate brownies later, I'm pumped for work, or maybe a nap from all that sugar.

We sit at the computer and Adrian shows me how to edit in Final Cut Pro. It's not too difficult once you get the hang of it.

I sort out the best photos and place them in the video timeline.

"Do you have any music?" Adrian asks.

"Crap. I forgot about that." I think for a second.

"What hip-hop songs are really popular?" He asks.

He opens up an internet browser and searches for top hip-hop artists of today.

"This one looks good," I say. "It's a new song released by the group, Black Eyed Peas."

"Are you sure?" He looks at me doubtfully.

"Yes, why?"

"I hate this kind of music," Adrian says.

I grab the mouse from him. "Well, this isn't for you anyway. It's for Jackie, and I need music that teenagers are going to like."

"OK," he says.

We download the Black Eyed Peas' song and save it to the desktop. Adrian opens the song file and places it in the video timeline.

A few cuts and edits later, the photo slideshow is done. He saves it as a QuickTime movie and we preview it.

"The photo slideshow looks really good," I say, watching the video two more times.

The video is four minutes long. I figure anything longer and the ADHD students might be falling asleep. They have such a short time span before getting bored!

"OK, are you ready to burn it?" Adrian asks, grabbing a blank DVD from his stash and inserting it into the computer.

"Let's do it!" I say eagerly.

He loads his DVD software and clicks the red burn button.

"OK, this shouldn't take long to burn," Adrian says.

"Great! Thank you!" I jump up and give him a kiss.

"So, when this is done, did you want to see a movie?" He asks.

Yes!

Oh, I know!

"Hey, what about that new movie my mom wanted us to see?" I ask.

"The alien movie?" He asks

"Yeah. It's called, '*The Fourth Kind.*' Do you want to see it?" I ask.

"Sure."

I give him a hug and he kisses me.

We head out the door and drive over to the movie theater. Of course, we're attending the cheap movie theater, which only costs $3 day or night.

Everything in California is so darn expensive. Like, for example, a movie ticket costs $10.75! At least in Michigan you can buy a ticket for a few dollars less and have money leftover for snacks. But I still miss Michigan . . . .

Yes.

No.

Yes, but I love the snow!

No wait, who am I kidding here?

Adrian and I walk up to the ticket counter and I reach for my wallet.

"I got it," he says, shoving my wallet back in my purse.

"Are you sure? I can pay. It's not a problem," I smile.

"Let's say it's a date. How's that?" He asks, smiling.

"Great idea!" I give him a kiss on the nose.

He pulls out his wallet and pays the cashier for the tickets. We head in and watch the movie.

When we leave the theater, I glance up at the late afternoon sky and wonder who's watching us. I swear I'm being followed by a UFO. I nudge Adrian on the arm and point to the sky.

"Where do you think UFOs come from?" I ask.

"The stars," Adrian says simply.

I roll my eyes. "Well, everyone knows that."

He laughs at me.

"Seriously, Adrian! I want to know."

"Call your Mom, then. She knows," Adrian says.

He has a point. My mom would know. She knows mostly everything about UFOs and aliens, which is pretty cool, considering her website is rated like number one around the world!

"If I were ever abducted, would you want me to tell you?" I turn toward Adrian.

"Would you want me to know?" Adrian asks, answering my question with a question.

"Would you want to know?" I ask.

"If you want me to know," he says playfully.

Grrr.

I roll my eyes. "Just answer the question, Adrian," I say playfully.

"Sure, if you want me to know." He chuckles and I hit him playfully on the arm.

What if I do get abducted? What if it happens tonight? I'll have to tell Mom immediately! Would they mind if I brought my cell phone with me on board? *I can't leave Earth without it!* Plus, how will Adrian know where to find me?

"I'll be honest, I'm a little scared to sleep tonight," I say. "Do you think we could pull an all-nighter?" I ask.

"I'm going to bed when we get home. I have to get up early and study in the morning," he says.

"Please?" I ask eagerly hoping he'll change his mind.

"You'll be fine. You have nothing to worry about," he says, pulling me closer and kisses me.

I hold him tight. "I hope you're right." But if I do get abducted tonight, I'm probably not going to tell anyone. I'm sure it will be too gruesome to even think about it. After all, Mom tells me about the horror stories she hears.

I think I'd rather just have the aliens swoop me up out of bed, take me to their craft, where I'll be met by a young, gorgeous alien man who'll smile at me. I mean, if you're going to get abducted, you do want to have a few requirements, right?

Here's mine. He has to be good-looking, not like a football player, but tall, athletic build, blonde hair (like Adrian) and pretty eyes and he can't have hair all over his back and shoulders! That is *so* gross!

He'll talk to me through my mind, since they communicate telepathically. We'll have passionate sex and hot kissing but he'll have to use a condom so I don't get pregnant . . . I'm not sure I feel comfortable carrying an orange or gray alien baby around in my body. Who knows what alien DNA could do to a human?

Although one time, I saw an *X-Files* episode where they injected alien DNA into children and it prevented them from getting sick.

Come to think of it, maybe it's not a bad idea to have an alien baby inside me. I'll never have to go to the doctor for a check up! The alien doctors will fly to me. They'll pick the baby up in the night and then bring him back. Oh, wait, what will Adrian say? I mean, the baby won't be his . . . .

"Jenn? Hello? Are you there?" Adrian waves his hand in front of me.

Huh?

"Oh," I look over at Adrian in the car. "Hey."

"We're here. Do you want to come in?" He asks.

"Why are we parked at Walgreen's?" I ask with confusion.

"Do you want to come in with me?" He asks again.

"What are we doing here?" I ask.

"We're getting condoms," he says.

"Oh, right! Great idea!" I forgot we needed to buy more. Wait, did I really forget . . . .

I open the Jeep car door and jump down. He grabs my hand and we walk into the pharmacy to make our purchase.

When we get home, I call Mom and we discuss the movie '*The Fourth Kind*.' I tell her Adrian and I really enjoyed the movie and she says she did, too.

"I saw it with your father," she says.

Huh?

"Why?" I suddenly ask.

"Because your brother didn't want to go with me so I asked your father." She says.

Since when is Dad into paranormal stuff? He never liked it when they were married.

"Dad says he misses you, Jenn, and you should call him more often." She says.

"Mom, why are you still hanging around with Dad?"

You two are divorced. Is this normal?

"Anyway, Mom . . . " I trail off, changing the topic.

"Your father enjoyed the movie," my mom says, sounding genuinely pleased.

"That's good, Mom," I say.

"Do you want to speak to your father?" She asks.

Is he there? Right NOW?

"David!" I hear her calling to him in the background. "Jenn's on the phone."

Why is *he* there?

"Jenn? Are you still there?" She asks.

"Yes, Mom, I'm still here." I say.

"Good because your father wants to talk to you."

I feel very uncomfortable being put on the spot like this.

"Hi, honey," I hear my father say cheerfully as he gets on the line. "So, honey," my dad continues, "How are you? Long time no see."

I don't know what to say.

"So," he says, "Mom said you enjoyed the movie?" He begins making small talk.

"Yep. It was great." I have nothing else to say since he was never into this paranormal stuff, except, "Why are you at Mom's?"

"Your mother and I are eating her delicious cheese-cake right now. I'm sorry you can't join us, sweetheart."

They just saw a movie together and now they're eating dessert together. Her homemade cheesecake! This is so weird!

"So Dad, how's work going?" I say, changing the subject.

"I was out on the road last week," he says.

I can't tell if he likes traveling as much as he used to.

"How's your boyfriend?" He asks.

"Adrian and I are doing great! Thanks!" This conversation has to end . . . quickly!

"How's the job going?" He asks.

Ugh.

"Great, Dad! I'll let you know if they ever make me director," I say quickly before he has a chance to ask.

"Well honey, they aren't going to ask you, they're going to expect you to work for it," he says encouragingly.

This conversation is going nowhere.

"Yes, I know! So, I have to get going," I say.

"Oh. Are you sure? I was just talking to—"

"Have a good day. Tell Mom I said bye," and I snap the cell phone shut.

"What's that all about?" Adrian asks, coming out to the living room.

"I think my father still likes my mother," I say.

"Aren't they divorced?" Adrian asks puzzled.

"Yes, but he and my mom went to a movie together," I say.

"Really?" Adrian asks.

"Yeah. She even served him her homemade cheesecake," I say.

"Parents are strange sometimes," Adrian says abruptly.

"Maybe you're right," I say, flopping down on the couch next to him.

"I know you don't want to see your mom get hurt," he says, "but she has a right to make her own choices."

"I know," I curl up next to Adrian on the couch.

"So, what do you want to do?" He asks.

"I want to have sex and forget about this," I say and he smiles at me.

"How did you know what I was thinking?" He teases.

Typical guy.

He lifts me up off the couch, carries me to the bedroom and closes the door.

Now we're on to something!

Nineteen

It's 7AM and here I am in my car, sitting in the high school parking lot, yawning and occasionally glancing out my rear view mirror.

I'm waiting for the maintenance guys to open the cafeteria doors this morning. On second thought, no, I'm not. The doors are probably already unlocked.

I look up and spot a few of the tutors walking in. It's Saturday Academy and all the parents and students of the Upward Bound Program are supposed to be here.

Ha! I bet only a few of them will come. What kind of parent would make their child get up at 7AM for a stupid meeting, anyway? I wouldn't. I would let my child sleep in. I'd make an awesome parent!

"Hello?"

HUH?

I jump out of my car seat, almost hitting my head on the top of the car roof. I look out of my side window and there's a face peering through.

"Monique?"

"Yo, you coming in *Jinn*?" Monique asks, pushing her hands away from the glass.

"Yeah. Give me a sec." I call through the car window.

She stands up and walks off. I glance back at my rear view window and basically, well, watch her until she gets to the front and walks inside.

Ugh. That was humiliating! I hope Monique doesn't tell anyone I was moping around in my car!

I unlock the car door, get out and walk briskly toward the front entrance of the school, well, more like the front entrance of the cafeteria.

I don't know why, but Jackie decided to have Saturday Academy in the cafeteria. Oh, wait, was it because she expected like a ton of parents to show up? Come on!

I swing open the doors and stop in my tracks. The room is completely filled with parents, teachers and students. I scan the room and do a quick count. There must be a least seventy people here!

I turn toward the middle of the room and see tables covered with black cloths and white plastic silverware and plates. Each table has a centerpiece with a single, silk rose in the middle. Balloons are scattered throughout the room.

I spot a projector screen in the front of the room. Oh, hey, that must be where my photo slideshow is going to be presented!

As I walk over toward one of the cafeteria tables, I spot Jackie wearing an Upward Bound shirt, khaki pants, and a scarf around her neck. Her hair drapes gently across her face and her make-up looks like something out of Vogue magazine.

I swear, Jackie's got to be my age. Come to think of it, I wonder how old she is? I know she's married because I hear her making personal phone calls to her husband *at least* four times a day. I know she has kids, but are they her step kids or "real" kids? I mean, one of them is eighteen years old, which would make Jackie almost forty! Yeah . . . right.

"Hello . . . Everyone!" A roomful of eyes look over at the microphone stand in the center of the room. The voice continues, "Please take your seats so we can begin," one of the tutors announces.

I quickly scan the room for a decent table with some empty seats. I find Vanessa and a few other tutors pulling out chairs from one of the back tables. I can hide over there. Perfect!

I rush over to their table, grab the last empty chair and sit down next to Monique.

"Hey," I smile over at her.

Monique grins, "Hey *Jinn*."

"Hey, Monique, have you seen Priscilla? She's wearing Victoria's Secret PJ's," Maribel says with her Spanish accent.

Monique turns around in her chair and I follow her gaze. I squint over at a far table in the corner and I can't believe my eyes. Priscilla, one of my students, is wearing slutty PJ's. Wait . . . didn't anyone tell her she was supposed to get dressed?

I notice all the tutors wearing their Upward Bound T-shirts. Then I look down at myself and realize I'm not wearing mine! I'm wearing a pink tank top with straps and khakis.

"Hey Monique," I whisper, "Was everyone supposed to wear their Upward Bound T-shirt?"

"Of course *Jinn*. Jackie expects everyone to wear their shirt for group events."

WHAT?

"Really?" I inquire further.

"Of course!" Monique says and turns away.

"Hello, everyone." I hear Jackie's voice echoing through the microphone. "Thank you for coming this morning. I'm so glad you could make it. Has everyone had breakfast?"

"No!" A few of the tutors at our table yell.

Breakfast? Oh, that's right!

"Oh," Jackie says, blushing. "Well, go eat and then we'll begin."

I watch as everyone races over to the buffet table. Wow. I didn't even see this when I came in. Off to my right is an enormous table and five platters . . . is that a fruit bowl? Sweet. Except, wait . . . it's probably non-organic fruit. Ew. But hey, it's free!

As I finally make my way through the crowd, I'm disappointed. There's absolutely nothing but pork. Pork sausages, bacon, Canadian bacon, tiny hot dogs and slices of ham. Slices of ham? Who eats all this meat for breakfast?

I don't eat Pork. I hate it. It's gross. Why would you eat something that's fatty and tasteless? OK, maybe it's not *tasteless* . . . as a matter of fact, some of it tastes pretty good!

I start reaching for the bacon but stop myself. No, I can't. I'd be breaking the Jewish kosher law. Oh, well, no one would notice, would they? There aren't any Jews here, are there? Well, this is Fresno. It's mostly Mexicans, Armenians, and Hmong people. I do a quick scan across the room, reassuring myself most of these people know Jesus and I don't. I'm safe!

I snatch a few pieces of bacon from the bowl and throw them on my plate. As I walk to the next platter, I grab one slice of ham, totally fattening though, and those cute little wieners wrapped in bread.

As I break away from the buffet table, I glance over at biscuits. Oh, I must have those! I grab three biscuits and five packs of butter.

"Excuse me?" A woman to my left interrupts.

"Yes?"

"Are you going to take that?" She points to the last piece of fruit in the fruit bowl. It's one little slice of honeydew.

I knew I forgot something. I have to have it. I grab the honeydew out of the bowl with my fingers and throw it in my mouth.

"Well, that's just rude," the woman says.

"Sorry," I say and head back to my table. Gosh, I really do feel guilty! Actually, if she wanted it, why didn't she just grab it?

"Jenn!"

I turn around and Rosaline is approaching me with a huge plate of food.

"Oh, hi Rosaline!" I say eagerly.

"How's everything going?" Rosaline asks and takes a seat at the table.

"So far so good," I say.

"How's the tutoring coming?" Rosaline asks.

"Oh, it's going great," I say. Except I really don't like the other tutors. They don't like me and never say "Hi" to me, and the students don't really need me.

"Are you thinking of applying for AmeriCorps next year?" Rosaline asks, stuffing her mouth with a biscuit.

For the same job?

"I'm not sure. Probably." Probably? Who am I kidding?

"That's great," Rosaline says. "We could really use your video talent here at the high school," she says.

"That would be wonderful. Where do I sign up?" What am I saying? I think I'm losing it.

"I'll give you more details in a few months after your term is over and we can start from there. Sound good?"

"Sure." I smile. What am I saying?

"Jenn, is that yours?" Rosaline asks, picking up a pink strap off the table.

"What is that?" I ask.

"It looks like it came off your shirt," Rosaline says.

What? I feel around my shoulders—yikes! One of the pink shoulder straps is missing!

"Do you have another shirt you can wear?" Rosaline whispers. "Because I can see your . . . " she motions with her hands over her chest.

Oh. My. God. She can see my boob!

I glance down at my shirt. "Is there a bathroom here?"

"Of course." She points to a door on the other side of the cafeteria.

I grab the strap and get up from the table and rush across the room.

"Jenn! I found you!" I hear Jackie's voice from behind me.

"Hey, Jackie." I say, holding my top up with my hand.

"Can you make a speech?" She asks.

Come again?

"I think it would be great if you made a speech before we showed your video. It would be nice to introduce you to the parents."

Now?

"Can you do that?" She asks.

"When?" I ask.

"Now," she says.

She has got to be kidding.

"I just need to run to the bathroom," I say, pointing toward the bathroom. I didn't even make it halfway across the room and it's still far away.

"Can you hold it?" She asks.

Wait . . . what?

"I really have to go," I say.

"Right now?" She asks.

"Yes, Jackie. I have to *go*." I make a tiny squeal like I have to go to the bathroom.

"Fine. Hurry up." She waves me off and walks back toward the microphone.

Inside the bathroom I stand in front of a mirror to fiddle with my broken right strap. I try tying the strap in a knot across my neck. OK, obviously that won't work. I need tape. Where am I going to get tape? Suddenly, I hear someone entering the bathroom. It's Maribel.

"Maribel!" I yell.

"Oh, hi!" She says.

"Can you help me?" I reach my arms up in the air holding the pink strap, like I'm ready for someone to change me.

"With what?" Maribel asks, looking puzzled.

I twirl the pink strap in my fingers. "It broke."

Maribel bursts into laughter. "Oh my God. Monique is going to love this!" She says, heading out the bathroom door.

Maribel?

I glance back at the mirror and try to tie the broken right strap again, this time to the other strap. It holds. For a few seconds. Then it falls to the floor. Ugh. What am I going to do? All of a sudden the bathroom door swings open again and Maribel and Monique walk in.

"*Jinn*, what are you doing in here?" Monique grins.

"You have to see this, Monique." Maribel approaches me. She glances down and picks up the broken strap from the floor. Then she lifts up one of my arms and holds the strap to my shirt.

"Wow!" Monique rolls her eyes and starts giggling. "*Jinn*, you're too much!"

"Isn't it funny, Monique?" Maribel says as they both burst into laughter.

Maribel turns toward me and throws the strap in my face. "Good luck, Jenn." She walks over to Monique, grabs her arm, and they head out the door still laughing at me.

Well, that didn't help.

"Jenn?" Jackie swings open the bathroom door and looks over at me. "Are you done? Let's go! We have parents waiting." She grabs my arm and pulls me out of the bathroom, while I hold the right side of my shirt up.

"Jackie. Wait." I say, yanking my arm away.

"Come on, Jenn. We don't have time for primping." She pushes me forward and eventually I find myself face to face with the microphone.

I'm in the center of the cafeteria and everyone is staring at me. My right hand is holding up my top as I step over to the microphone.

Jackie walks over and steps in front of the microphone. "I would like to introduce you to our AmeriCorps VISTA volunteer, Jenn." Jackie signals the audience to applaud as she steps away from the microphone.

A few people applaud and suddenly the room is silent again. I'm standing alone at the microphone.

"Well . . . hello everyone." I can do this. Easy as pie. "I'm Jenn and I'm from Michigan, which is very cold by the way . . . anyway . . . I'm from Michigan, which has four seasons. Fall, winter, spring and construction season." Apparently, these Californians don't understand this classic Michigan joke. Everyone stares at me. "Well . . . um . . . and here's my photo slideshow of the ropes course event." I say, pointing to the projector screen.

I dart from the microphone toward one of the back tables. I find an empty seat by a few Hmong students, who glance over at me giggling. One of the Hmong girls points at my shirt which is folding down over my bra.

Oh. My. God. You can see the top half of my boob. I quickly put my arm over my chest and pretend to hug myself. I must look super ridiculous or super infatuated with myself.

"OK, I'm turning off the lights." I hear Jackie calling from across the room. "This is a photo presentation of the ropes course activity your children participated in last week."

The Hmong girls glance away and everyone turns toward the projector screen. My video finally loads and starts playing. The music sounds pretty good and I notice the students across the room bouncing their heads up and down and tapping to the hip-hop music of the Black Eyed Peas. I knew they would like this song!

When the video ends, everyone claps. The cafeteria is filled with excitement. They liked it!

Jackie walks back to the microphone. "I hope you all enjoyed the video slideshow that was prepared by our

AmeriCorps volunteer. Let's give her a big round of applause."

I blush a little as everyone claps, turns around and looks over at me, except the tutors, who are having their own conversation and not clapping.

It figures. I'm not even supported by the tutors.

"So, thank you all for coming. This about wraps up our program for today," Jackie announces into the microphone.

A few parents get up from their tables and make their way out the door. I look over at the Hmong girls sitting at my table still giggling.

Good grief!

They get up, shove their chairs in, and walk off.

"Hey, Jenn!" I hear a familiar voice call out.

I glance over and Vanessa is walking toward my table. "Hey," I say.

"Sorry I couldn't sit with you. Jackie made me sit with some of the parents," Vanessa says apologetically.

"No problem," I say.

Vanessa gives me a hug. "Your video was awesome, by the way. You did such a good job."

"Thanks, Vanessa."

"So, how are you and Adrian?" Vanessa asks, changing the topic.

"Well—"

"Wait, don't tell me! You guys broke up?" She asks, sounding too pleased.

"Huh?" I ask.

"It's OK, you don't have to tell me how it happened. Listen, Jenn, I'm here for you, you know that, right?" She puts her arm around my waist and gives me a gentle squeeze.

OK, whoa there!

I'm feeling a tad uncomfortable.

"Do you want to talk about it? We could go to my place," Vanessa suggests.

Why do you sound so eager all of a sudden? "I'm OK, thanks, Vanessa." I gently shove her hand away and throw it to the side.

"I know it must be hard," Vanessa continues, "being a girl is hard but Adrian's a guy and all guys are losers, so, I was thinking . . . "

I don't want to know what you were thinking!

"We could hang out at my apartment. Are you game? They have a really cool hot tub," she says.

Now I'm feeling *very* uncomfortable.

"Vanessa, I think you have the wrong idea, here." I try sounding friendly, without hurting her feelings.

She leans in like she's about to kiss me on the cheek. "I know, Jenn."

I quickly pull away and she blushes. I look around the room to see if anyone is watching. The only people left in the cafeteria are a few tutors, Jackie, Rosaline and Vanessa. All the parents and students have left.

"What's wrong? I thought you liked me?" Vanessa asks, her face turning red.

"I do," I say.

"Vanessa!" I say a little too loudly and a few of the tutors look over.

Grrr!

Vanessa looks at me surprised. "What did I do?"

"I'm not a lesbian! I have a boyfriend!" I whisper.

"You're just in denial, Jenn!"

"No, I'm not!" I look back toward the tutors and they turn away.

"Obviously you're upset and I understand," she reaches into her purse and pulls out a business card.

"Vanessa, listen . . . . "

"Here." She hands me her business card, "In case you lose my phone number."

"I'm not going to call you," I say firmly.

"Like I said, you're new to this. You'll come around," she persists.

"No, I won't," I say, putting the business card in my purse.

"Whatever. It's your call," Vanessa says.

I walk past her toward the buffet table, grabbing a biscuit and stuffing it in my mouth. I head out the front doors and leave the cafeteria, not looking back.

Twenty

It's the first week back from "break" or rather, my personal vacation with pay, which was awesome after I found out the money was still being directed into my direct deposit. I made $389 without doing anything. I love AmeriCorps!

Not really.

It's only one of the few side perks to the job. Except, not really, since it depends on whom you "work" for. So, I guess, I got lucky.

"Hello? Monique?" Comes a girl's voice.

I turn around and this short, young Hispanic girl, about four foot nine walks in with a navy blue tank and fitting jeans. Her hair drops to her shoulders and the blonde highlights fall across her face.

"Yo, girl!" Monique calls across our table. She's sitting across from me, tutoring a Hmong student.

"Hello?" The girl asks again.

Monique turns around in her seat and looks at the girl with the blonde highlights.

"What Carissa?"

"Um . . . hello? I'm here. Pay attention," Carissa says, grabbing a chair from a student at a nearby table.

"Hey, watch it!" A black student says, falling off his chair. "What the hell are you doing? I was using that chair."

"Not anymore," Carissa grabs the chair from him and slides it over to our table and pulls up on the other side of Monique.

"Girl, can't you see I'm tutoring?" Monique asks politely.

Carissa throws his hair back. "So?" She tosses her backpack on the computer keyboard.

Monique pushes her bag off the keyboard and turns toward her, "Carissa, I'll be with you shortly."

"Shut up and tutor me," Carissa demands.

"Are you for real?" Monique asks.

"I'm here and I want you to tutor me *now*!" Carissa demands, dragging her chair closer to Monique.

The Hmong student looks over at Carissa and makes a disgusted face.

"What's *your* problem, honey?" Carissa asks the Hmong girl.

"What . . . you . . . doing?" The Hmong girl asks.

"Your English sucks. Don't talk," Carissa insists.

"Carissa!" Monique says defensively, "apologize to my student Emily."

"Emily's not a *Hmong* name. It's a *white* girl's name." Carissa says, glaring over at Emily. "Your name can't possibly be Emily. How about I give you a name? I'll call you Huong or Yang, or what about YinYang?"

"Carissa, enough!" Monique shouts, pointing to the door of the Career Center. "Get out!"

Carissa rolls her eyes. "Tutor me right now and then I'll leave you alone," she says with arrogance.

"You . . . mean . . . girl." Emily mutters.

"What was that?" Carissa glares over at her.

"Enough, girls." Monique's voice overrules. She turns toward Emily. "Listen, how about we reschedule a meeting for next week and we'll finish your project then, OK?"

"But Monique—" Emily begins.

"I'm sorry, Emily," Monique says.

Is Monique seriously giving in to Carissa? I can't believe this! I would never do such a thing! Since when is it OK for a student to sass a tutor? Carissa's like seven years younger than us. Monique and I are the same age.

"Beat it, *Huong*," Carissa snaps at Emily.

Emily grabs her book from the table and throws it in her backpack. She gets up and storms out of the Career Center.

"OK, what do you want, Carissa?" Monique asks.

"I want you to tutor me in math. I need someone to do my homework." Carissa throws her math book on the table, almost smashing the keyboard. Carissa grabs a stack of notes and throws them at Monique.

"Give me those," Monique says, grabbing the stack of notes and skims through them.

What is wrong with Monique?

For the next few minutes, I replay this scene in my head over and over again. I can't believe this! It's incredible how Monique let's these students walk all over her.

"I'm here," A girl's voice says, interrupting my thoughts.

I look up and Priscilla is standing over me with a tight pink cami shirt and a jeans skirt.

"Hey, Priscilla. How's it going?" I ask.

I knew Priscilla was coming today but was hoping she would forget.

Priscilla takes a seat next to me and folds her arms across her chest.

"Let's work on FAFSA, today, OK?" I ask, cheerfully.

Priscilla gives me a dull expression.

"Did you already apply for FAFSA?"

She shakes her head, "No."

"Great! So let's work on that, then," I say.

"I don't want to," Priscilla says.

"Why not?"

"I don't want to, OK?" She says angrily.

Fine.

OK, have it your way.

I don't understand her. It's *her* college career, not mine.

"Let's work on some scholarships today, OK?" I ask, smiling.

Priscilla meets my gaze.

"So," I begin.

Priscilla's still staring at me.

I look away and open a new internet search engine. I type in *Zinch.com* and wait for the page to load.

"So, do you have a Zinch account?" I ask, staring at the computer screen.

Silence.

"I was thinking we could work on scholarships, today," I say, knowing I'm repeating myself.

"You already said that," Priscilla points out.

Great, she's paying attention!

I turn around and smile brightly at Priscilla. "What kind of scholarships do you want to apply for?"

"What kind of scholarships do you want me to apply for?" She mimics without changing her expression.

Priscilla's not smiling and she's not frowning. She's sitting there with her purse in her lap and her backpack resting by her feet. I glance down at her shoes and they're adorable! I'm not much of a shoe person but they're pink with little bows on top.

"I love your shoes," I say. Maybe if I compliment her, she might pretend to like me.

"I know you do. Everyone does," Priscilla says apathetically.

Priscilla reminds me of a robot. She has no smile and she has no frown. She's neither happy nor sad. Just pissed. OK, maybe she's not a robot. What robot looks pissed? Hmm . . . Oh, I know! Maybe she's tired?

"So," I begin again.

"What?" Priscilla asks defensively.

"Do you want to sign in with your account?" I ask, pointing to the Zinch.com sign in page which reads, "Type in your name and password."

"Whatever," she says, rolling her eyes.

"OK, I'll use mine then." I turn to the computer and type in my username and password.

I don't have a lot of scholarships under my account but hey, they'll have to do.

I wait for a new page to load and then a list of twenty or so scholarships appear on the page. Oh, I have more scholarships than I did a few days ago! How cool! I scan the page and an icon appears next to ten scholarships marked "new."

"OK, let's apply for this one," I say, scanning the page and choosing the video contest.

"What is that?" Priscilla asks, looking bored.

Her attitude reminds me of a geology professor I had in college who was annoyed by everyone's questions.

"How about a video contest?" I inquire with a smile.

"Do I look like someone who makes movies?" She throws in, sounding annoyed.

I dare not look at her.

"Sorry," I say and click back toward the first page with all the scholarships listed.

I scroll down the list and find an essay scholarship contest. I click it and wait for the page to load.

"This is boring." Priscilla says with frustration.

I'm going to ignore that.

Finally the page loads and I read through the scholarship. "Hey, this sounds great. If you win this scholarship, you get a free iPad, and you win $2,000." I turn toward Priscilla and she's leaning in toward the monitor, reading the screen with me.

"1,500 words!" She says, her eyes widening.

I look back at the page. "It's only about—"

"Do I look like someone who writes four page essays?" She interrupts, sounding sarcastic.

Fine! You don't like video contests and you hate long essays.

I hit the "back" button and scroll further down the list of scholarships. Oh, here's one I know she'll enjoy. Anyone as lazy as her and without a brain will like this scholarship.

I open the scholarship and instantly the page loads with images of the American flag.

"What is that?" She leans in and reads through the scholarship rules.

"It's pretty easy. All you need is a camera. You take a snapshot of something patriotic to you and send it in." Honestly, what could be easier than that? I mean, the sponsors of this scholarship are offering $500, just for taking a photo! How easy can it get?

"That's too hard."

What? WHAT? I'm SORRY?

"Hey, Priscilla," I say, turning around in my chair, facing her. "What about—"

"No!" She interrupts me.

"Look Priscilla—"

"Look, Jenn, you're wasting my time!" She says unhappily.

Oh. My. God.

"I don't want to apply for these stupid scholarships. OK?" Priscilla says sarcastically. "I'm getting married. Doesn't that mean anything to you?"

Calm down. Breathe in. Breathe out. Relax.

"Are you there?" Priscilla says, interrupting my silent meditation.

"Yes," I mumble.

"I'm getting married," she says with certainty.

"I know," I manage a tiny smile. "Congratulations."

"You're *not* invited."

ARGH!

I mean, OK, I know I'm not invited. Duh! I hardly know this student. But come on, she doesn't have to be mean to me! What did I ever do to her?

I don't want to come anyway. I totally wanted to say this! But I decided against it. Damn it! Sometimes I wish I could speak my mind to these students.

Except I kind of want to keep my job . . . .

How about something better, someone that won't piss her off.

"I'm so happy for you, Priscilla," I say with a fake smile.

"Why?" She asks sarcastically.

Gosh! What *is* her problem?

I'm trying to be super nice and all she does is complain and be mean! Is this how she treats everyone?

"Are you excited for your wedding?" I ask, trying to sound cheerful.

"What do you think?" She asks with an attitude.

OK. That's it.

"Let's schedule another time to meet." I really can't sit here another thirty minutes. I want her out of here before I start pulling my hair out!

I reach for the school planner out of my shoulder bag and flip the page to next week. "When are you free?"

"I'm not." She states.

Ignoring her I say, "Next Tuesday will work. I'll see you at 3PM."

"Fine." She yanks her bag up over her shoulder, grabs her purse and storms off.

Twenty-one

I hear my cell phone ringing and I scramble around the bedroom looking for it. I finally find it under a huge pile of Adrian's dirty underwear. I keep telling Adrian to put his dirty laundry in the hamper! ARGH! Men!

I grab my cell phone and check the Caller ID. I no longer use my voice for ringtones since Adrian insisted I stop using them. Now it's hard to know who's calling me when the phone rings.

"Hello?"

"Honey! Hi! It's your mother."

"Hi Mom," I say.

"How're you? How's Adrian? When are you coming home? I miss you—"

If I don't stop her, she'll start asking twenty questions.

"I'm good. I'm doing really well, Mom. How's it going back home?"

"Actually, I'm at your grandmother's house with your father and Barbara and the rest of the family," she says.

"Really?"

This is news. She can't possibly be serious.

"Yes, we're here celebrating your aunt's birthday," she says.

"Did you drive in with Dad?"

"No, we drove separately," Mom says.

"Why did you go?" I ask.

"I'm still part of your dad's family, even if we are divorced," she says, "anyway, when will I get to see you?"

"I don't know, but I saw a UFO," I say, knowing this will get her mind off the subject of asking me when I'm coming home.

"Oh, really? Where at?" She sounds excited.

"Actually I've seen several since I've been out in California."

"How many UFOs did you see?" She asks.

"No, I mean, I only saw one at a time. I saw them on different days."

"Tell me what you saw," she says.

I hear her tearing off a sheet of paper. She's going to be taking notes so I better remember all the details.

"Well, one of them was gray or black and the other one was yellow."

"Start with the first one," she says.

I told her about both sightings and she said they could've been UFOs.

Oh well, at least now I can tell Adrian I'm an abductee. On second thought, maybe I shouldn't. I don't want to sound like an abductee wannabe. All I can say is, I saw several UFOs and they were cool. I wasn't even scared!

Now, where was that gorgeous blonde, muscular Nordic alien who was supposed to pick me up an hour ago?

Twenty-two

As I walk into the Career Center the following week, I spot
Priscilla and Monique sitting together at the front tutor table.
Monique keeps pointing at the monitor and Priscilla laughs in
response. What's going on? I mean, what's Priscilla doing
hanging around Monique? It's not like they're friends or anything. And it's not like Monique tutors Priscilla! *I'm* her tutor!

OK . . . don't panic . . . I'm sure it's nothing personal.

I walk over and take a seat close to them at the tutor
table. I log on to one of the computers. I look up occasionally
at Priscilla. She doesn't bother looking back and I think
Monique is either ignoring me or too focused. I can't see
what she's looking at on her monitor. Grrr.

"I'm on time, right?" I hear a girl say, plopping down
at an empty seat next to me. "I'm Sonia, remember?"

"Of course." It's Sonia without her clone Kavita.

"How's it going?" She asks.

"Great! How's class?"

"I got an A on my Biology paper," she says.

"Really? That's terrific."

"I was wondering, could you help me with my math
homework?" Sonia asks.

Um . . . no? I'm supposed to help her with college prep, not schoolwork.

"Jenn?" I hear someone calling me. "Can you come in my office for a second?" It's Jackie.

"Hang on a second." I tell Sonia as I get up from my seat. I walk toward Jackie's office.

"Hi Jenn. Take a seat," Jackie says.

I sit in front of Jackie's desk as she leans forward. "So, here's the deal. I really need these students to apply for scholarships. The deadlines are approaching quickly. So can you make a list of the students you're meeting with and another list of scholarships you're helping them apply for?"

Um . . . what if I can't remember?

Yikes!

"Sure. I can do that," I say, dreading the thought of making such a list.

"I want to make sure you meet with Kavita. She needs to pass all of her classes this year," Jackie says, "Have you met with Greg?"

"Yes, I did. We went over a few scholarships and he mentioned he was going into the Army," I say.

"Great. Well I know it's exciting for him but I still want to make sure you advise him about college in case he chooses to apply in the future, after he gets out of the Army."

"What does he need scholarships for? I thought the Army pays for everything. So you still want me to meet with him?" I ask, sounding surprised.

"Well, of course! If you aren't meeting with these students, what would be the point of having you work here?"

"OK," I nod.

"Great. That's all." Jackie turns back toward her computer and that's the signal for me to leave.

I get up and walk out of her office as Kavita runs toward me, panting. She's wearing her varsity tennis outfit and her hair is a mess.

"Hey Jenn, I need to talk to you," Kavita says.

"Sure, what's up?" I ask.

"I can't meet with you anymore," Kavita says.

"Why not?" I ask.

She pulls me into the hall outside the Career Center and we stand in a corner near the secretary's desk.

Susan the secretary gives us a puzzled look and glances back toward her computer.

"What's up?" I ask Kavita.

"You can't tutor me anymore. My coach is really upset with you."

Wait, WHAT?

Why do volunteers like me get all the blame?

"So, what's the matter?" I ask.

"He's like really pissed because you keep taking me out of tennis practice after school for tutoring," Kavita says.

"But I'm not forcing you to skip practice," I say.

"Listen, I know. I don't think it's your fault, but he says it is and you have to stop."

"So can we meet at lunch for tutoring?" I ask.

"I can't. I'm busy," she says.

Naturally, she probably wants to hang out with her friends. Doesn't she realize she's failing all her classes?

"You need to speak to my coach, Jenn!" Kavita insists.

"OK, where can I find him?" I ask.

"Well, right now he's at the tennis courts."

"Yeah, I know, but like, where is that?" I ask.

"Oh . . . um, it's near the basketball courts," she says.

"Right, well . . . where is *that*?" I ask. "Can you take me there?"

"Now?" She asks.

"Yes, now!" I say.

"Um, yeah, I can take you there," she says. "Practice is almost over so we better hurry."

I walk back into the Career Center and find Sonia, chatting on instant messenger.

"Hey Sonia, I need to go talk to Kavita's coach, so can we reschedule?"

Sonia shrugs her shoulders. "I guess."

"I'm sorry to do this at the last minute but it's *really* important for Kavita." I turn around and Kavita is out in the hallway, waiting for me.

"Sure. Text me next week, OK?" Sonia asks.

"I will, definitely," I say as Sonia packs her things and leaves.

The two girls exchange a quick chat, hug in the hallway and Sonia walks away.

I grab my shoulder bag and follow Kavita toward the tennis courts.

We walk past the cafeteria and classroom buildings. I've never actually gone past the high school administration building before. This school is huge! There are buildings everywhere and it looks more like a college campus.

We finally reach the tennis courts. There's a huge grassy field along the courts and we stop there. Kavita points to her coach. His back is turned away from us and he's having a serious conversation with a student athlete.

"That's Ian," Kavita says.

"Your coach?"

"No, Ian's one of the best tennis players we have on the team but he's such a jerk sometimes. Coach always gives him a hard time."

"So when should I walk over and introduce myself?"

"I'd go up there right now," she says.

NOW? "Sounds good."

Crap.

I'm scared.

I mean, what do I *say?*

"Wait!" Kavita tugs at my arm. "Don't tell Coach what I said to you, OK?" Kavita asks.

"I won't, don't worry," I say, reassuring her.

"Thanks. See ya!" Kavita says and she takes off.

Wait you're leaving me here . . . by myself? I watch as she runs off toward the locker room.

Ugh.

I stand up tall, my bag pulled back over my shoulder and I start my walk over to the tennis courts. I can do this. I need to support my students. What good is an education if all you know is *tennis*? On second thought, could you get an athletic scholarship, go to college for free and then become a Wimbledon championship player?

I watch as the coach blows his whistle and everyone grabs his or her racket and heads over to the locker room. Now's my chance. I speed up and when I'm almost twenty feet away, the coach turns around and looks directly at me.

Oh. My. God.

Tall?

Athletic?

Hot!

Wait . . . is that a *six-pack?* Oh my smokin' Jesus! He's gorgeous!

I immediately turn back wondering if I should talk to him later. Except I only make it a few feet before I turn around again to face him. I stop dead in my tracks. He has a California tan, short black hair, and a cute goatee. And did I mention how tight his ass looks in those tennis shorts?

Oh, gosh, is he looking at me?

I quickly turn my face away thinking he can read my mind.

Oh my God, what if he likes me! I mean, he only looked at me once!

Wait, what am I saying? I have a boyfriend!

Here's the deal. If he asks if I'm single, I say, "Yes." No . . . no, I say "No." What's wrong with me?

I love Adrian, I would never do anything to hurt him and he knows that! Maybe this is just a fantasy or something . . . I mean, maybe Adrian should try on some tennis shorts and see what happens?

Note to self: After tutoring, go out and buy Adrian tennis shorts (and whipped cream).

I look back . . . the coach is walking toward me! And he's waving!

I glance behind me to see if he's waving at someone else. Nope. I'm the only one on the field. It's just the coach and me.

"Hi," he says.

Did he just say *hi* to me?

"Hello," I say when I'm finally three steps away.

"I don't think we've met," he says.

Oh, trust me, I *know* we haven't met.

When I get closer, I notice he has blue eyes and dimples on his cheeks.

"Hi, I'm Coach Bailey," he says, extending his hand.

"I'm Jenn. I'm with Upward Bound." I shake his hand and smile.

"Oh, welcome," he smiles. "So, what can I do for you?" He asks.

Well . . . could you take off your shorts . . . ?

I really need to get these images out of my head!

No . . . I really need to ask him about Kavita. She's counting on me! Take a deep breath.

"We need to talk about Kavita," I say. Shoot, what's her last name?

"Kavita Gupta?" He asks.

"Yes, that's her."

"Sure, what's on your mind?" He asks.

"Well, here's the thing," I say. "She really needs a lot of tutoring in her classes and if she doesn't get help, she's not going to be eligible to graduate," I quickly explain.

"Um, OK? How does this involve me?" He asks, looking confused.

Dude, she's failing *all* her classes, as in "D's" and "F's." And you're pulling her out of tutoring! What's there not to get?

"I'm Kavita's tutor and I think you need to let her get some help with tutoring. I'm afraid she's going to fail all her classes because of tennis practice."

"Why's that?" He asks.

Is he really this clueless?

"I need to tutor her after school when she has tennis practice," I say.

"But she has tennis practice everyday," he says.

"But you have to let her come to tutoring! It's the only time I can see her. She needs to go to college and—"

"Listen here, I don't know who you are or—"

"I told you, I'm her tutor from Upward Bound," I persist.

"I don't care who you are," he says, "but she has got to come to tennis practice."

Are all hot guys this stubborn?

"She needs to come to tutoring. I was hired to tutor students like Kavita and I need to do my job," I say.

"And I'm not? I'm her damn coach for crissakes. I'm the one who could get her into college with a tennis scholarship, young lady," he says condescendingly.

I suddenly realize I've upset him.

"You're assuming she'll even qualify for a tennis scholarship, but her grades aren't good enough," I say.

"I refuse to let a student tutor tell me what to do," he says defiantly.

Are all hot coaches assholes?

"Well fine," I snap back. "I can see you don't care about her grades." I turn away, and head back toward the Career Center.

I walk back to the Career Center. When I arrive, Jackie is standing in the door of her office, hands on hips, waiting for me. She has a disgusted look on her face.

Oh, no. Does she know, *already?*

Everyone is turning their attention to me, including the tutors. Yikes!

"Into my office, Jenn. *Now.*" Jackie practically yells at me as I follow her lead into the office.

I take a seat as she slams the door shut behind me, rattling the certificate frames on the walls.

"I want to know what were you doing over at the tennis courts?" She barks.

I gulp . . . how do I get out of this situation? Last time I said I had surgery—

"This is serious, Jenn," Jackie says, hovering over me like the Washington Monument. "You spoke to a coach about one of my students without my permission," she says.

I try to say something. "Um, well—"

"Did you ask to have Kavita removed from tennis practice?" She asks.

"I was only trying to find time to tutor Kavita," I murmur, "and tennis practice was in the way."

"Your actions are uncalled for. Next time you have a problem with a student, you *need* to see me first!" She shouts, leaning closer to me as she takes her hands off her hips.

"I was just trying to help," I say, knowing everyone in the Career Center can probably hear her.

"How could you *not* know?" She snaps at me.

"I thought I was doing the right thing," I say.

"What you did was completely inappropriate!" She screams with her face getting red.

"But I did it because Kavita wanted my help," I quiver.

"Just go." Jackie says after a long pause. "I think you should just leave for the rest of the day. We'll talk some more tomorrow," she says.

WHAT?

No, way! If I wait until tomorrow she might decide to fire me!

"Jackie, I would prefer to discuss this right now," I say.

"Fine!" She says, throwing her hands up in the air. "I think what you did was really stupid. I think you should consult me before talking to any of our teachers or coaches. I'm surprised you would do such a thing. I wouldn't expect this from you."

"But I—"

"You need to grow up and act like an adult, Jenn!" She exclaims.

"Well I—"

"Jenn, I watch you. You always come into the Career Center and check your email, and you rarely interact with the tutors or students."

How does she know what I'm doing when she's sitting in her office?

Have you seen these tutors? They're not friendly at all. They laugh at me and hurt my feelings. *I wanted sunshine* which is why I came to California, *but ran sideways* trying to find my way back home.

I grab my shoulder bag and stumble out of Jackie's office.

Today was nothing but trouble. I get in my car and head toward Walgreen's to buy the best Belgium chocolate, Ferrara.

Twenty-three

Adrian and I are finally grocery shopping and with our very own food stamps! We had to wait a full month to get them. It's so cool since it's a plastic debit card, and all you have to do is swipe across the pad and type in your pin number. It's super easy!

"Hey, Jenn, how about this?" Adrian holds up yummy looking cinnamon bread.

"Oh that looks delicious," I say.

He turns the bread over and spots the price. "It's seven bucks a loaf," he shrugs.

"Throw it in the basket. It's not like we're paying this out of our pockets," I say with a smile.

Ever since we received food stamps, I've been completely addicted to Whole Foods and Trader Joe's. They're the best places to shop for organic food, except Whole Foods is much more expensive.

"We need to get squash and asparagus," I read from our grocery list. I saw this really great article the other day about how to make a delicious organic meal only using a few vegetables.

"Jenn, can we get this, too?" Adrian asks eagerly holding up a huge tray of chocolate cookies and putting them in the cart. "They're organic," he says, half convincingly.

"Sure!" I've said *yes* to just about everything today. We have loads to spend and now we'll never run out. It's great! I wish I could live like this forever! Now I understand how difficult it is to get people off food stamps. Who would want to?

We stare at the dessert counter for at least five minutes. Gosh, don't those fruit pastry treats look delicious? Every . . . single . . . one of them!

I turn to Adrian, "Sweetie, do you think we should buy some?"

"Yummy," he says, grinning and licking his lips. "Look at the delicious cheesecake with sliced strawberries on top."

"But they're not on the grocery list. We have a budget, remember?" I say.

"I thought we had food stamps and could buy anything?" He asks in despair.

Adrian grabs the cart and we manage to pull ourselves away from the tempting desserts. Maybe another time . . . like next weekend?

As we approach the seafood counter, I can't help but drool over the salmon and shrimp and oh, are those scrumptious crab cakes?

"Let's get one of each," Adrian suggests.

"That's a lot of seafood," I say. "Do we need all of that?"

"Of course!" He says.

"Fine, you get what you want. I'm going over to the produce department," I say.

"OK," Adrian says, walking up to the seafood counter.

As I walk over to the produce department, I see all sorts of fruit that I don't recognize from Michigan. I see weird looking fruit that other shoppers are putting in their carts! I spot watermelon and honeydew sitting in the bottom of a barrel. How yummy! Maybe we could get a few of these to eat. I reach for a watermelon at the bottom but a hand grips my arm. It's Adrian.

"Let me get that for you," Adrian says, lifting the heavy watermelon out of the barrel.

I never thought shopping with food stamps could be so much fun! I could become a *food* addict.

When we get home, I help unpack the food into the fridge and open the package of organic chocolate cookies from Whole Foods.

"Oh, Adrian, you have to try these," I say, stuffing my mouth with a second cookie.

He takes a cookie from the package and chews it slowly.

I wait for his reaction.

"Not bad," he finally says.

"Not bad? It's delicious!" I say.

"Just kidding!" He snickers, reaching for another cookie.

"Hey, so what are we eating for dinner tonight?" I ask.

"How about that pasta thing we bought?" He asks, taking it out of the grocery bag and putting it on the counter.

"Oh, hey I'll be right back," I say.

"Where are you going? I thought you were going to help me prepare the meal," he says.

"I am, I just need to check and make sure I got paid this week. I'll be back." I head down the hallway toward the bedroom.

I turn on the computer and load Firefox and type in my bank website. I wait for the page to load and type in my username and password.

Once it loads, I scroll down the page to my checking account and click on it. I look for a new biweekly deposit of $389.

Hang on . . . where is it? I look through the previous deposits and the only paycheck I received today was for $364. What happened to $25? Where did it go?

I rush back toward the kitchen, grab my cell phone and dial the 1-800 number for the VISTA Member Support Unit.

"Jenn, aren't we starting dinner?" Adrian calls out.

"Those stupid people never gave me all my money! Can you believe that?" I say to Adrian.

"So, does this mean you want me to start without you?" Adrian asks.

I call back out to him, "Can you? Please? If I call later, they'll be closed and I really need to reach someone during business hours." I wait for the phone to start ringing on their end.

An automated recording says, "Thank you for contacting the VISTA Member Support Unit. Please stay on the line and a representative will be with you shortly."

A man's voice answers, "Hello, VISTA Member Support Unit. How can I direct your call?"

"Hi! Can I speak to someone about my paycheck?" I ask.

"Sure, can I have your name?" He asks.

After giving him my name, he says, "Please explain the reason for your call, Ma'am."

"Well, I was supposed to get paid this week for the full amount of $389 like I always do, and well, I only got paid $364. My paycheck is short $25."

"Please hold and I'll check your account." He puts me on hold and classical music plays in the background.

This is so frustrating! Where is my money?

"Ma'am?" The man's voice comes back on the phone.

"Yes?"

"I'm not sure why you didn't get paid. But it does say on here that you owe $25," the man says.

What? Why do I owe AmeriCorps money?

Come on!

"I don't owe AmeriCorps any money. You guys owe *me* money!" I explain to the man.

"Well, I'm not sure why you didn't get paid. Please hold," he says.

What? Why can't I just speak to the manager or someone who knows what they're talking about?

"Ma'am?" He asks.

"Yes? What did you find out?" I ask urgently.

"It seems the Payroll Department has made a little goof," he chuckles.

What does he mean, "a little goof?" Doesn't he take me seriously?

"I'm so sorry for the silly mistake," he says slightly amused.

"When do I get my money?" I say, not seeing the humor in getting shorted $25 on my paycheck!

"You should receive it on your next paycheck," he says.

So I have to wait another two weeks for the $25?

That's *so* not fair.

"Can I talk to the Payroll Department?" I ask.

"I'm sorry, Ma'am, but we don't give out that phone number," he says.

What? They don't give out the phone number for the Payroll Department? Is this guy seriously for real?

"Is there anything else I can do for you?" He asks cheerfully.

Yeah, give me the phone cord so I can wrap it around your neck.

"Ma'am, are you there?" He asks again.

"Hello? Yes. I'm here," I say.

"Well," he says with an upbeat attitude, "Is there anything—"

"No!" I say and close the phone.

Oh my God, these AmeriCorps people are ridiculous.

I storm out of the bedroom and head down the hall toward the kitchen. I smell pasta cooking with eggplant and Italian seasonings.

I hear a male voice stutter. "Well . . . well why? She's . . . she's stupid."

I stop walking and tiptoe slowly toward the kitchen to eavesdrop. When did Jason get home?

I hear Adrian muttering, "Jason, all I'm asking is that you get off the TV once in awhile."

"Why?" Jason asks.

"Look man, Jenn wants to use the TV just as much as you, but we have to share it," Adrian says.

"So . . . so tell her . . . tell her to get . . . tell her to get off the TV," Jason says.

What is he talking about? I never *get* to use the TV!

"Dude, you need to share, OK?" Adrian asks.

"Look, man . . . look . . . if she . . . if she has a problem with . . . with me using the TV . . . then, then she . . . she should tell me," Jason says.

Oh please, Jason! If I actually told you to get off the TV once in a while, do you really think you would listen?

"All I'm asking is that you use the TV for only a few hours a day and then let Jenn use it the rest of the day. OK?" Adrian asks.

"But . . . but I only . . . I only use it . . . I only use it for like . . . for like three hours a day," Jason says not realizing he's on the TV all day long.

Wait! I know! I should set up a hidden video camera in the living room and record every time Jason uses the TV to play his stupid video games. It would be at least six or seven hours a day! Then I could submit it to the *Dr. Phil* show and he could set Jason straight.

"Well, Jenn said you're on the TV at least six or seven hours a day," Adrian says.

Adrian! Why the heck would you tell Jason what I said? Now Jason's going to get all upset with me.

Argh. Men!

"Wait . . . wait, what? She said that?" Jason says.

OK, now I'm going to interrupt their conversation.

I walk into the kitchen, past Jason, who is now sitting at the dining room table. I spot Adrian standing over the stove, stirring the pasta.

"Hey, sweetie, do you need my help with anything?" I ask Adrian, opening up the refrigerator door.

"No, I think I got it," Adrian says.

I close the fridge and walk over to the stove. "Oh, that smells good."

"Ew!" Jason says in response, and gets up from the dining room table. He walks toward the living room.

Figures. He's like a magnet to the couch to play video games. He turns the TV on. Not a surprise.

"Doesn't he ever leave the apartment?" I whisper to Adrian.

Adrian shoots me a strange look. "I don't think so."

"Oh my God, Jason needs to get out more!" I say.

I really wish I could be more like Jason's mom who's the only person who can get him to do anything! I mean, come on, the guy never moves farther than ten feet in any direction.

"Hey, Adrian, I'm . . . I'm going to . . . I'm going to watch . . . watch some TV . . . OK?" Jason calls from the living room, turning up the volume to loud.

"OK," Adrian says.

Grrr. "We were supposed to have the TV tonight!" I say, nudging Adrian in the arm and shoot him a nasty look.

Adrian peers into the living room. "Actually Jason, we're about to have dinner. Can we use the TV for an hour?"

"Now?" Jason asks defensively.

"Is there a problem?" Adrian asks.

I hear Jason turning off the TV, walking out of the living room and stomping down the hall to the bathroom.

Good boy.

"Great! Yay, we have the TV," I whisper to Adrian.

I help Adrian spoon out the pasta meal on our plastic plates. We sit on the couch and he flips through the channels. This is so relaxing, sitting here, eating food, watching TV and feeling a breeze come through the open balcony door. This is the life.

"Hey . . . hey Adrian!"

Not Jason. Again!

"What?" Adrian calls back, leaning over the couch.

I hear Jason turning on the shower. He opens the bathroom door. "Why . . . why is it torn?"

Adrian and I exchange confused looks. What is Jason talking about? We jump up from the couch and walk over to the bathroom where Jason stands next to a dangling shower curtain.

"What is this crap?" Jason asks, holding up the ripped, plastic shower curtain.

"Oh . . . that. Well, Adrian and I bought a very cheap shower curtain at the Dollar Store," I say. "We're trying to save money."

"It looks fine," Adrian says. "Here." Adrian grabs the shower curtain, ties a knot in one corner over the rod and strings the torn part through three available shower rings.

"What . . . what are you doing?" Jason asks, looking upset.

"I'm tying up the shower curtain for you," Adrian says.

"Can't . . . can't you . . . can't you just . . . just buy a new one?" Jason asks.

"Dude, look, I fixed it. It works just fine." Adrian says, sliding the shower curtain back and forth.

"It . . . it looks like . . . looks like shit," Jason says.

"Listen, Dude, if you don't like it, you can buy a new shower curtain," Adrian says.

"Can't she buy it?" Jason asks.

Um . . . sorry? I know I buy toilet paper, but come on! Are you trying to get yourself smacked now or later?

"Jason I'm not buying a stupid shower curtain when we already have one," I hiss.

Adrian gives me a disapproving look and turns back to Jason. "Look, Jenn and I bought this shower curtain. Even if it's torn, it still works. Just take a shower."

"Why . . . why can't . . . can't you buy . . . buy a new one?" Jason asks Adrian.

Jason persists and refuses to give up.

"Look, we don't have a lot of money, OK? Jenn told you we bought the shower curtain at the Dollar Store," Adrian says.

"What?" Jason looks appalled. "You . . . you bought this . . . bought this at . . . at the Dollar Store?"

"Look, we've been trying to save money. We go to the recycling center to earn extra cash. We use the money to buy things for the apartment like the shower curtain," Adrian says.

Which is true, for the past few weeks, we've been trying to save every can, pop bottle or juice bottle we buy. We buy water from the Dollar Store with food stamps and then recycle those cans and get money for it, so we found a way to profit from food stamps.

"Whatever," Jason says, rolling his eyes.

Adrian wiggles the shower curtain. "Are you going to take a shower or not?" Adrian asks.

"Fine," Jason says. "Get out," waving us out of the bathroom.

Adrian and I leave the bathroom, closing the door behind us and head back to the living room. It's too bad we can't lock him in there!

"Anymore interruptions from Jason and I'm going to—" I say to Adrian.

"Jenn," Adrian stops me before I can say anymore and kisses me on the cheek. "Let's just finish watching TV. OK?"

"Adrian, I hate Jason."

"Please, Jenn," Adrian says, "Can we just eat and watch TV?"

I grab my plate from the coffee table and start chowing down on pasta which is now cold.

Twenty-four

I arrive at the high school around noon. A few tutors are sitting around the tables typing on their laptops or reading. I look over and as I'm about to sit, I realize Priscilla and Monique are chatting, and Priscilla is laughing! She's smiling! I mean, isn't this the mean girl who hated me? Wait, why is Priscilla even sitting near Monique? I take a seat near them at the same table.

"So, this is what I need you to do," I hear Monique saying to Priscilla. "Log in to your Zinch.com account."

I take a quick glance at Monique's monitor. Huh? Why are they working on Zinch.com? I already worked on this with Priscilla.

Monique hands the keyboard and mouse to Priscilla and I see Priscilla typing something on the keyboard.

Hey, wait a minute. Priscilla is actually cooperating? How come she isn't giving Monique the cold treatment she gave me?

"Excuse me?" I realize I just spoke.

Monique looks over at me.

"What are you guys doing?" I ask politely.

"Hey *Jinn*," Monique says, "I'm just helping Priscilla with some scholarships."

Right, well, I already tried that and Priscilla didn't want to work on scholarships. So, what's the use?

"Oh, so how's it going?" I ask.

"It's great. Priscilla's already applied for several scholarships on Zinch.com," Monique says.

"That's *my* job," I say.

"Well, *I'm* helping her," Monique says.

"You're supposed to help her with homework," I say.

"*Jinn*, just let me worry about Priscilla, OK?" Monique tells me.

"I'm supposed to work with her on finding scholarships for college," I say.

"Well *Jinn*, she doesn't want your help," Monique says.

Well fine, if Priscilla doesn't want my help then she can just stay there with Monique.

I get up from my seat and change tables. I need to be by myself in the back corner.

Just then students come piling into the Career Center by the dozen and sit near their assigned tutors.

Sonia is my next student. Will she find me tucked in the corner? Before I can even think the thought, I feel someone pat my shoulder. I turn around.

"Hey, Jenn," Sonia appears behind me and takes a seat. "How's it going?" She asks cheerfully.

"Pretty good," I say, feeling like it couldn't get worse.

"So, did you want me to log into Zinch.com, then?" She asks.

"That would be great, thanks," I smile.

After an hour, Sonia applies for a few scholarships. But boredom strikes and she wants to leave early to hang out with Kavita at the mall. Ugh. I'm super jealous. I want a shopping buddy! Do you think I could invite myself along?

Definitely not. They would think it was too weird. I want these students to think I'm cool and reserved. I want

them to idolize me . . . no, wait, scratch that, that doesn't
sound very good. I mean, I want them to worship me . . . no,
to respect me.

I look over toward the front of the Career Center and
find Monique and Priscilla laughing and having a good time.
Why can't I be more like them with a circle of friends?

Later that day, I end up checking my email three more
times and doing a Google search on, "How to be liked by
high school students."

I even meet with Arianna, too. She shows up for ten
minutes and says she applied for like a zillion scholarships.
She hands me the proof—the application packets she filled
out, and completed essays to mail in tomorrow. I'm really
proud of her. Why can't more of my students be like her?

So far I've met five out of my seven students, but
have not seen Alejandra Garcia or Zachary Stone. I remember Jackie mentioning to ask for help, so I head toward her
office and knock on the door.

"Come in," I hear her call out.

I walk in and find Jackie typing at her computer.

"Jackie, I have a quick question for you," I say.

"Sure. What is it?" She asks, looking up at me from
behind her computer.

"I'm having a really hard time trying to schedule
Zachary Stone and Alejandra Garcia. Do you have any
ideas?"

"Have you tried pulling them out of class?" Jackie
asks.

Whoa. Is she kidding? After the incident with Coach
Bailey, I hesitate to ask any faculty for help.

"No, I don't think that will work," I say.

"Fine, then call their parents," she says.

"OK," I say, turning around to walk out of her office.

"Oh and Jenn?" She asks.

I turn around to face her. "Yes?"

"Thank you for asking first," Jackie says and then returns to her work at the computer.

Well, I survived that without more humiliation.

I walk back toward my seat and pull out the list of contact information from my binder for all the students. I look up Alejandra Garcia and only a home phone is listed. Yikes. I'm really scared to call her parents. What do I say?

I could explain I'm their child's tutor and I really need them to pass all their classes this year so I don't get in trouble with Jackie and lose my job. Do you think that would work?

Shoot!

I walk out of the building to get some privacy for making a cell phone call and dial the number to Alejandra Garcia's home.

"Hola!" I hear an elderly woman's voice with a Spanish accent answer the phone.

"Hi, can I speak to Alejandra Garcia?" I ask.

"Hola?" I hear the woman asking again.

"Hi! Hello there!" I say, realizing this isn't going according to plan. I guess I forgot half of California is made up of Spanish-speaking families!

"Hi, my name is Jenn Ruben," I say louder and more slowly as if speaking to a deaf person.

"Jenn . . . Ruben . . . " she says, as if learning the syllables.

"Right!" I answer eagerly. OK, who am I kidding? She imitates what she hears trying to understand it. I decide to speak in short phrases. "Speak to Alejandra Garcia?"

"Oh? Alejandra Garcia?" She repeats my words and I hear her put down the phone.

There's a long silence and then I hear someone picking up the phone.

"Hola?"

"Yes?" I was hoping for Alejandra, but it's the same grandmotherly voice.

"She no home," the woman says in broken English.

"She is not at home?" I ask.

"No," the woman hangs up.

Argh. This is more difficult than I imagined. I wish someone would have warned me about the language barrier. That beginning Spanish course I had over at the community college, well, geez, it didn't help much!

I go back inside and find Zachary Stone's contact information on the student list. Two numbers are listed, his dad's office phone and his home phone. This ought to be easier. At least I know he's not Mexican.

I walk back outside and sit down on the pavement in front of the building. I dial the first number listed, which is his dad's office. I wait for the ringing and someone answers.

"Dr. Stone's office. How can I assist your call today?" A pleasant, young woman answers.

"Hi, can I please speak to Dr. Stone?" I ask.

"Did you have an appointment with him today?" She asks.

"No."

"Then, I'm sorry, Dr. Stone is very busy. Is there anything else I can do for you today?" She asks.

"Yes, I really need to speak to Dr. Stone," I say.

"But you don't have an appointment. You need to have an—"

"OK. Thanks." I hang up the phone. Well, that didn't go well.

I dial the home phone number next and hear the ringing.

A woman's voice answers, "Hello? Stone residence."

"Hi, is this Mrs. Stone?" I ask.

"Why?" She asks.

Great, now I definitely sound like a telemarketer.

"Hi, this is Jenn Ruben, I'm a tutor for the—"

"Are you an advertiser? I really don't want you selling me stuff. Didn't I tell you to take me off that stupid telemarketer list?" She slams the phone down.

Wow. OK, let's try this again, shall we?

I flip open my phone and dial her number again. Gosh, I really hope she doesn't have Caller ID, or I'm screwed.

"Hello?" She answers cautiously.

"Hi, I'm from the high school, and I'm calling on behalf of Zachary Stone."

"Oh, that would be my son. Did you need to speak to him?" She asks.

"As a matter of fact, yes." I say.

"Well, unfortunately he's not here right now. Is this the principal's office, because I know my son is a very, *very,* good student," she replies.

"No, this is not the principal's office."

"Then who is this?" She demands.

"I'm one of his tutors from the Upward Bound Program here at the high school."

"I'm sorry, the *what* program?" She asks.

"The Upward Bound Program," I repeat slowly.

"And what is it that you do?" She asks.

You have to be kidding me! This lady has never heard of the Upward Bound Program that her son is involved with?

"I'm a high school tutor helping students apply for scholarships," I say.

"OK," she says, "but he's not mentally challenged or physically handicapped or anything like that."

Oh. My. God. Does she think the only school programs are for helping the handicapped?

"This is a tutoring program that helps students with their homework and prepare for college," I tell her.

"My son does not *need* your help," she says.

She's kidding, right? "Mrs. Stone, the program is to encourage students to go to college and to help them apply for loans and scholarships," I say, sounding like a brochure.

"My son won't be needing financial aid or scholarships," she says emphatically.

Wow.

"Are we clear on this?" She asks.

"Yes," I say. "Well, thanks."

She hangs up the phone.

Another call to a parent that ends abruptly.

I walk back into the Career Center and put the contact list back in my binder. Well, that was disappointing.

Twenty-five

A few days later, I receive an email from Nancy, a California State Supervisor. She wants all the AmeriCorps VISTA volunteers of Fresno to meet today for an official meeting.

A few hours later, I receive two more emails on this same subject. One message is from Rosaline and the other is from Jackie. Both messages inform me the meeting is mandatory for everyone, so I must go. Either way, I get the day off from tutoring and I still get paid! You can't beat that!

I head out of the apartment and walk to the meeting. Since the meeting's only a few blocks away, I don't have to waste gas driving. The weather is wonderful. It's only seventy degrees out here!

I walk past a few streets and then I arrive. Well, I'm at correct street address, but I don't see the building. Hmm . . . that's weird. I'm looking for a number that reads "4545." Rosaline said it was a whitish, yellow building. Oh, that must be it over there.

I look straight toward a large building with lots of windows on the side. I start walking toward it. When I get closer, I see a sign that says, "Closed." What?

I glance across the street and see a banner floating against a door reading, "Volunteers Welcome." Is that it? I glance up at the building. Hey! That isn't a building. It's a church!

Huh? Is the AmeriCorps meeting in a church? Oh, no! I look down at myself. I'm wearing jeans and a T-shirt. Definitely *not* church attire!

I locate the front doors and walk in. There are a few desks on the right hand side and a blue couch on the other end of the wall. The carpet looks like it hasn't been vacuumed in ages. It looks nothing like a church from the inside. It looks more like an office.

Where is everyone? The church is completely quiet, except for a few voices whispering down the hall. I walk down this incredibly long hallway.

I finally come to a small open room with four couches in a square. A few VISTA volunteers are sitting on the floor playing cards and a couple of guys are playing with a Hacky Sack. Another volunteer is reading in the corner.

OK. Now, I'm nervous. Not about the meeting, but about meeting Nancy, one of the state supervisors. I had problems at my previous AmeriCorps job and Nancy was supposed to support me, but didn't. I called her several times, sent her emails, and she never called me back! And now, today, I finally get to meet her, face to face.

I take a seat on a mahogany couch perched up against a white wall.

"Hello?" A young woman peers out of her office. "Hey, I'm Tammy. Are you here for the AmeriCorps VISTA meeting?" She asks.

"Yes, I am. I'm Jenn."

She walks over and extends her hand. "Hi. Nice to meet you. I'm here for the meeting, too. How long have you been volunteering for AmeriCorps?" She asks.

"For several months," I say, "but it feels longer."

She sits down next to me. "I've been here for three years," she says.

"Really?" I ask.

"Isn't it great!" She says.

"Wow," I say, not knowing what's an appropriate answer. "I love the free food," is all I can think to say.

"What do you mean?" Tammy asks.

How about getting food stamps and being able to afford to shop at Whole Foods?

"I receive food stamps," I say.

"Oh, aren't they great?" She asks. "But I feel bad."

"Why?" I ask.

"We're using taxpayer money. My cousin, he's a lawyer. He always complains about paying high taxes and paying for free government services like food stamps," Tammy says.

"Well, I don't feel bad," I say. "It's not like we can help it if we're poor. Right?" Poor people don't have a choice. I mean, look at all these free services! Who needs a job when you can get free money?

"But we choose to move out here to volunteer, didn't we? We have a choice," she says.

"Exactly. This is one of the best jobs I've ever had," I say, trying to sound supportive.

"What's in it for you?" She asks.

Well, let's see, besides the free food, there's cheap electricity, and not having to pass a California driver's test, and getting paid not to work.

"Everything!" I say, sounding enthusiastic.

"Same here!" She glances down. "It would be so wrong to take advantage of the free services, you know?" She asks, looking at me for confirmation.

"Um . . . right. I couldn't agree more!" I lie, realizing I can't tell her about the reduced electric bill or getting paid for not working.

"Hello?" A woman's voice calls out down the hall.

"Oh, hello," Tammy says to a female supervisor.

"I'm Nancy, one of the California State Supervisors."

Yikes!

Tammy walks over to Nancy and shakes her hand. Wow. Nancy is definitely much older than I imagined. She's very thin with gray hair, carrying a heavy, blue tote bag over her shoulder.

The volunteers realize Nancy is in the room. Nancy walks over to the students and introduces herself. As she goes around the room, she greets everyone for the first time. Then she comes to me.

I smile. "Hi, Nancy, I'm Jenn Ruben," I say, holding out my hand.

She pauses for a second, shaking my hand. "Oh, so *you're* Jenn Ruben?"

I nod my head. So this is Nancy. I will not lash out at her. I will stay calm. I need to stay calm.

I hate you, you old lady!

"Nice to meet you, Jennifer." Nancy says and takes a seat at a blue couch across the room. At least she's far away from me.

"So, shall we begin the meeting then?" Nancy asks.

Tammy takes a seat next to me while the other volunteers spread out across the room and take their seats on the couches.

"Today, I want to go around the room and ask each and everyone of you about your AmeriCorps job here in Fresno," Nancy says.

That's a really bad idea.

I have a better idea! How about we get some pizza and watch a movie! Or, better yet, let's go home and skip the meeting altogether! Then I can grab Ben and Jerry's, go home and watch a movie with Adrian!

Oh, wait . . . Jason's there.

Argh!

"So," Nancy says, looking around the room. "Let's start with you." She points to the bookworm in the corner.

He has a beard and glasses and looks intellectual. He begins by telling us his age, who he is and why he's here.

He begins, "Um, I love working at the homeless shelter. So far the experience has been really rewarding. Even though the pay isn't great, I still love what I do. I really enjoy helping someone get a new start in life and I'm really looking forward to doing this again next year."

I wonder, did they reduce his paycheck by $25, too?

"Well, I'm so glad you're having a wonderful experience with AmeriCorps." Nancy smiles over at him and pulls out a notepad and a pencil from her tote bag and starts taking notes.

Is she writing down everything he said? Why?

What if his comments get sent to the AmeriCorps Washington, D.C. office? I can't possibly say anything bad about AmeriCorps. I might get fired.

"Jennifer?" Nancy says.

My turn already?

Nancy looks over at me. "Would you like to go next?"

Can I say, no?

Oops! Look at the time! I think we better reschedule and finish this meeting another time.

"Jennifer?" Nancy repeats again.

"What?" I ask.

"Can you tell us a little about your AmeriCorps experience?" Nancy asks.

What do you want to know that you don't already know, Nancy? Didn't you get my calls or emails?

"Jennifer, are you ready?" Nancy asks again.

"I tutor students in the afternoon. We go over scholarships and loans and it's great," I smile.

"What else?" Nancy asks.

Is she looking for more than that?

Oh, right.

"Everything's going well in the program so far," I lie.

However . . . the Payroll Department owes me $25, and the AmeriCorps health insurance won't reimburse me (even though they said they would) for $26. Why should I be paying out of pocket costs for stupid TB tests especially when I have negative results? Why do I have to spend my money to get a California ID card when I could easily use my Michigan driver's license? Doesn't my California ID look like a driver's license anyway? Why do I have so many supervisors? Why do I have to tutor ungrateful students who hate me anyway? Why doesn't anybody like me?

"That's wonderful to hear, Jennifer. I'm glad you are enjoying your AmeriCorps job," she smiles. "See me after the meeting," she says.

What's *that* supposed to mean?

Nancy turns toward Tammy, who is smiling brightly. Tammy explains her love for AmeriCorps and how much she wants to apply again next year.

Pardon me while I gag.

After Tammy finishes, Nancy turns toward another VISTA volunteer and interrogates him the same way. At last everyone tells their stories and explains their jobs.

I still can't get over how many people actually said they enjoy AmeriCorps. One girl said she didn't like her experience, and received nasty stares from the group.

Nancy concludes the meeting by saying she's grateful everyone came today and she hopes we have a safe trip back home.

I can't wait until I'm done with my term of service!

"Jennifer?" Nancy walks over to me as the volunteers make their way out of the room. "Shall we have that private chat now?"

Before, or after I have Ben and Jerry's ice cream?

"So, tell me," Nancy says, taking a seat next to me. "What was the problem you were experiencing in your other job?" She's referring to my last AmeriCorps job in a neighboring town of 12,000 people.

"Oh you mean—" I begin.

"Before you begin, let's not point fingers at people," she says.

"So I can't say who—" I begin.

She interrupts. "I don't want you to complain about anybody and bring up the past. Just tell me what happened and let's not jump to conclusions, OK?" She asks.

Why not? What better way to start a meeting than by gossiping about the people we hate! I would consider it a good bonding experience.

"So, tell me, Jennifer, I'm listening," Nancy says.

"OK," I begin. "The experience first started when I moved in with a Mormon family."

She nods her head. "Go on. I'm listening."

"I was going to get an apartment when I moved out to California but they were all filled. Anyway, I rented out a room and stayed with this Mormon couple and it got all weird."

"Tell me more," she says, folding her arms across her chest.

"Well, almost every week, a bunch of Mormon school boys wearing dark pants, white shirts and ties, stopped over, handing out Jesus books. And I almost got killed."

She puts her hand over her mouth. "You almost got killed? What happened!" She seems surprised.

Read the emails.

"I was attacked by a bat one night in my bed. It swooped down on my head and I nearly—"

"Oh my goodness. That must have been difficult. Let's move on and discuss your job at City Hall," she says.

Don't you want to hear more about the bat? Don't you want to know the Mormon wife told me the bats had cute little hands and had been in the house for thirty years? She said they had as much right to live there as I did, and that I should get used to them.

"So, Jennifer," Nancy pauses, "Would you like to begin with telling me about your supervisors?"

Am I being interviewed?

"Well, I didn't like any of my supervisors. I had too many people supervising me. That was the problem. They were snotty and mean—"

"Why don't you tell me about your job duties first," Nancy says.

Ugh! So what do I talk about then?

Nancy pulls out her notebook and starts writing something down. She looks up at me. "Now, your information is very valuable. I need to have it for my records." She says, "Go on, I'm listening."

This is too stressful. I really need chocolate—

Now.

"Well . . . um . . . I did a lot of secretarial work . . . for them," I say, unenthusiastically referring to my many supervisors. "They had me fax papers, fill out forms, and print brochures. They gave me loads of work to do. They—"

Nancy interrupts. "Well that's wonderful to hear. It's always good to keep our volunteers busy," she says.

What planet is she from?

"But they made me do all *their* work," I whine. "They decided I should answer all their phones, too. That wasn't part of my job description. I didn't like how they took advantage of me since I was the youngest—"

"Now, Jennifer, let's not be so irrational—"

She should try working with supervisors who monitor your every trip to the bathroom!

"Tell me, was there anything you liked about your supervisors?" She asks.

Nothing! Haven't I said that enough?

"Jennifer?" She taps her pencil on her lap. "It's OK. If you feel the need to talk about your supervisors, then fine. Go ahead." She doesn't look pleased!

"Which supervisor?" I finally ask. "I had *four* supervisors, you know. Actually come to think of it, I had *five in five months.*"

"Continue," Nancy says, jotting down some notes.

OK . . . I liked James, my first supervisor. He was the Economic Director at City Hall. He was fun except he retired during my service. Total bummer.

And . . . let's see. I hated Beth, the second supervisor. She drove a Mercedes and used federal grant money to buy herself three Blackberry cell phones. Now who needs three? And why did she always dress like she was attending a funeral? I didn't know anyone could wear that much black who wasn't Jewish!

The third supervisor was Freddy. He made personal calls to his wife continuously, checking in with her because he was bored. Freddy wore polo shirts which made him look like a golfer, instead of a Marketing Specialist for City Hall. And by the way, where are the business cards he promised to make for me?

Which brings me to Victor my fourth supervisor, the City Hall Director. He was too busy for me. All the meetings I scheduled with him were canceled since everyone else was more important. Then he blamed me for not meeting with him more often. *If they hired me, why didn't they have time for me?*

Eventually the first supervisor was replaced with a young, blonde woman named Candy. She was from the East Coast and was my fifth supervisor in five months. She wore classy, slim-fitting clothes, matching handbags, and designer sunglasses.

Candy was the closest to my age. She wore her skirts above the knee and attracted stares from male co-workers. I was told my skirts had to be worn below the knee. At age 27, Candy was earning $35,000. At age 24, I barely cracked $10,000 and mine was just a living allowance. I wanted to be friends with Candy, but I didn't have money to spend as her shopping buddy.

"Oh, I had issues with most of my supervisors," I finally blurt out to Nancy.

"I'm sure you don't mean that," Nancy says.

It was really bad. Every time I left work, I would walk over to Walgreen's which is one of only three franchise shops in the city. I would buy a bag of Ferrara Belgium chocolate and eat the entire bag in about thirty seconds. Now that's called *stress*.

"Jennifer, you should have tried harder to get along with your supervisors," Nancy says. "Even if the tasks were not in your job description, you should still have done them."

I wonder if Nancy would answer phones and do other people's jobs if it weren't in her job description?

"I heard about your situation through Adam, over at the Economic Development Department in Fresno," Nancy says.

What? She knew this already?

"Right. Well, Candy was best friends with Adam, but I didn't know it. He would ask me questions about how the job was going," I explained.

"So, you shared your concerns with Adam?" Nancy asks.

"Yes, I was told to speak to Adam if I had any problems with my supervisors. Occasionally, I would drive into Fresno to meet with him," I explain.

"Then what?" Nancy asks.

"After Candy was hired, I started having problems with Candy, which I told Adam. Candy treated me like a child even though I was only three years younger. Later on, I found out Adam and Candy were best friends. I mean, everything I told Adam *in confidence* was being relayed to Candy," I say.

Is that even *kosher?*"

"Sometimes supervisors need to discuss concerns with other supervisors," Nancy says.

"Anyway, one day after I complained about Candy to Adam, she gave me a huge list of projects to do *that same day*," I say.

"Supervisors have the right to assign projects as things come up," Nancy says.

"I still don't think that's fair," I say.

Breaks and lunches were an issue with staff at City Hall. The staff worked a 10 hour day and took a one hour lunch. Candy told me, that as a volunteer, I was only allowed a thirty minute lunch for working the same 10 hour day.

Candy made personal calls during work and scolded me when I did so. One time I was outside making a personal call home. Candy stormed outside, upset I wasn't working on a project. She said I needed approval *first* before taking a break. She rarely let me take any 15 minute breaks.

"After I learned Candy and Adam were best friends, I asked Adam if I could change jobs," I explained.

"So, that's why you changed jobs," Nancy says.

"I tried calling you months ago to tell you about this, but you never returned any of my calls or emails," I say.

"I had a lot of things going on and I was very busy," Nancy says.

I wish Nancy would just sympathize with me instead of telling me about supervisors' rights.

"Well, I'm glad we had our little discussion today," Nancy says, wrapping things up. She puts the notebook back in her tote bag and stands up.

"There's more—" I begin, catching her off guard.

"Look, Jennifer," Nancy says, opening the front doors. "I need to go." She picks up her tote bag and hurries out the church.

I'm so stressed out my head's going to explode!

I need ice cream.

No, I need chocolate.

No, I definitely need sex . . . Adrian?

   I turn around and walk back toward my apartment, stopping at the local 7-Eleven store along the way to get my Ben and Jerry's ice cream, a bag of M&M's and a donut . . . do you think they have Ferrara Belgium chocolate there?

Twenty-six

A few months pass by. The weather is getting warmer. The temperature rises in Fresno and the weather reporter says it's going to start hitting the hundreds. Ugh. It's getting hotter and hotter and still we haven't turned on the air conditioner. I glance over at the thermostat hanging on the wall.

"Adrian!" I yell out.

He comes sprinting out the bedroom in his boxers. "What's up?"

I point to the thermostat on the living room. "Does it really read 90 degrees?"

He leans in closer to read the thermostat. "Holy shit. Let's turn on the air conditioning."

He switches the button to "air" as we wait by the vents for the cool air to rush through.

"What does the temperature say now?" I ask a half hour later, propping myself up from the couch.

Adrian walks over and takes a look. "It says 88."

Oh my God, it only went down two degrees in a half hour?

"Do you want to go swimming?" I ask.

"No," he says, coming over to the couch, "it's too hot."

"That's the point of swimming, Adrian," I say.

"Yeah, but I'm not even motivated to go outside. It's a hundred degrees outside."

Wow. It's going to hit exactly a hundred degrees today. Back in Michigan, it rarely gets hotter than ninety! And if it does, it's in August. Ugh. I feel sticky in this apartment.

I sit at the computer and check my email. There's a new message from AmeriCorps. It says they updated my living allowance status, which is my paycheck. I login to the AmeriCorps website and scroll down at the bottom of the page.

I notice a new comment posted under "Resolved Issues #801234." So they solved the problem of my missing money? This is great! I click on the highlighted post and read the comment.

So it says the VISTA Member Support Unit looked into my issue further and contacted the Payroll Department in Washington, D.C. They said there was a mix up and now they owe me $50 on top of the usual paycheck, meaning they shorted me $25 on two paychecks.

This means they shorted me on two paychecks! In the last line of their message, it says they reimbursed me. I need to check my direct deposit statement.

"Hey!" Adrian says, walking into the bedroom. "What's up?" He asks.

"Plenty . . . like keeping tabs on AmeriCorps."

"What do you mean?" He asks with a puzzled look.

"I went online and it says AmeriCorps paid me the $50 they owed me."

"Isn't today payday?" He asks.

"What's today?" I ask.

He points to the calendar hanging on the wall, "Friday."

"Oh, that's right. Hang on a sec," I say, logging into my online bank statements. "Hey, look," I say, grabbing Adrian's arm.

"What am I looking at?" He asks.

"Oh my God, I don't believe it!"

"Jenn?" He asks. "What is it?"

"They shorted me another $25!"

"So, is this the third time?" He asks.

"Yes, I can't believe they're doing this!" I say.

"You better call them back!" Adrian says.

"You're right," I say, jumping up and giving Adrian a kiss, "but first I have to go to tutoring."

I head off for tutoring to meet with Arianna. When I arrive at the Career Center, Jackie isn't in her office. Actually, none of the tutors are here except Monique, and I really don't want to talk to her. After the whole Priscilla incident, we haven't been getting along. I mean, Monique doesn't even say *hi* when I walk in the room.

Ugh. I really need to find Jackie so I can figure out if she has any projects for me to do.

I take a seat near Monique at the tutor table.

"Hey Monique," I say, interrupting her online shopping.

She gives me a quick look and then stares back at her computer. "What's up, *Jinn?*"

"Hey, do you know where Jackie is?" I ask.

"Nope." She returns to shopping on the computer.

"Do you know what time 'after school tutoring' ends?" I ask her.

"4PM . . . everyday," she says not looking up.

"Right, well . . . I know that."

"Why are you asking me?" Monique looks up confused.

"I'm sorry," I smile. "I mean, when does school get out?" I ask.

"June," she looks back at the computer.

Right, well, I already know school gets out in June! Doesn't almost every school get out then?

"Do you know what day school gets out in June?" I ask.

"Look, *Jinn*," Monique says annoyed with me, "if you really have so many questions, go ask Jackie. I'm *busy*."

"But she's not in her office," I say.

"So call her," Monique says as if giving me an alternative.

"I'm sorry, I was just—"

Monique interrupts. "*Jinn*, I'm trying to buy some shoes here, OK?" She points to the computer. "I'm really busy and can't talk now," Monique turns back to the computer as Maribel walks in.

"Hey Monique!" Maribel says, carrying her Gucci handbag and wearing cowboy boots.

Monique looks up. "Yo, Girl! You look cute today."

"Thanks," Maribel says, swinging the Gucci handbag like a fashionista. "Don't you love my new handbag?" She shoves her handbag under Monique's nose.

Monique strokes the leather handbag. "Is it fake?"

"Um no, it's real," Maribel insists.

"Girl, you really need to stop spending money," Monique says.

Maribel takes a seat next to Monique and points at the monitor. "What are you buying?"

"Oh, just some shoes. Here. I'll show you," Monique says, gesturing toward the DSW shoe page on the computer screen.

For the next few minutes, I watch as Maribel and Monique giggle over shoes that well exceed my budget allowance of $10. Didn't these girls ever hear of *thrift* shopping at Goodwill or Salvation Army?

I wait a few more minutes for Arianna to show up. Why are my students always late? Arianna was supposed to be here already and meet me during lunch!

I hear the lunch bell ring and several students walk in, carrying their backpacks and listening to their iPods. Most of these students rarely do homework anyway. They come to the Career Center to hang out with friends, eat lunch, or watch videos on YouTube.

Today looks like an average day. For the past several weeks, I've come mostly during lunch and after school hours. I rarely arrive in the morning since all the students are in class.

I check my email for a few minutes and watch a few videos on YouTube to pass the time. I glance over at the clock on the computer. There're only five minutes left until lunch. Wow. Time slows down when you're not having fun.

Where is Arianna? She's like a half hour late. I pull out my phone and send her a text message asking where she is. Immediately I get a response back. *What?* She's at a doctor's appointment and can't come in today. Why couldn't she tell me this before? Argh.

I send another text. This time I address it to Sonia. "Can you meet me after school today?" I wait for her to text back. Nothing.

"Yo, *Jinn*," Monique calls.

I look up.

"Yo, I meant to tell you, I'm working with Priscilla from now on," Monique announces.

"Do I need to tell Jackie?" I ask.

"No, I've already taken care of it," Monique says.

Why is Monique stealing my student? I mean, why does she even *want* to tutor Priscilla?

"So . . . what about the scholarships and FAFSA stuff I'm supposed to work on with Priscilla?" I ask.

"Oh, don't worry, girl, I'll help her with it," she says.

"Are you sure?" I mean, this *is* Priscilla, the girl with the vacant stare who never says hello and only makes insults.

"We work great together. She even asked me to help her out with her wedding!" Monique says, emphasizing her role as the favorite tutor.

Well, fine. I don't want to go to her stupid wedding anyway. It'll probably just be girls wearing jeans one size under, Abercrombie and Fitch tight fitting shirts with their boobs hanging out. And, I mean, who wants to get drunk at a wedding reception with high school seniors?

"Did you know Priscilla's dad is throwing a huge wedding?" Maribel asks. "I heard it's going to be awesome. She invited me too. It's going to be huge, with lots of food."

Monique interrupts. "Really? Girl, we should go shopping together and find you a cute dress."

"Yeah, we should. Oh, Monique, did I tell you that Priscilla's dad is paying for an open bar?" Maribel says.

Wow.

"Seriously? Damn, girl. That's awesome," Monique says.

Bzzzz. I feel my cell phone vibrating on the table. Finally, something to distract me before I even feel more left out than I already do. I open up my phone and there's a new text message from Sonia. "Sure. C U 2PM." Great. It looks like I do have tutoring this afternoon. Now it's not a wasted trip! I mean, it's a twenty minute drive and there's no reimbursement for gas. Do you think they have *gas stamps*, like food stamps?

After lunch ends, the students head back to class and Maribel, Monique and I are alone in the Career Center. Jackie still hasn't shown up. I've already checked my email like a dozen times and really wish I could get into Facebook. I'm so bored! Monique and Maribel are watching something on YouTube and laughing hysterically.

"Hey girls," a pleasant voice calls out.

Monique and Maribel look up as Jackie walks through the door.

"Hey Jackie," Monique glances my way and grins.

"So, girls, I got us some candy," Jackie says, waving a mini Snickers bag at Monique and Maribel. Jackie walks over to her office.

"Those Snickers look delicious, Jackie!" Maribel calls out.

"Come on in, let's have some," Jackie calls from her office.

I follow Monique and Maribel into Jackie's office like hungry puppies. They take the only two chairs in Jackie's office as she rips open the candy bag.

"I've been craving chocolate all day," Jackie says, pouring the Snickers bars on her desk.

Monique and Maribel are sitting in chairs within reach of the candy. I'm standing awkwardly behind them. Should I reach over their heads and just grab a Snickers?

"Oh, hi Jenn," Jackie says, noticing me finally. "Did you need something?"

I stammer, "Um. I—"

"Was there something you needed?" Jackie asks again.

"Do you want a Snickers bar?" Maribel asks, turning around with a bar in her hand.

Monique grabs the Snickers out of her hand. "Yo, girl, of course *Jinn* doesn't want one," Monique says, ripping open the wrapper and throwing the Snickers bar in her mouth.

"Well, I—" I say.

"So, are you all set?" Jackie asks. She seems really annoyed by my presence.

I fidget. "I was wondering if you had any projects for me for the next few weeks or so?"

"Such as?" Jackie asks.

"Oh, I don't know," I say.

"How's it going with the students?" Jackie asks.

"It's going great," I lie.

The school year's almost over and I haven't met on a weekly basis with most of my students. They never show up since they always seem to have doctors' appointments or after school practice.

"So, have they finished FAFSA?" Jackie asks.

"Actually we're already working on scholarships," I say. How do I tell her their parents did FAFSA for them?

"Well, that's wonderful. So you're almost done." Jackie says, looking pleased as she unwraps a Snickers bar.

I really want a Snickers. I feel a chocolate binge coming on. "So, is there anything else you want me to do here?"

"Nope. Tutoring and that's about it," Jackie says. "Well, I'm sure you need to get back to work."

I smile politely and walk out of her office. I take my seat at a computer. I feel like crying. Was Jackie trying to kick me out of her office? I mean, was I really not invited? I feel so left out and *I didn't even get a Snickers bar!* Argh.

I grab my shoulder bag and leave. I drive the half block to Walgreen's and grab the last Ferrara Belgium bar on the shelf. I pay the $1.30 and eat it in my car. I grab my cell phone and dial Adrian.

"Hello?" Except it's not Adrian who answers the phone.

"Hello? Who is this?" I ask.

"Who . . . who wants . . . wants to know?" Jason asks.

"Jason!?"

"No!" He shouts.

He's such a liar. "Why did you answer Adrian's phone?" I demand.

"Is . . . is this . . . is this Adrian's mom?" Jason asks.

"Are you kidding? This is Jenn."

"Who?" He says, teasing.

"This is Jenn," I say louder.

"Who's *that?*" He asks, pretending not to know.

"I want to talk to Adrian," I say into the phone.

"HE'S NOT HERE!" Jason yells into the phone almost deafening my ears.

Good grief. "Where is Adrian?" I yell back.

"Get . . . get off . . . get off the phone! Adrian is . . . is waiting for some girl to call," Jason says.

What? What girl?

"Get off Jenn!" Jason yells back into the phone.

"Why?" I ask. I'm confused.

"Hang up, Jenn!" Jason yells.

"No!" I demand.

"Is this Wendy?" He asks.

Hello?

Are you retarded? You already know it's me, you stupid idiot! It's so difficult getting Jason to hand over the phone to Adrian when I'm sitting in my car in the Walgreen's parking lot.

"THIS IS JENN!" I yell. I'm going to kill you Jason, if you don't get off Adrian's phone and stop pulling pranks.

"Adrian . . . doesn't like . . . doesn't like you. OK? He's . . . he's talking to . . . to another girl on . . . on my phone."

What?

What other girl?

This has to be some sort of joke.

"Put Adrian on the phone, Jason!" I practically scream over the line.

"Bye," Jason says, hanging up the phone.

Excuse ME?

Now I dial Jason's cell phone.

"Hello?" A voice whispers.

"Adrian?" I ask.

"Hey," Adrian says.

"Adrian, what's going on?"

"I'm on the phone with my mom, Jen. What's up?"

"Why are you using Jason's phone?"

"Because he gets phone reception over here and I don't. He has a Verizon phone, remember?"

No, I don't remember. Why would I?

"Where are you?" I demand.

"I'm in the mountains," Adrian says.

That explains why he doesn't get reception.

"What are you doing there?" I ask.

"I can't talk much right now," Adrian says.

"Well, I just called to let you know your stupid friend Jason said you were on the phone with another girl and that you hated me and wanted to break up and—"

"What?" Adrian sounds genuinely surprised.

"I told you, I don't like Jason."

"Hang on, he's right here next to me," Adrian says.

I hear the line go dead. What happened? I try dialing the phone again, but it's turned off. OK, this is too weird.

I check the clock in my car and it's twenty minutes before 2PM. Sonia said she would meet me right after school. I drive back to the school and take a seat at a computer in the Career Center. Monique and Maribel are still in Jackie's office. They're having such a good time.

Argh.

The school bell rings.

Well, that was earlier than expected.

In just a few short minutes, students swarm into the Career Center carrying their heavy backpacks and dumping them on chairs and tables. They immediately sign onto the computers and start giggling with their friends and munching on snacks.

I decide to check my email again. Nothing new. Ugh. This day is really dragging.

Suddenly, my cell phone vibrates. I glance at the Caller ID. It's from Sonia. I flip the phone open and it indicates a new text message, "Sry at doctors appt."

Is she really at a doctor's appointment? Why did she say she was coming if she wasn't? I don't get it. Doesn't she like me?

I can't really tell Jackie since she'll expect me to make the students come and I can't. Somehow, she'll turn this into *my* problem.

I reply to Sonia's text message, "OK. C U next week." Except I probably won't see her next week. Or, the week after that. I haven't seen any of my students this week. They all have excuses.

Bzzzz. My cell phone vibrates again and it's a new text message from Sonia, it reads, "Sry. Can't come next week."

Exactly.

I immediately text her back, "Why?" Is she planning ahead not to show?

My phone buzzes again. A new message from Sonia reads, "dentist appt." Will it be an eye appointment next? But it puzzles me since Sonia seemed to like me. Well, nothing I can do about it now. I log off the computer, grab my shoulder bag and head out the door.

I almost expect Jackie to scold me for leaving early, but I don't hear anyone chasing after me.

Half a bag of M&M's and thirty minutes later, I arrive home at the apartment. I climb up two flights of stairs in the heat. The temperature is supposed to be a hundred today.

I unlock the door and walk inside. It's dark . . . and quiet. Everyone's gone. I forgot, they're in the mountains!

I drop my purse on the floor and plop down on the couch. I turn on the TV. There are no zombies and gunshots to disturb the serenity. I enjoy the freedom of channel surfing.

As I'm about to watch Comedy Central, I hear music. I mute the TV and the music gets louder. I get up off the couch and walk toward the bedroom. Is the music coming from the bedroom?

I open the bedroom door and turn on the light.
Oh. My. God.

Adrian is lying under a sheet. There are red hearts made from construction paper taped to the walls. A huge sign reads, *Happy One Year Anniversary*. Yay! It's our anniversary today! It's been one year since we had our *first kiss*.

In the middle of the mattress, I spot a huge flower arrangement of the most dazzling yellow lilies ever!

"Adrian . . . " I feel tears running down my face.

"Close the door," he says softly.

I close the door, and lie down on the mattress next to Adrian. "Happy Anniversary," he says, handing me the flowers.

They smell wonderful. "Thank you," I say and put the flowers on the computer desk. "I thought you were in the mountains?" I ask.

"I was. I just got back," he says. "I bought the best flowers from a gift shop in the mountains," he says, proudly.

Awe! He drove forty five minutes to find me flowers! How can any girl refuse a guy like that? Isn't he sweet?

Adrian pulls me toward him and gives me a kiss. He puts his arm around my waist and throws me on the mattress. He gets on top of me, kicks off his shoes and pants, starts kissing my neck as he peels off my shirt and unbuttons my pants. Oh my God! I can feel the adrenaline rush through my body! Yes! I love this feeling. He pulls me on top of him and rubs against me.

Are you . . . ? Ready?

Wait! *Wait!* My eyeglasses!

Too late.

Twenty-seven

The next morning, I wake up feeling incredibly sexy and confident. That was the best night of my life. *Ever!* I lost track of how much sex we really had. Other than that, I feel so great that I almost forget to tell Adrian about Jason's prank over the phone.

I have two glasses of milk and Whole Foods' cinnamon bread for breakfast. I finally tell Adrian about the phone conversation yesterday with Jason saying Adrian was waiting for a call from another girl.

Adrian is furious when he hears this. It's the last straw with Jason. Adrian jumps up from the couch and pounds on Jason's door, demanding an explanation. Jason comes out and gets defensive, denying the entire conversation.

Jason blames it on his Asperger's Syndrome as if he has a split personality disorder instead. Jason storms out of the apartment to call his mom. Later, his mom phones back wanting to speak with Adrian. Adrian explains Jason is too difficult to live with and that's the reason he has to move out.

Adrian tells Jason to pack up and leave today.

Jason hisses loudly to anyone listening, "Why can't Jenn leave?" and "Everything would be better if she left instead!" Jason throws his clothes and games into the back of his truck and then leaves.

I breathe a sigh of relief after Jason drives away. Finally, I get my car stall back. Plus, the living room is once again ours! Yay! Life couldn't be better!

I begin to feel guilty for breaking up this longtime friendship between Adrian and Jason. What will Adrian think? Will he blame me for damaging his relationship with Jason?

"Jenn," Adrian says, coming up from behind, folding his arms around my waist.

I turn around and we kiss. Adrian pulls me toward the couch. Yay, we're going to have sex! On the couch! He lies down, his back against the couch and pulls me close, toward his chest. Is this a new sex position? Hmm. I'm not familiar with this one.

"Jenn, I've been wanting to ask you something for a while now."

"Oh?" I ask, looking up at him.

Oh my God! We're not going to have sex! No wait, he's going to propose instead!

And then can we have sex?

YES!

Where are we going to get married? I mean, I'm from Michigan and he's from Fresno and that's like a $500 plane ticket per person and who's going to pay? And I haven't even thought of a wedding theme—

"When are you telling your parents about AmeriCorps?" He asks.

Huh?

"It's been a year. When are you telling them the truth about what you're doing here in California?" Adrian asks.

Wait, no marriage proposal?

Darn.

"Jenn?" He asks.

"I meant to call them," I say, "like one of these days."

He smiles, "No you didn't."

I smile back. "You're right. I have no intention of ever telling my parents the truth."

"You know what I think?" He asks.

You want to marry me I hope?

"I think you should call your parents right now and tell them the truth."

Adrian pulls his cell phone out of his pocket.

"Why do I need to?" I ask.

"It's gone on long enough," he says, "and your AmeriCorps term of service is ending soon."

"I was hoping my parents would never find out," I say.

"Your parents have a right to know and they're going to find out anyway," he says, handing me the phone.

My heart starts to race. I hesitate for a few moments. I really can't call Mom or Dad, can I? I mean, what if Dad gets really upset and wants the money back he gave me to move out to California? I never made it to Hollywood. I never made it as a director. I was never on a movie set. I never really told my Mom what I was doing.

Ugh.

"Jenn?" Adrian frowns.

Huh? Oh. "I'm thinking," I say, still tapping the phone in my hand.

"When are you going to tell your parents?" He asks.

"Why are you so persistent? They don't really need to know."

He grabs my hand and kisses my fingers. "Jenn, you really should tell them so they can be proud of you."

I meet his eye. "Huh?"

"Because you independently chose to move out here to California. You left your family behind to take on a volunteer job," he says.

Only Adrian could make AmeriCorps sound like a good job.

"Leaving my friends was hard," I say, looking down.

"How about your parents?" He asks.

I look up. "I think my mom can handle the truth better than my dad," I say.

"So what are you going to do?" He asks.

"Maybe I'll tell them in a book," I say.

Adrian gives me a hug and kiss.

Twenty-eight

So, OK, here's the deal. It's been two weeks and I've been on the phone constantly with the VISTA Member Support Unit. They keep telling me the AmeriCorps Payroll Department has underpaid me.

AmeriCorps did reimburse me for two of the paychecks. I got a check for $439. Except I haven't received any reimbursement for the third paycheck.

Ugh.

I mean, when you only get paid $4 an hour, $50 is considered a crap load of money! Think about it. With that $50, I could buy out a whole row of clothes from Salvation Army. OK, well, I could buy like two rows if I go on half price day!

Plus, I'm living on food stamps which is really great since I love shopping at Whole Foods which is *so* expensive.

I live in this old apartment which never cools down in the summer. I absolutely die in the heat. It's like a hundred degrees in here!

Hello! This is the Central Valley—almost desert. It takes real determination to tolerate the heat. But Adrian and I promised each other we would save money by keeping the air conditioning *off* for most of the day.

Where is that reimbursement? I need it so I can keep the air conditioning on even longer. I *must* have it!

I called the VISTA Member Support Unit and told them the reimbursement wasn't added into my last paycheck. Needless to say, they were confused.

The help desk woman told me to call Debra, a payroll technician for the VISTA Member Support Unit.

So I called Debra and we've been on the phone the past two weeks. She's been extremely helpful.

Debra reassured me she sent the issue to the Ameri-Corps Payroll Department and she's been contacting the Payroll Supervisor daily to follow up. Except they haven't called Debra back. So now I have to play the waiting game.

So, here I am, sitting in the hot living room contemplating my next move as I wipe sweat off my face.

Hmm.

I hear someone outside the apartment, unlocking the door. It's Adrian!

"Hey," he says, walking in and throwing down his backpack on the floor.

"Hey yourself," I say, smiling.

"What's up?" He asks.

"I'm frustrated," I say.

Adrian walks over and gives me a kiss. "What's going on?" He asks, taking a seat next to me.

"Remember when I told you that AmeriCorps owed me money?"

"Yeah, what about it?" He nods.

"Well, I just got off the phone with a payroll technician and she said my money *really* will be on my next paycheck."

"Great!" Adrian says.

"But what if it's not there? What happens then?"

"Why wait?" He asks.

"What do you mean?" I ask.

"Well, why do you have to wait? Why can't you just call the Payroll Department directly?" He asks.

"I already thought about this, but the VISTA Member Support Unit refuses to give me the phone number," I say.

"Look Jenn, I really think you should talk to someone higher up about this. I'm not trying to sound mean, but look, it doesn't look like anything's getting done," Adrian says.

Which is true. Why would it take two weeks for a Payroll Department to figure out how to pay me $50?

"Jenn, why don't you do a search for the Payroll Department phone number?" He asks.

"I already tried searching for it online and I can't find anything on Google," I say.

"Don't they have a staff directory?" He asks.

"That's a great idea! I didn't even think of that!" I say.

"Let me know what you find out. I'm going to take a shower, OK?" Adrian says, getting up and walking into the bathroom.

I grab my laptop from the bedroom, flip it open and wait a few seconds for it load and the screen to appear. I open up Firefox and navigate to the AmeriCorps website.

I click on *AmeriCorps VISTA* on the far right and then a new page loads. I scroll down the sidebar and look for anything that says something like, *Staff directory*.

Hmm . . .

Where is it?

Then I see it.

On the left hand side is a tab that reads *About us*. I click on it and scroll through the choices underneath it.

I click on *Contact us*. The first option underneath *Contact Us* reads, *Staff Directory*. Bingo! I found you! Ha!

I click on the link and wait for a new page to load.

A search field in the middle of the page appears sorted by department.

I scroll through all the choices and then decide on *Accounting and Financial Department*.

A new page loads with many names and phone numbers. Wow, this is so amazing! Interesting how none of this was mentioned during training.

I scroll down to the bottom and select one of the names at random, *Frank Adams*. I don't know who this is at all, but I like the sound of his New England name. I dial the office number listed underneath his name.

I wait for a few seconds while it rings.

On the second ring, a voice picks up.

"Hello? Frank Adams here," I hear a husky male voice answer.

"Hi," I say, "I'm currently an AmeriCorps VISTA volunteer in California and I have a question regarding my paycheck."

"Oh, with regards to what?" Frank asks, shuffling papers on his desk.

"Well, I'm trying to get a hold of the Payroll Department," I say.

"Then you want to speak to the Office of Budget," he says.

Oh, right! Exactly! Office of the Budget sounds so formal. So official!

"So, would you like me to transfer you to the Payroll Supervisor?" Frank asks.

"Yes, please!" Gosh, isn't he helpful?

"Hang on," Frank says as the line clicks and a few seconds later, I hear another line ringing.

Gosh, I'm so nervous, what am I going to say? I don't even have a speech prepared.

Wait, I don't need a speech. I just need to yell at these stupid people for messing up my paycheck!

"William Peters here," an older man answers.

"Um . . . uh . . . hello?" I ask nervously.

"Who's . . . who's calling me?" He has a thick East Coast accent.

Gosh, I can barely understand him.

"Who's calling?" He asks again.

"Hello, my name is Jenn Ruben and I'm currently an AmeriCorps VISTA volunteer in California."

"Why are you calling *me*?" He demands.

Oh. Um . . . oh no! He sounds upset that my call interrupted him.

"*Hello?* You there? Why are you calling me?" He demands.

OK. Now I'm worried!

He's really pissed.

I need to relax so I can explain to him what's going on with my paycheck. I need him to fix it for me!

"Hello, Sir?" I ask.

"What?" He barks.

"I'm calling you in regards to my paycheck. I need to talk to someone in the Payroll Department," I say.

"I'm the Payroll Supervisor. However, I suggest that if you have a problem with your paycheck, you need to contact the toll free number of the VISTA Member Support Unit. Do you need that number?" He asks.

"No, I don't," I say immediately. "I already called them and they can't help me. I was shorted $25 on three paychecks, and I want to know where's my money for the third paycheck?" The words rush out before he has a chance to interrupt me.

"What's your name?" He asks.

I give him my first and last name *again* and wait for him to speak. I think my forcefulness works with him since now I hear him typing.

"I'm going to look up your payment history," he says.

"Great, thank you," I say.

There's silence and a few seconds later I hear more typing and the clicking of a computer mouse.

"Hmm. I'm looking through your payroll records. Where does it say your paycheck was shorted?" He asks.

"Well, here's the thing. Three of my paychecks were shorted $25, and I finally got reimbursed for two of the paychecks but they still owe me for the third paycheck. I've been on the phone many times with the VISTA Member Support Unit and they *told* me to call you," I say.

Well, OK, the VISTA Member Support Unit didn't exactly *tell* me to call Payroll. It was actually Adrian's idea.

I mean, think about it, why mess with the middle man, the VISTA Member Support Unit, when you can go straight to the top of the Payroll Department in Washington, D.C.? Isn't this like the central location for the U.S. government, right?

I hear William return to the phone. "Jennifer, as I'm reading your account here on my computer, I'm looking through your earning statements. It seems you were actually overpaid."

Huh?

"I don't think that's possible—" I start to say, remembering the three shorted paychecks.

"I'm looking at your earning statements right now. It shows an overpayment of $25 for each of the three paychecks. But you were only entitled to $25 for each of the two supplemental paychecks. So, you were overpaid $25," he says.

I'm *so* confused. He throws numbers at me like he's reading balls from the lotto machine.

So, I had three paychecks that were short $25 each, and he says they only owed me for two paychecks?

I feel like I'm repeating myself. I already went over this with Debra, a payroll technician. So, if I have three screwed up paychecks, then shouldn't I receive three supplemental paychecks?

One of the VISTA Member Support Unit members even told me, "Wow, that's weird. I've never heard of a volunteer who didn't get paid the full amount. Are you sure you checked your earnings statements correctly?"

Hello!

What is this? Of course I check my statements. I always verify my direct deposits.

Am I the only volunteer with such problems? This can't be possible. I mean, how many thousands of volunteers serve in AmeriCorps every year?

"*Hello?* Are you there?" William asks over the phone.

"Yes, sorry," gosh, I almost forget I'm still on the phone!

"Jennifer, the bottom line is you were overpaid!" He says.

"What? But you guys screwed up on my paycheck like three times!" I say.

Grrr. I'm so mad at them!

"We didn't *screw up* on anything, Jennifer," he pauses. "Didn't we pay you the additional supplemental amount for two of your paychecks?" He asks.

"Yes, but you still owe me for the third paycheck. Why were my paychecks shorted in the first place?" I ask.

"We paid you, didn't we?" He asks, sounding impatient.

"Yes, you paid me for two," I sigh.

"So what's the problem?" He asks.

Come again? "Sir, the problem is that you still owe me for the third paycheck."

"But you weren't owed for the third paycheck," he says.

"Yes, I am," I say.

"You were overpaid for the third check which you did not receive because it was an overpayment," he says, sounding like he understands his own words.

Huh?

"*Jennifer?*" He raises his voice.

"Yes, I did get paid for two supplemental checks."

"So, then, what's the problem?" He asks.

"Well, I want to know why my paychecks keep getting messed up and where's my other $25?" I say to him, wondering why I have to re-state the obvious?

Goodness, you would think a Payroll Supervisor would know what his employees were doing.

"You need to talk to another department who deals with that sort of thing," he says.

"Can you give me their phone number? I want to know *who* typed up my paycheck wrong."

"Payroll checks are computer generated," he says flatly.

What?

Come again?

That can't be right.

Debra at the VISTA Member Support Unit, told me the Payroll Department manually types in paycheck amounts and the computer does the rest.

"Sir, I was told that someone manually has to type up my paycheck." I say, knowing I have him there!

"This is not my area. You need to speak with another department," he says.

Wait a second.

"Aren't you the Payroll Department?" I ask, not wanting to surrender this quickly.

"Yes!" He says.

"Aren't you the Top Guy?" I ask.

"Yes, I'm the Payroll Supervisor for the Payroll Department."

Exactly my point!

"So, if you're the guy I speak to about my paycheck, then why are you telling me to speak to another department?" I ask, beginning to understand why they call these government employees *bureaucrats*.

"Jennifer, you are not owed any money. Is it possible the money you thought you were owed was already paid to you?" He asks.

I need some chocolate to clear my head. This is too much stress for one day!

"I have to go to a meeting," William says finally. What?

"Good day," he says, and the line goes dead.

Good grief! Are all payroll departments like this?

I scroll to a tab in Firefox and Google "AmeriCorps complaints about paychecks and who to call." It says I should call the VISTA Member Support Unit number. No kidding! I feel like I'm going in circles. Argh.

I scan the web page and notice a link to the Office of Inspector General for National and Community Service. This sounds very *federal* and *official*, plus they have a hotline, too.

The hotline is for *volunteers and others to report instances of fraud, abuse of authority, and mismanagement.* I know right away these people can help me!

Wow, I can't believe my good fortune. Here's a 1-800 phone number right out in the open for the whole world to see!

"Hey Jenn. You want to eat some lunch?" I hear Adrian calling from the bathroom.

"In a minute, sweetie, I really need to call the OIG."

"The who?" Adrian asks.

"The Office of Inspector General," I say.

"Who's that?" Adrian asks, walking out of the bathroom.

"They're the people who handle fraud complaints from AmeriCorps volunteers," I say.

"Sounds like you finally found someone who can help you," Adrian says, walking down the hall with a bath towel wrapped around his waist. "Good luck then," and walks to the kitchen.

I immediately dial the 1-800 hotline number.

After one ring, a middle aged woman answers the phone. "Hello. OIG, Holly speaking."

I introduce myself and tell her I'm a volunteer over in Fresno, California and I explain my situation.

"I see," she says. "So, you're owed $25 and they haven't paid you? I need to know who exactly hasn't paid you."

"AmeriCorps," I say.

"When you say AmeriCorps, do you mean the grant organization you're working for?" Holly asks.

"No, I mean I'm having problems with my paycheck," I say.

"Oh, so this would relate to the Payroll Department then?" She asks.

"Yes, I'm having problems with my actual living allowance paycheck. I was shorted on one of my paychecks and am owed a $25 supplemental check," I say.

"So you're telling me the AmeriCorps Payroll Department did not pay you correctly for one of your checks?" She says.

"That's correct," I say.

"Well, I'll get right on this. Volunteers need to get paid," she says, hanging up the phone.

What if William the Payroll Supervisor is right? What if I was actually overpaid? But wait, didn't he say I was overpaid on the third check but that it was never sent to me?

Argh.

I glance over to Adrian who is standing at the kitchen counter. He looks so sexy from the back with that wet towel wrapped around his waist. I wonder what he'd say if I came up behind him and pulled it off?

"How about if I make us some sandwiches?" Adrian calls out.

"Sure, that sounds great," I say.

I hear my cell phone buzzing on the couch. I quickly flip it open. "Hello?" I ask.

"Hello? Jennifer? This is Nancy!" She makes more of a declaration than a question.

Nancy? What does she want?

"What did you find out about the paycheck issue?"

"Well, I first called—"

"Tell me, why did you call the Office of Inspector General?" Nancy demands.

Nancy's question catches me totally off guard, like maybe my conversation with the OIG was recorded by the FBI, and maybe that woman Holly was never planning to get right on my problem?

I just spoke to Holly a few minutes ago! How did Nancy find out?

"That was a very *poor* decision on your part, Jennifer," Nancy scolds me.

What? WHY?

"Do you realize what you have done?" She demands to know.

No. What did I do besides call a government hotline and ask for help?

"I cannot tell you how many problems you are going to cause," she says. "The OIG will now be calling our office nonstop for the next month because of your complaint. I'm already so busy and now I have to drop everything and deal with your problem. Are you listening to what I'm saying?" She pauses. "You made a very, a *very* poor decision. You should never have called the OIG."

"But—" I start to say.

"They have already started reviewing the case regarding your paycheck."

Already? Wow. I'm impressed. Too bad Nancy's so upset, but I should've called the OIG first!

"I don't think you realize what an avalanche you triggered, but the OIG will be on top of us, questioning us," she says, sounding very irritated.

"I didn't realize—" I begin.

"Jennifer. I'm going to make myself clear. If you have any more doubts about your paycheck, you must call me first. Never, ever, call the OIG. Do I make myself clear?"

Oh. My. God. Is she seriously talking to me like this? I mean, if I wasn't actually *allowed* to call the OIG, then wouldn't they have told us this in training?

Likewise, I was never told not to call the OIG for questions and concerns regarding the Payroll Department or my paycheck.

"Jennifer? Do I make myself clear?" Nancy asks.

"Yes. I —"

"If you have any more concerns regarding your paycheck, you must contact me first. And if you have any questions regarding anything else associated with your position, you must contact me, and only me. Do I make myself quite clear?"

"Yes."

"Goodbye," she says, hanging up.

Wow.

Nancy makes it sound like I committed a federal crime by calling the OIG.

"Jenn, who was that?" Adrian asks.

"It was one of the California state supervisors. She was really upset with me," I say.

"Why?" Adrian asks.

"Because I called the Office of Inspector General and it got her in trouble," I say.

"Geez Jenn, why does this stuff always happen to *you?*"

"Maybe I need some help from a higher power. I even called out to God and Jesus a couple of times, but they didn't help," I say.

"You should pray to those *Hindu* Gods," Adrian says. "They have Gods for almost everything."

"Do you think it would help?" I ask.

"Wouldn't hurt to try," Adrian suggests.

"Well, I guess I can't do anything about the $25 now," I say.

"I think you have the right idea," Adrian says. "I'm sorry it didn't work out."

"Gosh, after all this stress, I could really go for some ice cream right about now," I say.

"But what about the sandwiches I made?" He asks.

"I'd rather have *you* for my sandwich, sweetie," I say, giving him a big hug.

Adrian grabs me and kisses me. "Hey, let's go get that ice cream instead."

"How about Ben and Jerry's?" I ask.